THE AUTHORS   SL 1992

Mark Hollingsworth is a freelance researcher and journalist. He has worked for Granada Television and the TVS current affairs programme *Facing South*. He has also been a regular contributor to the *New Statesman* and the *Observer*. He is the author of *The Press and Political Dissent* (Pluto Press, 1986) and was the researcher for *The Miners' Strike* by Geoffrey Goodman (Pluto Press, 1985). Born in 1959, he was educated in South Africa and lives and works in London.

Richard Norton-Taylor has been Whitehall and Security correspondent of the *Guardian* since 1975. Before that he was the paper's European correspondent in Brussels. He is the author of *Whose Land Is It Anyway?* (Turnstone, 1981) and *The Ponting Affair* (Cecil Woolf, 1985). In 1986 he won the Freedom of Information Campaign's media award. Born in 1944, he was educated at Oxford University and at the College of Europe, Bruges.

BLACKLIST

The Inside Story of Political Vetting

Mark Hollingsworth
and
Richard Norton-Taylor

'I'll be judge, I'll be jury,' said cunning old Fury. 'I'll try the whole cause, and condemn you to death.'
Lewis Carroll – *Alice in Wonderland*

THE HOGARTH PRESS
LONDON

Published in 1988 by
The Hogarth Press
30 Bedford Square
London WC1B 3SG

A CIP catalogue record for this book is available from the British Library.

ISBN 0 7012 0811 2

Typeset in Linotron Palatino
at The Spartan Press Ltd,
Lymington, Hants
Printed in Finland by
Werner Söderström Oy

Contents

Acknowledgements

Towards the end of *The Front*, a film about McCarthyism in Hollywood in the early 1950s, there is a scene in which Woody Allen is summoned before the House Un-American Activities Committee. Allen plays a character who has allowed his name to be used as a 'front' for a Hollywood screenwriter who has been blacklisted. At first Allen is scared and decides to collaborate with the Committee. But as the questions become increasingly intolerant and authoritarian, he changes his mind. When told to inform on his friends, he pauses ruefully, tells the Committee to 'Go to hell,' and storms out. The film ends with Allen being jailed for contempt of court but hailed as a popular hero.

That scene illustrates how one BBC producer always felt when told to blacklist someone he had just appointed. Fortunately, there have been other executives, personnel directors and industrial relations managers who have felt equally affronted by secret political vetting. They have spoken to the authors at some risk and we are very grateful to them, although obviously we cannot mention their names.

However, there are some people who deserve a special mention. First and foremost is Jon Eric Lewis, our outstanding researcher, whose work was meticulous, precise and first-rate. We are also most grateful to Mark Leopold for his expert help and advice with the British Telecom chapter. For the Private Security section we were fortunate to have Gary Murray as a special consultant who provided priceless evidence on how private detectives have gained illegal access to the Police National Computer.

We are also indebted to Tony Watson (now Deputy Editor of the *Yorkshire Post*) and Charles Tremayne of Granada Television's *World in Action* for their investigations into the Economic League. Their programmes produced some remarkable new

evidence about Britain's largest private vetting agency. At the
BBC, Michael Barnes, producer of *The Secret File on Citizen K*, a
documentary about the blacklisting of the American journalist
Penn Kimball, was very helpful.

The National Council for Civil Liberties and the Labour
Research Department were also very co-operative, particularly in
providing useful documentation.

In addition we would like to thank the Transport and General
Workers' Union, particularly Steve Riley, the construction workers' union UCATT and the civil servants' First Division Association, notably Sue Corby.

Finally, we would like to thank Jenny Uglow and Robert Lacey,
our editors, for their faith and, above all, their patience.

Mark Hollingsworth and Richard Norton-Taylor, London 1988

Introduction:
The Reality, The History and
The International Experience

'We do disagreeable things so that ordinary people here and elsewhere can sleep safely in their beds at night. Is that too romantic? Of course, occasionally we do very wicked things . . .'

John le Carré – *The Spy Who Came in From the Cold*

This book examines the history and current extent of political vetting and blacklisting in the private and public sectors in Britain today. Vetting is more than a 'system' – it is, rather, a network of official and unofficial security agencies who weave a web in which many individuals are trapped, and from which they cannot escape. As we have pieced together numerous case histories, from private interviews and conversations, and from published and broadcast material, a highly disturbing pattern has emerged. Each example, each case history has its own story to tell.

The range of political beliefs of potential victims of the blacklist is enormous. In the eyes of the security service (MI5), for example, active trade unionists like Jack Dromey are 'potentially subversive'.

Dromey is a national officer for the Transport and General Workers' Union, representing 300,000 manual workers in the dockyards, local government and the civil service. Like hundreds of other trade union officials he is an active supporter of the Labour Party. During the 1987 General Election campaign he worked at Labour's headquarters, playing a key role in projecting the party's new 'moderate' image.[1] He has little time for Marxists or what he calls the 'ultra-left'.[2] To this day he remains unaware that the State has branded him a 'potential security risk'.

MI5 has compiled a permanent file on Dromey, chiefly because of his union activities – he co-ordinated picketing during the bitter 1977 Grunwick dispute.[3] But it was during his chairmanship of the National Council for Civil Liberties (NCCL) that the security services first saw him as 'a potentially dangerous subversive'. In the mid-1970s, according to former senior MI5 officer Cathy Massiter, the NCCL was targetted as 'a subversive organisation' because of its criticism of the police and other state institutions.[4] Files were opened on its senior personnel, including Dromey, who was also on the Executive Committee, and legal officer Harriet Harman.

While he was at the NCCL Dromey met and later married Harman, now a Labour MP. But even had she not been the NCCL's legal officer Harman would still be considered 'a potential subversive' – merely because she was Dromey's wife. The shadow extends beyond the couple themselves to their three young children. Being the son or daughter of a 'subversive' can cause considerable doubt about a person's 'reliability' for a job – the 'sins' of the parents are often visited on the children.

Dromey and Harman are just two entries on MI5's computer of one million 'subversives'. But this is just one aspect of a much wider and more dangerous phenomenon in British society: the secret blacklisting and vetting of thousands of ordinary citizens.

Blacklisting is an issue which, because of its secret nature, is rarely discussed publicly. When MPs raise the matter in Parliament, Ministers either refuse to comment or cite 'national security'. The general view of employment blacklisting is that it was a feature of the 1950s Cold War and was largely the product of the American Senator Joseph McCarthy. Britain, according to conventional wisdom, has escaped relatively unscathed from the scourge of the political witch-hunt, with our civil rights intact. How wrong that analysis has turned out to be. In fact, the only real difference is that blacklisting in the United States has been a much more open affair. It is also easier to detect in America because of their Freedom of Information and Privacy laws. By contrast, the essential and recurrent characteristic of blacklisting in Britain is its hidden nature, protected by the assumption that 'it couldn't happen here'. This has resulted in the lack of public and political scrutiny of an issue which can affect the lives of almost every working person in this country.

The essence of blacklisting is that it prevents people from being employed for reasons unrelated to their ability to do the job. In most cases, the decision is based on their alleged political views and trade union activities. Entirely personal information is also used against people.

There are three forms of blacklisting. Firstly, the vetting of applicants after they have been offered jobs and then blocking their appointments. Secondly, sacking employees after they have started work. Finally, placing peoples' names on blacklists, thereby barring them from future employment with other companies.

Some vetting – like the 'positive' vetting of civil servants and other public employees – is openly acknowledged. But much is secret, especially in the private sector. It is a remarkable fact that it is not actually illegal for an employer to sack an individual because of his or her political views. Even if an employee succeeds at an Industrial Tribunal case for unfair dismissal, the company or government department is not obliged to reinstate them. The best that he or she can hope for is financial compensation.

Clearly, for the ordinary victim of the blacklist there is little protection.

In recent years the practice of blacklisting has increased in both scope and frequency. Private companies have tempting commercial motives for using personnel vetting procedures. One way for them to increase profitability and broaden their corporate base is to curb high wage rises and prevent potential industrial disputes. They could achieve this by improving their industrial relations strategy and developing a constructive dialogue with their employees. But more frequently the management's solution is to sack trade union activists or to blacklist prospective employees before they join the company.

In order to avoid industrial action over such practices, personnel departments implement their vetting procedures in great secrecy. Many companies have their own security officers, the vast majority of whom are ex-policemen. Part of their job is to check the criminal records of prospective employees by using their old police contacts. Even though this is illegal it is a common practice. They also employ professional vetting agencies. By far the largest of these is the Economic League, although some companies use private investigators and security firms. Their services are used particularly extensively in the construction, engineering and car industries, where there is a long history of poor industrial relations.

While profit, commercial expansion and a compliant labour-force remain the prime motives for big businesses, vetting within government departments has more overtly political connotations. Civil servants have, of course, been subject to positive (i.e. 'open' and acknowledged) vetting procedures since 1952. The procedure was intended to reduce the risk of secrets being leaked as a result of an individual's political and personal beliefs. Similar procedures are now used for employees in the nuclear industry, the Civil Aviation Authority, the Post Office, police forces (including civilian employees) and members of the Territorial Army. Private companies with classified government contracts such as British Telecom and defence firms are also subject to vetting.

Positive vetting for employees who work in areas genuinely involving national security is perhaps necessary. But all too often these procedures are carried out with excessive secrecy, which lays them open to abuse. The government, British Telecom and many defence contractors now have personnel policies which are a combination of overt and covert vetting. This can lead to political factors creeping into a system ostensibly based only on security considerations. A good example of this has occurred at the BBC. For nearly fifty years the BBC secretly vetted a large number of its employees. This policy was theoretically justified by the BBC's potential role as the wartime broadcasting station, and the fact that some employees in the Overseas Services had access to 'sensitive information'. Yet, in practice, the BBC vetted *all* their journalists, even producers and directors on drama and arts programmes. Although these people were hardly in need of vetting, many of them were blacklisted.

The BBC experience, described in Chapter 5, shows how easy it is to use the premise of 'security' for political or ideological reasons. The danger inherent in all personnel vetting is that political views and activities become the criteria, rather than genuine security factors. This danger was highlighted on Wednesday 3 April 1985. On that afternoon, just three hours before the parliamentary recess for the Easter holidays, Mrs Thatcher announced revised security vetting procedures in a written answer to the House of Commons.

The timing and method of the sudden announcement meant that the Prime Minister could not be questioned by MPs about the new guidelines, which had far-reaching implications and which, she said, had 'immediate effect'. Neither the employees covered by the rules, nor the trades unions representing them, nor the senior civil servants in the Cabinet Office responsible for vetting, were consulted or informed of the initiative beforehand.

The new security vetting system was to cover over half a million civil servants and many thousands of people working in the nuclear industry, British Telecom, the Post Office, the police forces and defence contractors. It also changed the terms of reference of the 'Three Wise Men' – the members of the Appeal Board: Lord Justice Lloyd, Sir Patrick Nairne (former Permanent Secretary at the Department of Health and Social Security) and Edward Hewlett (former Deputy General Secretary of the Institute of Professional and Civil Servants). Under the traditional practice, a public servant would put his case before this Appeal Board, who would then adjudicate and send their recommendation to the Minister concerned. Now their role would be merely consultative. Ministers would, in effect, be judge and jury, themselves determining the definition of a 'subversive' or 'subversive activities'. A Minister alone would make the ruling. The previous success of the Whitehall establishment (supported by governments of both parties) in keeping Ministers and politicians at arm's length from the purge procedures had ended.

But the key feature of the 1985 guidelines is the new, and broader definition of 'subversion' (which still has no legal definition). The term 'subversive' was traditionally taken to mean a link, direct or indirect, with communist or fascist groups. Lord Denning, former Master of the Rolls, defined a subversive in 1963 as someone who 'would contemplate the overthrow of government by *unlawful* means' (our emphasis).[5]

Mrs Thatcher went much further. She stated:

'It is the policy of Her Majesty's Government that no one should be employed in connection with work the nature of which is vital to the security of the state who:

1) Is, or has recently been, a member of a communist or fascist organisation, or of a subversive group, acknowledged to be such by the Minister, whose aims are to undermine or overthrow Parliamentary democracy in the United Kingdom of Great Britain and Northern Ireland by political, industrial or violent means.

2) Is, or has recently been, sympathetic to or associated with members or sympathisers of such organisations or groups, in such a way as to raise reasonable doubts about his reliability.

3) Is susceptible to pressure from such organisations or groups.'

When pressed to explain the first part of this definition, the government said that it had merely adopted the form of words used in a speech in 1975 by Lord Harris, then a junior Home Office Minister, during a debate on the security services.[6] But when Harris used that form of words – borrowed from an informal definition used by M15 and the Special Branch – he was not announcing new government policy or making an official statement, and his phrase had no special status.

In an attempt to calm some of the fears raised by the new procedure, Leon Brittan, then Home Secretary, told Peter Jones, Secretary of the Council of Civil Service Unions, in August 1985:

'Both main elements of the definition must be met before an activity may be regarded as subversive i.e. there must be a threat to the safety or well-being of the state and an intention to undermine or overthrow Parliamentary democracy. The definition therefore imposes strict tests which ensure that . . . ordinary political or trade union activity cannot be taken to constitute subversion.'[7]

The government also claimed that the new guidelines followed logically from a report by the Security Commission in 1982. The Commission noted that 'the internal threat has altered considerably' since 1962, when the formal description of subversive was limited to communism or fascism. The 1982 report added:

'The fall in Communist Party membership has been accompanied by the proliferation of new subversive groups . . . whose aim is to overthrow democratic Parliamentary government in this country by violent or other unconstitutional means.'[8]

But there was no mention in the Report of 'undermining' by 'political or industrial means', as stated in the new 1985 definition.

What is completely new in the 1985 statement are the second and third parts of the definition of subversion. The inclusion of the phrases 'sympathetic to or associated with' or 'is susceptible to pressure from' places a huge number of people in the 'subversive' ranks. It therefore gives M15 and the Special Branch the power to blacklist individuals who are engaged in perfectly lawful, non-violent political activity. This policy of guilt by association also means that groups such as CND, Friends of the Earth, the Anti-Apartheid Movement and trades unions can be deemed 'potentially subversive' by the State. Mrs Thatcher herself has suggested that membership of a trade union is itself cause for suspicion. During the controversy over her decision to ban unions at GCHQ in February 1984, she said: 'There is an inherent conflict between the membership of a trade union and the defence of national security.'[9] In effect, this hands a blank cheque to the security services.

Another key feature of the guidelines is the power they give to Ministers. The new guidelines to the Board of Appeal state: 'A decision of what employment is to be regarded as involving "connection with work the nature of which is vital to the security of the state" or on what constitutes "classified work" or "access to classified information" is not one for you but for Ministers in charge of Departments.'

In the past these issues were considered by Whitehall permanent secretaries in consultation with union leaders, in a climate of consensus. This sweeping extension of their power now leaves the way open for Ministers to use the procedures against political opponents. As Larry Gostin, then General Secretary of the NCCL, said on the day after the policy was announced:

'It gives a Minister general authority to suspend those individuals who he or she believes to be undermining the Minister's actions by political or industrial means. This places at risk active trade unionists and civil servants who take differing views from the Minister and who may feel as a matter of conscience that information should be disclosed in the public interest.'[10]

Terms like 'security of the state' and 'national security' are, like 'the public interest', extremely vague, and give a Minister an enormous amount of discretion and power. As John Ward, General Secretary of the First Division Association, which represents senior civil servants, said in January 1988: 'Civil servants know at first hand that it is no longer acceptable for a government Minister alone to be able to decide unilaterally what constitutes national security.' Just how vaguely 'national security' is defined is evident from the answer Mrs Thatcher gave to the Labour MP Ken Livingstone in January 1988. 'This term,' she said, 'is generally understood to refer to the safeguarding of the state and the community against threats to their survival or well-being. I am not aware that any previous administration has thought it appropriate to adopt a specific definition of the term.'[11]

The judiciary have made it clear that it is up to the government to define 'national security'. During the *Spycatcher* case the courts refused to accept the government's appeal on the grounds of 'national security' at face value. But that was a special case – Peter Wright's book had already been published, thousands of copies had been imported into Britain and the 'damage' had been done. The traditional approach of the judiciary was reflected in the Law Lords' judgement on the GCHQ union ban in 1985. Lord Fraser, then the senior Law Lord, stated:

'The decision on whether the requirements of national security outweigh the duty of fairness in any particular case is for the government and not for the courts. The government alone has access to the necessary information, and in any event the judicial process is unsuitable for reaching decisions on national security.'

The current definition of a 'subversive' is now so wide and vague that it is dangerously open to abuse. It is interesting to note that, while the British government was extending its definition, the Australian administration was doing precisely the opposite. The Australian Security and Intelligence Organisation (ASIO), the equivalent of MI5, dropped the term 'subversive' on the grounds that it was far too general. They replaced it with 'politically-motivated violence' – a more specific phrase. The public, ASIO's Director-General Alan Wrigley said, does not expect its security services to be concerned with left-wing trade unions. The definition of the word 'subversive', he warned, could be 'endless'.

There has been no proper explanation of why the British government chose to announce the new security procedures when it did. One Whitehall view is that the government wanted to 'legitimise' activities disclosed by Cathy Massiter, a former MI5 officer, the previous month. Massiter revealed that the Security Services had placed trade unionists and the NCCL under surveillance and had tapped the telephone of CND activists. The government may have decided to argue, retrospectively, that 'subversive' activity in fact covered many more people and groups than the public assumed.

The History of Blacklisting

It is often thought that the phenomenon of the political and industrial purge stemmed from the Cold War years. In fact, the origins of blacklisting can be traced back to the time when trade unions first became active – in the seventeenth century.

Among the best-organised groups of workers at that time were the feltmakers and craftsmen. Their union, the Journeymen Hatters, became particularly militant in the 1690s over low wages. And so the employers took action. In 1697 the Feltmakers' Company introduced the 'character note' or 'leaving certificate' system. Under this scheme a master could refuse to employ a journeyman who failed to produce a 'character note' from his previous employer.[12]

But it was not until the Industrial Revolution that blacklisting became widespread. It was particularly prevalent in the railway industry. The big companies would send secret letters to each other enclosing the names of employees they had dismissed. One such letter was written on 7 November 1839 by Mr E. J. Cleather, Chief Engineer of the Grand Junction Railway, on behalf of the directors of his company, to the Secretary of the Stockton and Darlington Railway. Cleather told him that they had 'recently been under the necessity of discharging several enginemen from their service for acts of insubordination.' He added: 'Feeling the importance of possessing efficient control over this class of men, in which all railways are equally interested, I appeal to you to co-operate by not readily giving employment to the men who have been discharged.' In a postcript to the letter Cleather provided the names of the three offending engine drivers – Evan Edwards, John Cant and George Summerdale.[13]

The 1840s were a time of great industrial expansion, especially for the railways. Numerous companies were set up, and they needed manpower for the construction of many hundreds of miles of track. But in order to ensure a compliant workforce, tough bylaws were passed, which made it very easy for employees to be dismissed for 'insubordination' or 'misconduct'. Some politicians wanted to extend this practice by legislation. For example, in 1840 Lord Seymour proposed that 'there should be a registry of servants employed on the railroads since it was by no means uncommon when a servant was dismissed by one railroad for neglect or misconduct at once to get employment on another railroad.'[14] Seymour's 'registry' plan was not taken up – perhaps because the companies already had their own records. But the climate of industrial relations in the nineteenth century was such that employers were able to use blacklists and 'character notes' to ensure that active trade unionists did not work.

There was little change during the next hundred years, except that blacklisting became increasingly secretive, mainly because employers did not want to provoke strikes over the issue by a stronger trade union movement which was growing in power. Ironically, it was this very secrecy which may have prevented a public outbreak of McCarthyism in Britain during the Cold War. The climate was certainly ripe for a witch-hunt. There was a rash of spies. Some, like Professor Alan Nunn May, Dr Klaus Fuchs and Bruno Pontecorvo, were convicted. Others, like Guy Burgess and Donald Maclean, defected to the Soviet Union. There was even an English version of Senator Joseph McCarthy in Sir Waldron Smithers, the organ-playing right-wing Tory MP. Every year from 1947 onwards Smithers would rise in the Commons to ask the Prime Minister of the day to set up a 'Committee On Un-British Activities' along the lines of the American model. Clement Attlee and later Winston Churchill always greeted this request with a brisk 'No, sir' at Question Time.

The way Ministers and senior civil servants dealt with Smithers's demands provides an insight into why McCarthyism did not break out in Britain. The lack of a strong select committee system in Westminster made it very difficult for Smithers to operate. While he was isolated in Parliament as an eccentric reactionary, the US political system has powerful Congressional committees which McCarthy was able to exploit for his campaign.

However, Britain was not entirely immune. In May 1947 Clement Attlee set up a Cabinet committee on 'Subversive Activities', the forerunner of the introduction of positive vetting and the 'loyalty programme' of civil servants in 1948.

One of the most disturbing effects was the reaction of private employers and local authorities. Many tried to take advantage of the Cold War atmosphere. In 1949 the John Lewis Group planned to set up political tests as a condition of employment at a time when their workers were demanding higher wages, and only backed down after angry criticism from all political parties and trades unions. But in the following year some local authorities began dismissing political extremists from teaching posts. One Scottish teacher was refused a job because she had a communist husband – even though the school was short of staff. Some, like London County Council, dropped this policy after protests. But others, like Middlesex County Council, continued the ban for several years.[15]

Perhaps the most remarkable incident occurred in 1952. That year the Admiralty removed Commander Edgar Young from their list of retired naval officers. This unprecedented decision was based on the Navy's view that Commander Young's left-wing activities were not 'appropriate' for a naval officer. Even pro-fascist officers who had been interned during the Second World War had not been treated in such a fashion. There were strong protests in Parliament. But the Admiralty stood their ground, and even refused to see a deputation of military and naval officers who wanted to speak on Commander Young's behalf.[16]

Such vetting practices continued through the 1950s, and in industry in particular it was carefully organised. The shipping companies were especially keen to blacklist trade union activists. Documents show that the ship-owners compiled blacklists of seamen and dockers with the assistance of Special Branch officers. One list contained the names of twenty-eight workers who had been involved in an industrial dispute. None of them were Communist Party members and one is now a Labour councillor.

This policy was mainly a response to the growing militancy of the seamen and the increasing radicalism of the National Union of Seamen (NUS). In the past the NUS had been run as a company union. But by the late 1950s the rank and file were growing restless. Masters and captains were still running the ships under the oppressive 1894 Shipping Act, and working conditions increasingly deteriorated. In 1960 the situation was so bad that the disgruntled seamen staged a nine-week unofficial strike.

After the dispute was settled there were fierce repercussions from the ship-owners. Many of the activists were imprisoned. Others, like their leader Jim Slater, who later became General Secretary of the NUS, were simply blacklisted. For fourteen months Slater could not get work. He then complained and eventually, in September 1961, he was summoned before an Employers' Special Committee to present his case. The Committee, in effect, admitted that he had been blacklisted. They told him he could return to work only if he agreed not to involve himself in union activities or provoke unofficial strikes. Slater refused. He told the Committee that the real problem was the appalling conditions on the ships. Much to Slater's surprise, the Committee then backed down and told him he would be able to go back to work.

But the ship-owners had prepared for Slater's return. On 30 October 1961, a marine superintendent of a major shipping company in the north-east wrote a confidential letter to the captain of a ship. It concerned the future employment of Slater and his fellow union activist John Appleby. The letter stated:

'John Appleby and James Slater have been reinstated as unestablished seafarers. You are hereby instructed that you are not to engage either of these two men under any circumstances. If you are presented with either of the above as the only choice, you are at liberty to reject him and obtain a replacement from another port.

This letter is not to be filed. After making a note of the names and discharge numbers, this letter should be destroyed.'

The International Experience

It is often illuminating to compare the experience of British victims of the blacklist with those of other countries. We can contrast, for example, attitudes to vetting in the United States and West Germany.

In 1980 a lawyer representing the firm Jackson, Lewis, Schnitzler and Krumpan spoke at an American management seminar. His brief was industrial relations. On the subject of trade-union activists, his advice was: 'Weed them out. Get rid of anyone who is not a team player. And don't wait eight or nine months. I'd like to have a dollar for every time there is a union organising and the employer says "I should have got rid of that rotten bastard three months ago."'[17]

Such is the reality of present-day blacklisting in the United States. The basic motive for the employer is a clear commercial one: sack the activists and you will remain a non-union firm. That means lower wage costs and higher profits.

However, in the USA there has also been a more fundamentally political purpose behind blacklisting. During the height of McCarthyism in the early 1950s the issue was seen as more to do with basic social and cultural values and ideas than with threats to national security. That is why the industry most under attack was the cinema, particularly its writers. The House Un-American Activities Committee (HUAC) began investigating allegations of communism in Hollywood in 1947. Congressman John Rankin said the HUAC was going to track down the 'footprints of Karl Marx'. He added: 'We are out to expose those elements that are insidiously trying to spread subversive propaganda, poison the minds of your children, distort the history of our country and discredit Christianity.' Rankin claimed that there were 'loathsome, filthy, insinuating un-American undercurrents that are running through various pictures.'[18]

Clearly the purge of 'communists' was about political ideas. It had little to do with security issues. Indeed, there was no documented evidence of a direct connection between the American Communist Party and espionage at any time during the post-war period. This has been confirmed by the anti-Soviet, anti-communist historian Theodore Draper.[19]

The chief targets of the HUAC investigators were people working for the RKO studios in Hollywood, who were suspected of holding communist views because many of their films were about social issues. When Howard Hughes bought RKO in May 1948 the purge intensified. Hughes hired a private investigator to delve into his employees' political leanings. One such agent was Kemp Niver, who compiled dossiers on everyone earning over $1500 a week. He inquired into their political views, how they spent their money and what they did in their spare time. 'The same thing the FBI would do today if they were an unfriendly person,' recalled Niver.[20]

Two victims of the RKO purge were the producer Adrian Scott and director Edward Dmytryk. They were sacked for being members of the 'Hollywood Ten' who, when summoned before the HUAC, refused to co-operate and were jailed for contempt. The HUAC also sent to prison the novelist Dashiell Hammett, author of *The Maltese Falcon* and *The Thin Man*. He was a member of the American Labor Party and an active supporter of many radical causes. He was put under surveillance by the FBI and blacklisted for several years.

They were far from alone. According to David Caute's *The Great Fear*, at least sixty-nine actors, directors and writers were victims of the Hollywood blacklist. And that was a conservative estimate. What was remarkable about the purge was the lack of radical content in the actual films. As the playwright Lillian Hellman said: 'There has never been a single line or word of Communism in any American picture at any time. There has never or seldom been ideas of ANY KIND.'[21] This was acknowledged by Louis B. Mayer, head of MGM Studios, in 1950: 'I have maintained a relentless vigilance against un-American influences. If, as has been alleged, communists have attempted to use the screen for subversive purposes, I am proud of our success in circumventing them.'[22]

But it was the authors and poets of America whom the US security agencies were particularly anxious to silence by using the blacklist. In 1952 the poet William Carlos Williams was rejected for the job of Poetry Consultant to the Library of Congress in Washington. He was not given a reason. But, according to his FBI file, he was turned down on 'security grounds'. A memo to FBI chief J. Edgar Hoover said: 'The applicant was not appointed because of an unfavourable report.' It transpired that the FBI had kept a substantial file on Williams since 1930, when he had written a letter to the radical *New Masses* magazine, enclosing a contribution.

The FBI kept records on as many as 134 writers. Many of the files released under the Freedom of Information Act do not show what the government suspected.[23] But they do reveal that the FBI compiled secret files on virtually every American Nobel prizewinner for literature. The first of these was Sinclair Lewis. His novel *Kingsblood Royal* was described by the FBI as 'the most incendiary book' since *Uncle Tom's Cabin*, because it constituted 'propaganda for the white man's acceptance of the negro as a social equal.' Another Nobel prizewinner, Pearl Buck, was also an FBI target because of her opposition to racial discrimination. Other authors put under surveillance included John Steinbeck, William Faulkner, Ernest Hemingway (because of his support for the Loyalist cause in the Spanish Civil War), Norman Mailer and Elizabeth Hardwick. Occasionally the FBI acted on their 'information', as in 1952 when novelist Graham Greene was almost refused entry to America – he had been a member of the Communist Party for four weeks in 1923 while at Oxford University.[24]

At the height of the Cold War FBI agents even tried to persuade librarians to inform on the reading habits of library users. Such was the paranoia of the time.

The most significant consequence of McCarthyism was that security files compiled at the time were to affect the future careers of many innocent people. One notable casualty was the distinguished journalist Penn T. Kimball, a writer with *Time* magazine and a reporter and editor on the *New York Times*. He was also an adviser to two State Governors and later Professor of Journalism at Columbia University.[25] It was while at Columbia in 1977 that Kimball asked to see his FBI file under the Freedom of Information Act. He had applied out of natural journalistic curiosity, but when the papers arrived he was stunned. The file was incomplete, but the documents clearly showed he was classified as 'a dangerous national security risk'. And the date stamps on the papers matched up with occasions when passports had been delayed and academic grants denied. More serious still were the job offers withdrawn because of the file's contents, including a top level post with the Kennedy administration in the early 1960s.

Kimball found that the dossier was opened in 1946, when he applied for a job with the US Foreign Service after serving as a Marine. It was full of memos from FBI investigators like: 'Kimball was seen drinking beer in the company of communists . . . Kimball was overhead saying something favourable about Tito.' Some informants referred to his liberal beliefs and independent thinking but acknowledged his patriotism. But others saw this liberalism as a sign of communist sympathies. One said of him: 'One of those young fellows who had received too much education and gone communistic or socialistic.'

In fact, Kimball was never a socialist or communist. He was a life-long member of the Democratic Party and a liberal. 'I had always been quite an outspoken individual in terms of whatever I felt was going on in the world,' said Kimball. 'But I had no conception whatsoever that I was really such a dangerous individual as the government files said I turned out to be.'[26]

The FBI dossier contained no hard evidence. It was a mixture of opinion, gossip and third-hand information. The State Department had also doctored the information to make it more damaging. Reports from local FBI agents were summarised and rewritten by State Department officials.

Kimball asked for his CIA file. At first his request was refused. But three years later, on 6 August 1982, the CIA report arrived with the 11 o'clock mail. It was not the best of days. He had just returned from the hospital where his wife Janet had died two hours earlier. He did not open the package until after Janet's burial several days later. But when he did pull out the documents and began reading he was in for a terrible shock. The CIA had also branded his late wife a 'national security risk', a charge based on the fact that Janet Kimball had spent a week's holiday with him in Mexico City in 1956 at the same time as the Soviet spies Alfred and Martha Stern.

Kimball decided it was now time to take on the US government. In 1984 he sued the State Department, the CIA and the FBI, demanding exoneration. It was not until October 1987 that he was finally vindicated. The government agreed to settle the case by admitting that their records 'reflect no information that Penn Kimball, or his late wife Janet, were ever disloyal to the United States.' They also agreed to destroy all the existing files. Kimball had won. But others were not so fortunate. Many careers and lives were ruined by the blacklist.

One of the most tragic cases concerned Sam Jaffe. For fifteen years Jaffe was a top foreign correspondent with CBS and ABC television news as a bureau chief in Moscow and Hong Kong. Like many journalists based in the Soviet Union in the 1950s, he was asked by the FBI to pass on information based on his conversations and meetings with Russians. Jaffe agreed to an arrangement similar to that which the CIA had with at least fifty other journalists, according to a Congressional Committee.[27]

But then the FBI began to ask him for information about his colleagues, and the CIA offered to pay him as an undercover agent. Jaffe refused on both counts. It was then that his troubles began. In 1965 the CIA began compiling negative security reports on him stating that he 'should not be used in any capacity'. In 1969 Jaffe was recalled by ABC to Washington from his Hong Kong post. He decided to resign his job, as he was confident of finding another foreign correspondent position, given his award-winning pedigree. But he was unable to get work. Initial enthusiasm at interviews always seemed to fade. It was only later that he was told privately by employers that he was not hired for 'security reasons'.

For the next sixteen years Jaffe was unable to obtain any regular full-time work. Eventually he took legal action, and in 1979 the truth finally came out. An FBI document from 1969 – the year Jaffe resigned from ABC – was presented to the court. It stated:

'The New York FBI office agreed with the Washington field office that the plaintiff [Jaffe] was an agent of a foreign intelligence agency, and even though the plaintiff may not have considered himself as such, there was no doubt that the foreign intelligence agency regarded him as their agent.'

The FBI also refused to release all of Jaffe's files despite six applications under the Freedom of Information Act. The CIA had sent him a letter in 1975 saying that a careful investigation had cleared him of being an agent for any foreign power, but still the FBI refused to admit their mistake in branding him a security risk.

It was not until 1984 that US District Judge Barrington Parker ruled that the FBI had 'no grounds' for ever having suspected Jaffe.[28] By then it was too late. He was a broken man, spending most of his time helping his wife Jeune in her flower shop. Eventually, in February 1985, he died of cancer. He was 55.

The FBI's defence in the Jaffe case was that 'national security' was involved. But as Arthur Miller, Professor of Law at Harvard University has said:

'"National security" is a convenient catchphrase for doing anything you want to do. You can make your career in national security as Joe McCarthy did in the 1950s . . . You can use national security concerns to justify wire tapping, searching, seizure, maintaining records, denying employment. You can use national security for anything you want because thus far the people who use those words are basically unaccountable. No one has really said: "Now, wait – prove to me there really is a national security interest here – prove it."'[29]

It is true that 'national security' is often given as the reason for personnel vetting. But occasionally the authorities are caught out compiling straightforward political blacklists. This happened in 1984 when it was revealed that the United States Information Agency (USIA) had produced a list of ninety-five people barred from their overseas speakers programme sponsored by the government. The USIA arranges for eminent citizens to lecture overseas about the state of America. But since 1981 the USIA, a government body, had been rejecting so many speakers on political grounds that their staff made a list of their names to avoid proposing them again. At first the USIA denied knowledge of its existence, but it was then forced to conduct an internal investigation. Two months later the Agency admitted the practice was 'initiated and employed by top management.'[30]

Most of the ninety-five blacklisted were Democrats and liberals. 'It was like a fraternity,' said one former USIA official. 'Anyone from a non-conservative persuasion was blacked.'[31] A USIA inquiry later revealed that thirty-eight people had been listed 'for partisan or ideological reasons.'[32] Among those banned were novelist James Baldwin, *Washington Post* editor Ben Bradlee, feminist writer Betty Friedan, liberal economist J. K. Galbraith, poet Allen Ginsberg, consumer campaigner Ralph Nader and Coretta King, widow of Martin Luther King. Also on the list were Jack Brooks, the Democratic Congressman and Chairman of the House Committee on Government Operations, and Gary Hart, the Democratic Senator who was then running for President.

In West Germany the government has incorporated a policy

based on ideology rather than 'security'. In 1972 the Prime
Ministers of the ten West German states, led by the then Federal
Chancellor Willy Brandt, introduced 'Guidelines on the Employment of Extremists in the Public Service'. Known as *Berufsverbot*,
this decree set down the 'basic principles regarding the loyalty to
the constitution of civil service employees.' Essentially, it meant
that 'radical' civil servants of both left and right could be refused
employment or dismissed from the public service. Those covered
by the 'Decree Against Radicals' include doctors, teachers,
lawyers, rail workers, postal workers and civil servants.

Berufsverbot was extended in 1975. The Federal Constitutional
Court – the highest judicial body in West Germany – ruled that
membership of a party which is not banned but is 'hostile to the
constitution' can be a factor when an employee is vetted. Under
the right-wing coalition government of Chancellor Kohl the use
of the decree has been intensified, with civil servants being held
more strictly to their duty of loyalty to the State. According to
government minister Herr Dreesmann, it was 'the obligation of
civil servants to stand up for the constitution of this State based
on the principle of freedom and democracy, always act accord-
ingly and defend it at all times.'[33]

Dreesmann argues that the courts have ruled that only the
German Communist Party (DKP) and the neo-fascist National
Democratic Party (NPD) pursue anti-constitutional objectives.
But in reality members of a whole range of radical groups have
been affected, including the Green Party, the peace movement,
anti-fascists, socialists and even the Church. By contrast there
have been hardly any cases of neo-Nazis or fascists being
disciplined.[34]

The spread of *Berufsverbot* has been immense. Since 1972 some
200, mainly communist, applicants have been refused public
service jobs. The political backgrounds of 3.5 million people have
been put on record with the help of the intelligence services. This
is done by the West German Special Branch (*Verfassungsschutz*) or
'The Office for the Protection of the Constitution' as the government calls it. The courts had also handed out disciplinary
measures, including dismissal, in 6,779 cases based on the
Berufsverbot law.

The postal workers were among the biggest casualties. In
October 1981 Hans Peter was dismissed from his job as a post
office engineer after thirty years of service. He was a member of
the German Communist Party (DKP). After several hearings and

trials he was sacked for being 'a security risk' to the Federal Republic. The court acknowledged that he was not a security risk 'at that time', but could be at some unspecified, future 'time of crisis'.

For Wolfgang Repp the process was much longer and even more painful. He had joined the Post Office as a 15-year-old apprentice in 1965. In 1974 he was elected as a local union official with an overwhelming majority. That year there was a wave of industrial action in the Post Office, particularly in Repp's home town of Frankfurt. In April 1975 he was summoned to a *Berufsverbot* hearing and questioned about his membership of the DKP – he had stood as a Communist Party candidate in the 1972 and 1974 local elections. This interview provoked a remarkable response – his colleagues, the union, MPs, and thousands of people demonstrated in protest. The proceedings were dropped.

However, in 1978 the *Berufsverbot* process was renewed, and Repp was offered continued employment, but on a lower grade. He refused. The case did not come to court until 1984, and Repp was not allowed to summon over fifty witnesses he had lined up in his defence. During the case he was suspended on a reduced salary. He was then asked to resign from the DKP and to give up his activities on the party's behalf. Again he refused. Eventually, in December 1984, another court ordered his reinstatement. But after five weeks back at work his suspension was reimposed. Further hearings are still pending, thirteen years after the first inquiry.

Herr Dreesmann, the government minister responsible for the postal service, said of the Repp case:

'For years he [Repp] has been an active supporter of the DKP. This means that he has violated his duty to be loyal to the constitution . . . Herr Repp could end the disciplinary proceedings if he voluntarily retired from the civil service. Since he is not prepared to do so, and is not willing to meet the obligation to be loyal to the constitution, the disciplinary proceedings must continue which may end with a decision to dismiss him.'[35]

Herr Repp said:

'They could find nothing to hold against me in the way I did my job as a postman, so they tried to discriminate against me on account of my political opinions. I was labelled as an enemy of the constitution, although no details have ever been given to me of exactly where and when I am supposed to have breached the constitution . . . I am not against the constitution of the Federal Republic of Germany. I am for its full implementation. We are a long way from that at the moment. The *Berufsverbot* against me is an example of that.'[36]

The most remarkable *Berufsverbot* case showed both its authoritarian nature and how the government uses it. In 1982 Dr Jochen Vollmer, a Protestant cleric from Baden-Württemberg, swore his oath of loyalty to the constitution. But he then added a rider that the State had no right to decide on 'the ultimate truth' that bound his conscience. The *Berufsverbot* machine was soon cranked into action and Dr Vollmer was promptly sacked. This is the reason given by the Freiburg court:

'An applicant who puts his duty to be loyal to the State under the proviso that his duties as an official should be compatible with his religious convictions does not – in the court's opinions – offer the guarantee that he will at all times actively support the free democratic basic order.'

Such a decision clearly shows that the West German government has been using *Berufsverbot* to stifle and suppress political dissent by non-communist radicals. That is the ultimate danger of all political vetting operations.

But at least in the United States and West Germany the process is relatively open. In America you can obtain your FBI and CIA files through the Freedom of Information Act. In West Germany the *Berufsverbot* is enshrined in law and can be fought through the courts. In Britain even that official acknowledgement is denied to people. Instead, vetting is shrouded in unnecessary secrecy. A secrecy which this book hopes to break down.

1

Vetting Our Servants: The Civil Service Since 1945

Positive Vetting

There are two systems of vetting in the Civil Service. They are 'positive' vetting, which is overt, and 'normal' or 'negative' vetting, which is secret. Here is an example of the first system.

In 1985, a young but senior civil servant was questioned about an official who had once worked for him and was undergoing a positive vetting investigation. 'I was appalled to be asked,' he said, 'whether he had strong views on nuclear disarmament. I asked why: I was told that those with "strong moral views" on the subject had shown themselves "ready to betray secrets".' He took this to be a reference to Sarah Tisdall, who was sentenced to six months in gaol in 1984 after passing documents to the *Guardian* which showed how the government planned to handle the public relations aspects of the arrival of cruise missiles at Greenham Common. He was also told that such people were ready to 'commit sabotage' – an apparent reference to the Greenham Common women.

He continued: 'I then asked whether this meant that officers who favour disarmament would fail their positive vetting; whether, in the light of Clive Ponting,[1] the PV-ers would now ask whether officers have strong views on accountability to Parliament; and whether, in the event of a unilateralist Labour government, they would weed out those *opposed* to unilateral disarmament. No answers, of course. And I was left wondering if something would now go down on *my* record.

'This is not the first sign,' he added, 'that this government, with the complicity of compliant senior civil servants, has deliberately blurred the distinction between the threat of espionage or sabotage externally directed, against which the Security Services are properly deployed, and internal political opposition. GCHQ was the other obvious instance.'[2] But it is disturbing to see that this has now been constitutionalised to this extent.

'I must say that, more generally, I find it increasingly difficult to co-operate with PV officers whose social, political and moral values seem to date from the mid-1950s. (My PV-er was ex-Indian Army, and showed it!) It is repulsive to find oneself almost unconsciously disguising radical views, tacitly agreeing that homosexuality is *prima facie* evidence of unreliability, accepting stereotypes of the "loony left" as potential "enemies" and so on.' He said he was 'frankly, frightened' of entering into what he called 'sensible discussions' with his investigating officer.

Positive Vetting, or 'PV', was introduced in 1952. Under the system civil servants and others working directly or indirectly for the government are investigated to see whether, for reasons that can be loosely summed up as 'sex, money and politics', they would be vulnerable to blackmail and could be trusted. The official criterion for PV is the likelihood that the individual concerned would have 'regular and constant access to Top Secret Information.'[3] Originally estimated to cover just 1,000 officials – mainly those working on the atom bomb project – the system now embraces about 66,000 civil servants and an identifiable number of other people working for companies included on what the Ministry of Defence, whose Personnel Security Investigating Unit (PSIU) is responsible for vetting throughout Whitehall, officially calls 'List X'.

The enormous expansion of the number of people caught in the PV net reflects the way in which more and more information is now classified. It also shows how a system, once installed, submits to the bureaucratic tendency not only to overclassify information, but to pry and control in a way which, spurred by the political climate, can be abused. But the PV system does not always work. It did not catch Geoffrey Prime, for example, the most spectacular spy in recent years. It did not catch Michael Bettaney, the MI5 officer who offered secrets to the Russians, nor did it save the government from the embarrassing case of the Queen's personal police officer, Commander Michael Trestrail.

Officials about to be investigated for PV clearance are asked to fill in a confidential form about their family and their political proclivities, and to give the names of two close personal friends (these are questioned, along with other referees such as a former employer). The official is asked whether he or she has any relatives in communist countries or has ever visited or lived in those countries. The official is then asked to answer 'yes' or 'no' (and if 'yes', to elaborate) to the following questions:

Have you ever been a member of or in sympathy with, any communist, Trotskyist or fascist organisation in the United Kingdom or elsewhere?

Have you ever had any connection with any group or movement associated, or in sympathy, with a communist, Trotskyist or fascist organisation?

Have you ever been a close associate of a person who to your knowledge is or has been, a communist, Trotskyist or fascist?

Have you ever been a member of, or in sympathy with, any organisation (not covered in previous questions) which advocates or practises unconstitutional activities in pursuit of its political activities?

In their answers, officials are advised to 'take into account not merely your own belief but also the opinion which is generally held of the organisation or persons in question, even if you do not endorse that opinion.'

One of the 700 or so PV investigators, who are employed by the Ministry of Defence but deal with all departments (other than the Foreign Office, GCHQ and the armed forces, which investigate themselves) described his work in this way: 'A file comes to us from whichever government department . . . We may get a file from say, British Telecom and that is passed through the Headquarters of PSIU to one of our team.' The team leader 'will draw the investigating officer's attention to any particular aspects. He may say; "I want you to probe the nationality of this man's wife," or whatever it may be.' The subject is interviewed for perhaps three hours. Investigations are then carried out, going back ten or fifteen years, to past employers and so on. 'So I would see, having seen the referees and the subject, as appropriate, school masters, university teachers, bursars or colleges, moral tutors at universities, all his employers, including part-time and moonlighting jobs, all his seniors in the Civil Service. If the senior, as very often happens, does not know an awful lot about him, then I see a colleague of the same grade. The senior may well say; "This chap has lunch every day in a pub with so and so . . ." Whenever we talk to referees and to all sorts of people we always say, "Now who else knows this chap? Who knows his wife? Who knows his family?"'[4]

So there are three stages to positive vetting: the security questionnaire completed by the subject, a field investigation including interviews with the subject's references, and a check on the files of M15 and the Special Branch (which, in turn checks the police criminal records). Within M15, C branch, responsible for 'protective security' will check with F branch, responsible for 'domestic subversion'. If there is anything adverse on record about the subject, a recommendation will go back to the Ministry of Defence and the individual's own department saying 'refuse vetting'.

'Normal' Vetting

This is the process that was, presumably, applied to Peter Staghniewski, an economics graduate of Edinburgh University. In 1978 he applied for a job at the Tropical Products Institute (TPI), part of the Overseas Development Administration (ODA). In December of that year he was offered a position as Researcher on the recommendation of the Civil Service Selection Board. He was told that the offer was subject to formalities – 'the satisfactory completion of enquiries into age, health and other matters.' A month later, he was informed that he would not get the job at all. The letter of rejection was sent on the very day on which he was being shown around the TPI laboratories at Culham, being told what kind of work he would be doing and being given advice about living accommodation. When he asked what had gone wrong he was told: 'We are not able to explain the nature of a rejection since information is given to us in confidence.' Staghniewski tried to find out why he had been turned down. The Civil Service Commission, responsible for overall recruitment, said that as far as it was concerned there was no problem – if his references had not been satisfactory, it told him, he would not have been invited to an interview in the first place. He was told by Edinburgh University that his former teachers and supervisors had not been approached. He approached his MP, Ted Fletcher, who, in June 1979, was informed by the ODA that the decision 'has nothing to do with the fact that his [Staghniewski's] father was Polish [he became a naturalised British citizen in 1954].' He remains none the wiser. He assumes that the decision may have had something to do with his politics. He had been a member of the Labour Party in 1974 and 1975, and a member of CND in 1975. He had participated in three 'student grant' marches, and a 'rent strike' at his university in the autumn of 1975. Was that the problem?

The NV process covers many thousands of people – it is impossible to be precise about the total number for, unlike positive vetting, it is covert. The PV system applies to senior public servants, those most likely to have access to highly classified information and those in particularly sensitive jobs. The tentacles of NV spread far and wide. This so-called 'purge procedure' was disclosed to Parliament in 1948 (though it began earlier). It has become a blanket system covering not only the Civil Service but also defence companies and other public corporations. It includes MPs' Research Assistants and even the government's Youth Training Schemes.[5] The NV process concentrates not so much on 'character defects', but on political associations and any evidence of past 'subversive' activities. It covers young people, whose careers may be blighted at the very start of their working lives, without their knowledge, and without them ever knowing why.

'Normal' vetting involves a sweep through the Criminal Records Office as well as a check with Special Branch and MI5 files to see that, as Whitehall puts it, there is 'Nothing Known Against' the individual who is being investigated. Potentially damaging information would include associations with organisations deemed to be 'subversive'. A significant elision is made here; subversion (of which there is, of course, no definition in law) is made synonymous with criminality. In other words, the government – any government – is free to classify a threat of open debate as a threat to national security. It can also use this argument to avoid having to answer awkward questions from independent-minded employees.

NV closely resembles the covert vetting processes carried out in the private sector, which we describe in later chapters.

The History of Positive Vetting

At the beginning – and for us that means the start of the Cold War – there was something unBritish, almost distasteful, about vetting. Everything was rather relaxed, informal and presumptuous; personal contacts and the Old Boys' Network was the key to recruitment. McCarthyism was alien to Whitehall's instincts and culture. This attitude was later to produce hypocritical and ironic results even at the sensitive heart of secret government, namely, the Security Service.

Both Sir Roger Hollis, Director-General of MI5 between 1956

and 1965, and his deputy, Graham Mitchell, backed away from witch-hunts. Both were accused after their deaths of having been Soviet agents (the former by Chapman Pincher and Peter Wright, the latter by Nigel West, alias the Tory MP for Torbay, Rupert Allason). Many of Kim Philby's M16 colleagues believed he was a victim of US-style McCarthyism when he was asked to resign after the defection of Burgess and Maclean. This attitude can, of course, be interpreted another way. Roy Hattersley, Labour's Deputy Leader, put it thus: 'There is a terrible truth about the security services; I mean, we believed for twenty-five years that if you were an old Etonian, you could not be a traitor.'

Discounting the allegations that a group of M15 officers plotted to destabilise the Wilson government of the mid-1970s, Lord Annan, the former university administrator and commentator on broadcasting, observed: 'There is another check on the operation of the Security Service: the establishment itself.' Despite the pressure from Beaverbrook and others on the right, there was no McCarthy witch-hunt in Britain. No dons were dismissed; no Angleton-inspired mole hunt (Angleton was the CIA's counter-espionage chief) within the security services that blighted many brilliant careers inside the CIA took place. Over the years only twenty-five civil servants were moved from their posts or – rarely – dismissed, whereas 25,000 in America were sacked or resigned. In Britain,' he claimed, 'the common law maxim of guilt having to be proved prevailed.' Churchill, who took a relaxed view of the Burgess/Maclean defections, had one eye on the US and McCarthyism when he said, in the coronation night broadcast in 1953: 'Parliamentary institutions, with their free speech and respect for the rights of minorities, and the inspiration of a broad tolerance in thought and its expression – all this we conceive to be a precious part of our way of life and outlook.'

Clement Attlee, who introduced the 'purge procedures' and the positive vetting system to Britain in the 1940s, partly as a result of pressure from the US, explained his attitude in Parliament after he had left office: 'We are pardonably annoyed at being in-structed by a beginner like Senator McCarthy. The British Labour Party has had nearly forty years of fighting communism in Britain, and, in spite of war and economic depression, the communists have utterly failed.'

What Attlee did not tell the Commons was that he had already set up a Cabinet Committee on 'subversive activities' in May

1946. The exercise was not prompted by Parliamentary pressure, but by the defection of a Soviet cypher clerk to Canada eight months earlier. Igor Gouzenko, who had sought asylum in Canada, provided information which led to the arrest of Dr Alan Nunn May, a British scientist who worked on the joint atomic power project at Chalk River, Ontario, during the Second World War.

The Attlee government also set up a committee of officials under Sir Edward Bridges, then head of the Civil Service, and including Sir Percy Sillitoe, head of M I5, John Winnifrith, head of Personnel at the Treasury, and Graham Mitchell, also from M I5. Although covert purging of civil servants had already begun, this committee marked the end of Whitehall's somewhat haphazard attitude towards vetting and the start of a new approach. In March 1948, Attlee announced to the Commons that the government had decided on a new 'purge procedure'. Under this, any civil servant deemed to be associated with communist or fascist organisations would be summarily removed from posts related to 'national security', and, if no alternative posting could be found, dismissed. Suspicion alone was a ground for transfer or dismissal, and it was not necessary for the government to prove any act of disloyalty had actually taken place. In the course of the Commons exchange following his announcement, Attlee stated: 'The general principle covers all those in service of the State where secrecy is involved.'

Scientists working on the atomic programme were divided; some accepted the new procedures as an 'unpleasant necessity', others asked why the Official Secrets Act was not sufficient. They warned that 'the new measures establish a dangerous precedent which allows persons to be penalised for associations and opinions not proscribed by law.' But, in an official statement, the British Atomic Scientists' Association said that there was a consensus among them that the new regulations should not be extended beyond the Civil Service or institutions directly involved in work on 'important military secrets'. They added, in a clear reference to the US: 'It is difficult to avoid the conclusion that even in friendly countries, individuals employed in universities and in industry have been penalised on political grounds.' It could lead, they warned, to a 'serious change for the worse in the intellectual atmosphere of our schools and universities to the great detriment of coming generations.'[6]

Individuals were not, and are still not, allowed to see the

evidence on which accusations were based. Officials do have a right to appeal to a Board of 'Three Wise Men', but their authority has gradually diminished, to the point that they are now little more than a rubber stamp. The purge procedure has been extended to cover more and more people (see Introduction), and those who fall victim before they have been formally accepted for a post are not told the reasons for the withdrawal of the job offer. They can only guess.

In the first year, seventeen cases came before the Three Advisers: in six no action was taken, and the rest were transferred to 'less sensitive work'. Six others decided not to take their cases to the appeal board. Over the following seven years, 167 civil servants were removed from their posts. Twenty-five of them were dismissed, twenty-four resigned, eighty-eight were transferred to non-sensitive work, and thirty-three were reinstated. In the US, 9,500 federal officials were sacked after the 1945 purge, and another 15,000 resigned. All were named. In Britain none were named. However, the real number of British officials barred from promotion or not recruited will never be known. Although Attlee did not say so, almost all of the officials affected were communists, or were alleged to be so. 'The security authorities were overjoyed when they eventually found a fascist in one of the service departments. It made the whole operation look even- handed.'[7]

The Extension of Vetting in the 1950s

In February 1950 the scientist Klaus Fuchs was arrested after he confessed to passing atomic secrets to the Russians. MI5 knew he was a communist and a potential security risk when he became a British citizen eight years earlier. Britain needed all the scientists it could get to work on its own atom bomb project, a project which, ironically, was kept secret from the public and was jealously opposed by the Americans. But Fuchs's arrest led the US to suspend all co-operation with Britain in developing nuclear weapons. Washington pressed Attlee to adopt a more aggressive purge procedure and to introduce a system of positive investigation into the private lives and political affiliations of officials involved in secret and sensitive work. So, just as Gouzenko's defection led to the first purge procedures – negative vetting – Fuchs's spying prompted Attlee to order his Cabinet Committee on 'subversive activities' to draw up proposals for a system of positive vetting.

An official committee under John Winnifrith was set up in April

1950 to initiate a PV system in Britain. Its report was ready by November, and was sent to the Prime Minister. This report remains classified, but Sir Norman Brook, then Cabinet Secretary, wrote to Attlee:

'The "positive vetting" which the report recommends involves primarily a change of attitudes and methods on the part of the departmental establishment authority concerned who "having first made sure that the security service has no adverse record of the candidate, should itself make a conscious effort to confirm his reliability." This is to be achieved partly by a check of personal records which will be kept in fuller form than hitherto, and partly – in a minority of cases – by specific inquiries undertaken by the security Service.'

According to Brook, the report suggested that the total number of posts for which PV would be required was unlikely to exceed 1,000. By 1982 the number of posts for which PV clearance was required stood at 68,000, a figure which the Security Commission itself said that it regarded as excessive.

US pressure continued. A tripartite conference on security with British and Canadian officials was arranged in June 1950, a few days before the start of the Korean War. American anxiety was fuelled by the defection of Dr Bruno Pontecorvo, one of Klaus Fuchs's colleagues at the Harwell Atomic Research Establishment, in September 1950, and the defection of Burgess and Maclean in May 1951. The British themselves were concerned about the communist threat in France. They called a meeting with senior US and French officers in Paris to discuss the problem. In the midst of the conference the British delegation learnt, to its embarrassment, that Burgess and Maclean had fled to France and were probably on their way to the Soviet Union. The US called a second conference with Britain and Canada in July 1951. A month later, another report from the Winnifrith Committee said that the proposed PV system would not be limited to people working on the atomic bomb project. It 'would have to be extended to all persons holding vital posts in government service.'

The Attlee Cabinet finally agreed to the principle of PV in October 1951. The system was introduced by the new Conservative administration in January the following year. The process was instituted, and two years later PV investigators were formally asked to look out for 'serious character weaknesses of a kind which might make a person liable or subject to blackmail.' In 1955, Prime Minister Anthony Eden appointed a Conference of

Privy Councillors to look at 'security procedures now applied in the public services'. This time the initiative was provoked by public confirmation that Burgess and Maclean were in Moscow and by a Commons debate on the whole affair. Setting up a committee, or asking the Security Commission to carry out an inquiry, has been the consistent, almost pavlovian, reaction by a government faced with an embarrassing incident or disclosure. The Conference completed its work in 1956, but a White Paper stated that it was not in the public interest to publish the full report. It said that in future emphasis should be placed on character defects – 'failings such as drunkenness, addiction to drugs, homosexuality or any loose living' – as well as communist sympathies. But the report also made clear that the Communist Party was being kept under close surveillance (we now know from the former MI5 officer Peter Wright that in 1955 MI5, in an operation called 'Party Piece', entered the flat of a rich CP member and photographed the files of the party's entire membership), as were those regarded as sympathetic to it. 'One of the chief problems of security today,' the White Paper said, 'is thus to identify the members of the British Communist Party, to be informed of its activities and to identify that wider body of those who are . . . sympathetic to communism.' It went beyond the concept of guilt by association, effectively stating that suspected officials were guilty until proved innocent. 'In deciding these difficult and often borderline cases,' the Privy Councillors said, according to the White Paper, 'it is right to continue the practice of tilting the balance in favour of offering greater protection to the security of the State rather than in the direction of safeguarding the rights of the individual.'[8]

The then Home Secretary, Major Lloyd George, told the Commons that 'with the assurances that the government intend to do all that they can to prevent their policies and procedures impinging unfairly on human rights, the House can rest content with the findings of the inquiry.' It was a presumption those outside Westminster were not prepared to make. MI5 and the police Special Branch had been steadily increasing their surveillance of political and industrial activists: their targets were no longer confined to espionage. The security guidelines and the government's defence of them led to the setting up of the Campaign for the Limitation of Secret Police Powers, whose supporters included the historians G. D. H. Cole and A. J. P. Taylor, the sculptor Henry Moore, the playwright Terence Rattigan, and Peter Ustinov. The Campaign uncovered many cases of discrimination against left wingers who were neither government servants nor communists (for example the ICI solicitor John Lang, whose case is discussed in Chapter 3). At the annual conference of the Association of University Teachers in 1957 there was a fierce debate on whether lecturers should give information to MI5 about their students.

The practice continues. In the present climate there is widespread concern about the use to which information, not only about students, but also about lecturers themselves, can be put, especially in light of new criteria for funding universities. And today it is also questionable whether safeguards against the political vetting of teachers and other employees of local authorities, including social workers, are sufficient.

In the mid-1950s, a man who became one of the country's leading industrialists and has since been knighted was forced to leave the Civil Service because MI5 said his wife was a communist. In a letter to the *Economist* magazine at the height of the *Spycatcher* affair, Aubrey Jones, a senior minister in the Eden and Macmillan governments, said: 'In 1955 I was appointed Minister of Fuel and Power. While occupying that post I was told that an official whom I held in high esteem could not be promoted because, so it was said, his wife was a communist . . . He was, quite clearly, unfairly treated. I'm fairly sure that he was never told why his career had been blighted, and the public service lost a very able official.' Some years later, as a Minister of Supply, Mr Jones said he was confronted by a similar case. He was told that a technologist at the Royal Aircraft Establishment at Farnborough had to be removed from classified work because he had started reading the *Daily Worker*.[9]

The Security Reviews of the 1960s

Two spy scandals – the discovery of the Portland spy ring in 1961, which ended in the arrest of George Blake and the civil servants Ethel Gee, Frederick Houghton, Gordon Lonsdale and Peter and Helen Kroger, led the government to set up yet another inquiry into security procedures. The result was the 1962 Report, much of which also remains secret, drawn up by a committee chaired by the Law Lord, Lord Radcliffe. The Report came up with a number of specific recommendations, notably that PV investigators of public servants should be carried out every five years (a procedure which soon became a victim of bureaucracy – there were, and are still, not enough investigators to carry out the job properly or consistently). It noted, however, that 'traces of communist association' were usually derived from intelligence records, rather than from field inquiries by PV investigators which tended, if anything, to concentrate more on character defects. Radcliffe recommended 'more frequent resorts to the purge procedure in marginal cases.' But it was the tone and intellectual contortions of the Report that were revealing. 'For the sake of brevity,' it said, 'we have followed the common practice of using the phrase "communist" throughout to include fascists.' Radcliffe acknowledged that 'it is not the policy of the [Communist] Party, according to our information, to give its members, open or secret, any encouragement to undertake espionage . . . The Party is treated as one of a number of political parties seeking the votes of the electorate.'

It also stated, however, that the 'sources from which the main threat to security come . . . are subversive organisations in this country, of which in current conditions the most formidable is the Communist Party of Great Britain, with its fringe of associated bodies and sympathisers.' Radcliffe also pointed a finger at the Civil Service unions. 'We understand,' his report said, 'that there is no evidence that the communists have made any exceptional effort to gain control of these unions . . . No evidence has been brought to our knowledge that communist union officers, whether serving on a paid or unpaid basis, have been detected in any form of espionage. Nevertheless, we regard this presumably deliberate massing of communist effort in Civil Service unions as most dangerous to security, however one defines it.' Therefore, it continued, it would be reasonable for any Whitehall department to 'deny access to or refuse to negotiate (either by correspondence or face to face) with a named trade union official whom it had reason to believe to be a communist under the definition used in the purge procedure.'[10] Again, the officials charged would not be allowed to know the nature of the allegations against them – or their families – and so would have no way of knowing whether they were accurate or fictitious.

The unions seemed to be resigned to accepting the Radcliffe Committee's arguments. One of its victims was Cyril Cooper. In 1963, Cooper, General Secretary of the Society of Technical Civil Servants (now the Institution of Professional Civil Servants) was barred from taking part in negotiations with Whitehall departments on behalf of his members. He appealed to the Three Advisers, telling them that he had left the Communist Party many years previously. He was asked about contacts with communist diplomats – he replied that he occasionally had drinks with them at receptions. He had had one with a Czech Labour Attaché, accompanied by another man who turned out to be a Czech journalist, at a TUC reception.

Cooper was reminded that he had been to Moscow and had gone to the Bolshoi Theatre several times. He recounted afterwards that he was asked, if he was interested in opera, why he had not gone to Vienna. He was then asked if he and his wife had artistic friends; he confessed that he had. To which a questioner on the board immediately asked him: 'Aren't all of those long-haired people of one political persuasion?' Cooper said he doubted that they were. The questioner disagreed. His appeal was turned down.

The next major review of security procedures was set up twenty years after Radcliffe – in 1982.[11] Yet again, it was a review prompted by an embarrassing incident; this time the allegation by Chapman Pincher in his book *Their Trade is Treachery*, that the former Director-General of MI5, Sir Roger Hollis, was a Soviet agent. The Report of the Security Commission chaired by Lord Diplock, a Law Lord – was not asked to look at Pincher's allegation; it was a broad analysis of the state of security procedures. It was, in many ways, an enlightened document. It began, however, by saying that although 'the external threat from Soviet intelligence services' remained undiminished since Radcliffe, 'the internal threat has altered considerably.'

It continued: 'The threat offered by the Communist Party of Great Britain has probably diminished as a result of the fall in the number of its members and the disillusionment of many of them with Soviet policy since 1961 in invading Czechoslovakia and, more recently, Afghanistan. The fall in CPGB membership, however, has been accompanied by the proliferation of new subversive groups of the extreme left and extreme right (mainly the former) whose aim is to overthrow democratic Parliamentary government in this country by violent or other unconstitutional means, not shrinking in the case of the most extreme groups from terrorism to achieve their aims. Membership of individual groups is small but, for the most part, active and conspiratorial. They might well seek to make public information injurious to the interests of this country, not at the behest or for the benefit of any foreign power, but simply to harm this country itself, whether by causing a rift between it and its allies or otherwise, and by these means to weaken its defences against the overthrow of democratic government here by force.'[12]

We quote this at length since it remains the state of the art of the security establishment's analysis. But the extracts of the Diplock Report which were published did not conclude that the PV system should be extended. Indeed, it said quite the reverse: that too many posts were subject to PV clearance, an implied criticism which was all the more significant given that the report also observed that 'character defects rather than disloyalty for ideological reasons or subversive tendencies have been the cause of all known cases of disclosure of information to hostile intelligence services' that had occurred since the 1962 Radcliffe Report. As we have already noted, negative vetting, or the purge procedure, was, and is, directed primarily at 'political subversion', whereas positive vetting is aimed at character defects. The Diplock Report recommended that the rule whereby all officials of the rank of Under Secretary or above were automatically subject to PV clearance should be abolished.

For the first time, the Commission also recognised the tendency of the vetting bureaucracy, like any other, to expand, and noted that this expansion led to less, rather than greater, efficiency. The PV process could take as long as three months. Not only was it expensive, it could also lead to the loss of valuable recruits, especially those with specialised qualifications.

One of the criteria for positive vetting is the likelihood that the person concerned would have regular access to highly classified information.[13] The fact that 66,000 posts, including 44,000 in the Home Civil Service, are subject to the PV system shows the extent to which information is classified. The Diplock Report made it clear that the Security Commission itself believed that too many documents were over-classified. It called for a 'thorough review' of Whitehall's classification system and added: 'Where the need to prevent an unauthorised disclosure is only temporary, as may often be the case outside the fields of defence and secret intelligence work, consideration could also be given to the possible advantage in the originator of such classified material recommending a period after which de-classification would be automatic.'

Decisions about whether to stamp documents 'Confidential', 'Secret' or 'Top Secret' are taken by officials, as well as ministers (officials are naturally cautious, and ministers, worried about being embarrassed and having to explain decisions to an informed public, welcome this caution).

The role of officials was made clear by the Ministry of Defence in evidence given to MPs. Ewen Broadbent, Second Permanent Secretary at the Ministry, was asked by the Labour MP, John Gilbert:

'What precise instructions do members of your Department receive in respect of their duties when they classify documents? Am I right in thinking the security classification of documents is determined by the originators of the document?'

Broadbent: 'Yes.'

Gilbert: 'He has total discretion at the level at which he classifies subject to the guidelines you have given him.'

Broadbent: 'Yes.'[14]

So the system is maintained, shielded from any sceptical scrutiny.

Character Defects

In a significant passage, the Security Commission said that in view of changes in the law which meant that homosexuals with an unconcealed and stable relationship were now less vulnerable to blackmail, homosexuality should not be an absolute bar to PV clearance. But it chose its words carefully. It said: 'In the Home Civil Service, male homosexual inclinations or relationships should not necessarily be treated as an absolute bar to PV clearance, but should be dealt with on a case by case basis, paying particular attention to whether the way in which the individual has indulged in his homosexual tendencies casts any doubt upon his discretion or reliability.' But this should not apply, it said, to the Diplomatic Service or the armed forces, where homosexuality remains a disciplinary offence.

Two months after the Diplock Report, Commander Michael Trestrail, the Queen's Police Officer, responsible for her personal protection, resigned following press reports that he had indulged in secret and promiscuous homosexual activities, mostly with prostitutes. The Security Commission, under its new Chairman, Lord Bridge, another Law Lord, was asked to conduct an investigation. He found that the Trestrail case showed that the criterion for PV – the protection of classified information – was both too narrow and too imprecise. Trestrail could have been blackmailed, not to leak secret documents to a potential enemy or subversive, but to give details of the Queen's movements. Bridge praised Trestrail's efficiency and 'unswerving loyalty' to the Queen. There had been no breach of security and security had not been put at risk, he concluded. He criticised the reaction of the Commissioner of the Metropolitan Police whose immediate decision after the scandal had broken was to impose blanket PV on the whole of the police Royalty Protection Group. 'PV,' Lord Bridge pointedly remarked, 'is no substitute for efficient personnel management.'[15] The clear message was that the PV system, which had in any case been applied only belatedly to Trestrail, was a blunt, mechanical instrument, when what had been needed were imaginative interviewers and a proper understanding of the man.

The shortcomings of the PV system were dramatically highlighted in the case of Michael Bettaney, which led to an indictment by the Security Commission of senior management of MI5. Bettaney was arrested in September 1983 and found guilty at an Old Bailey trial, most of which was held in camera, of ten counts under the Official Secrets Act, including sending a secret MI5 assessment of the KGB's order of battle in Britain to an official at the Soviet embassy. He received a twenty-three-year jail sentence for what some of his former colleagues believe amounted to a nervous breakdown. He had retained his PV clearance despite bouts of heavy drinking, in public as well as in private, and despite an offer to resign after a conviction for drunkenness in October 1982. He had had a particularly stressful period of duty in Northern Ireland, and the Security Commission commented that his heavy drinking should have provided 'the most significant pointer to his instability of character' as far back as 1980. Had an investigation taken place in 1982, it added, 'we think it highly likely that a decision would have been taken to withdraw his PV clearance.' His colleagues reported his drinking to their superiors, but all the warnings were ignored. Late in 1982 Bettaney was posted to MI5's Counter-espionage Section. The Security Commission's report suggests that if something had been done to help him, Bettaney would not have done what he did. In the course of an unprecedented attack on MI5 management, the Commission said that 'the very fact of the service's comparative isolation makes it all the more important that those responsible at the higher levels of management should maintain a self-critical attitude.'[16]

Successive governments have repeatedly said that positive vetting is not meant to catch spies: it is meant to catch all those who could be vulnerable or who might be tempted to spy. It has had some notable failures. John Vassall, the Admiralty clerk blackmailed by the KGB, passed his PV when he was posted to naval intelligence after his tour of duty at the British Embassy in Moscow in 1956.[17] Geoffrey Prime, the GCHQ official who spied for the Russians between 1968 and 1978, passed all his vetting examinations – at one stage towards the end of his GCHQ career he was made a Personnel Security Supervisor, responsible for drawing up reports on other GCHQ staff. He was arrested in the course of an investigation by the West Mercia police on sexual attacks on young girls. He then confessed his espionage activities to his wife, Rhona, and it was she who told the police. In November 1982 he was sentenced to thirty-five years in prison for espionage, and three years for sexual assaults.

The Security Commission inquiry into the affair, published in May 1983 (as Official Command paper 8876), said that 'no fault can be attributed to those responsible for the operation of the PV system in relation to Prime.' It added that GCHQ did not see any scope for significant improvement by prescribing new criteria to govern the type of person recruited for PV investigating work. 'We do not,' the Commission said, 'see how any investigator could have been expected, purely by question and answer, to penetrate the calculated mendacity of Prime . . .'

GCHQ, like MI5, vet themselves and do not rely on the Ministry of Defence like other government departments. GCHQ was reluctant to criticise its own procedures. However, MI5 suggested in the wake of the Prime affair that PV investigators should come from a wider background, at the same time proposing that former Special Branch officers – as opposed to ordinary police officers – should be recruited for the task.

The truth is that, in a democratic, pluralist, society there can be no absolutely foolproof way, short of subjecting those who work in the security and intelligence agencies to intolerable pressures, of preventing determined spies. According to the Security Commission, 'the really important revelations were based on information in his [Prime's] memory.' The Commission, which has, over the years, produced thoughtful, even sensitive reports (and, as a result, has been attacked by the more hysterical elements of the media and the House of Commons) mentioned that Prime had sought psychiatric advice for severe depression in

1972, yet had not reported this to the GCHQ authorities. It suggested that in future GCHQ staff should give their consent to Civil Service medical advisers having access to their doctors' reports. It accepted that this 'would not catch cases such as Prime if the individual failed to give information about his visits to a psychiatrist.'

The Commission also proposed a system of random exit searches at GCHQ sites. But it acknowledged that 'such procedures would be unlikely to frustrate the trained and determined spy.' Management, at GCHQ and elsewhere in the Civil Service, should promote an atmosphere of trust, respect for their workforce, and high morale (including good pay and conditions), an atmosphere of collegiality – devoid of unnecessary secrecy. Enlightened personnel management would help to frustrate or prevent disloyalty provoked by resentment, and thus decrease the number of people susceptible to blackmail. It could even help to reduce the opportunities of 'spies' motivated by ideology.

Not long after Prime was gaoled, eight young RAF servicemen based at GCHQ's listening post at Ayios Nikolaos on Cyprus were arrested under the Official Secrets Act. They were charged with a number of security offences relating to documents and tapes collected and processed at the base. Most of the trial was held in camera, but the official claims, which the prosecution failed to prove, included the allegations that thousands of Secret and Top Secret documents had been leaked, and that the servicemen had indulged in sexual orgies described in part of the trial which was held in public as 'splash parties'. In October 1985 they were all acquitted by a jury. The embarrassment of this acquittal led to four separate investigations into security procedures, as well as an inquiry under David Calcutt QC into the behaviour and role of RAF Provosts at the Cyprus base (there were allegations that the servicemen had been subjected to unacceptable treatment under interrogation). But the lessons of the affair – the trial was mainly held in camera – seemed clear enough: do not put young servicemen, some of them in their teens, in charge of protecting potentially sensitive material in an unrewarding, even boring, job in a foreign country and a strange environment without families and without sufficient recreational facilities. They were vulnerable, and vetting their backgrounds was irrelevant to the potential temptations of the lonely Cyprus base. Even if the story given by the military authorities had been true, the existing vetting procedures, whether positive or negative, did not prevent, indeed could not have prevented, the situation. Sensitive and imaginative personnel management could have done so. And there was another factor: the Ministry of Defence attempted to give the impression that the documents involved were all highly sensitive, so as to create an aura of mystique and to impress the jury. As one commentator has said: 'A gigantic amount of information and paper is produced daily in signals operation rooms – and every bit is highly classified, whatever its intrinsic importance.'

Early in 1985, Rex Davie, the Cabinet Office official responsible for security and personnel, told Peter Jones, Secretary of the Council of Civil Service Unions, that the government had decided to reduce the number of PV posts by 2,000 (out of a total of 44,000 in the Home Civil Service). He refused to identify the posts involved 'on security grounds'. But there is no evidence that the government has implemented any of the other recommendations of the 1982 Security Commission Report or accepted its general tenor. What evidence there is suggests the reverse.

In 1987, a number of senior civil servants approached their union, the First Division Association (FDA). They were concerned that, after having openly declared their homosexuality, they were refused PV clearance although they were either celibate or had stable relationships.

Richard X volunteered the information that he was a homosexual. As a result he was told that he would not, after all, be promoted to the post he had previously been offered as a Private Secretary in a Minister's office.

Michael Y, a government lawyer, openly acknowledged his homosexuality in his PV questionnaire. He was told that he could not be promoted even though his Permanent Secretary said he had complete trust in him and had no doubts about his discretion or reliability. He was told that he could be 'vulnerable to pressure' because he had yet to find a partner and his lifestyle was not 'settled'. He was also told that assessments made about him had to be 'subjective'.

The FDA was concerned that, while in theory homosexuality was no bar to PV clearance, the impression was being conveyed that if an official admitted to being gay, clearance would not in practice be given. This would only discourage openness – officials would wonder whether honesty really was the best policy – and this would in turn damage security. Michael said that his colleagues had told him that he should never have admitted his homosexuality. Yet trust and truthfulness, according to those officially responsible for PV policy, is more important a consideration than 'extreme political views'. When it was put to him by the Commons Defence Committee in 1983 that 'surely the crucial element is the desire to conceal . . . that is what makes a man blackmailable, is it not?' Ewen Broadbent replied on behalf of the Ministry of Defence: 'That is the key point.'[18]

One of the ugliest episodes involved Sir Maurice Oldfield, former head of MI6. Oldfield is recognised as one of the most successful, thoughtful and imaginative heads the secret intelligence service has had. Mrs Thatcher brought him out of retirement in 1979 to co-ordinate security and intelligence in Northern Ireland, where different factions – MI5, MI6, the RUC and the Army – were squabbling over policy at a time when the British government wanted to forge better links with the Republic. Oldfield believed that a priority was to try and get the nationalist community to support the security forces in their struggle against terrorism. He cultivated Catholic priests, influential opinion leaders in that community. A smear campaign against Oldfield soon began, suggesting that Oldfield was a homosexual. Many people, including Oldfield himself, believed the campaign to have been originated by MI5 and the RUC, both of which resented Oldfield's appointment and his policies. According to Colin Wallace, a former Army Information Officer in the province who had links with MI5, Oldfield 'had a "Mr Clean" approach in Northern Ireland, particularly against assassination plots and the dirty tricks war.'

In 1980, when he was already showing signs of the stomach cancer which was to kill him early the next year, Oldfield was asked by Sir Robert Armstrong, the Cabinet Secretary, whether there was any foundation in the rumours. Oldfield confessed to having lied in previous PV investigations: he had had homosexual relationships, but only at school and at university in Manchester more than forty years earlier. He said he did not know whether he was a homosexual or a heterosexual. In any event, he had had no physical relationships for a long time and no homosexual encounters since he was a student.

He left Northern Ireland in 1980, a broken but an honest – perhaps, too honest – man. The allegations against him were revived in 1987 in the book, *Traitors: The Labyrinths of Treason*, by Chapman Pincher. They were denied by Oldfield's lifelong friend, the former MI6 officer, Anthony Cavendish, in *Inside*

Intelligence, a book the government tried to ban. Mrs Thatcher told the Commons that Oldfield could have been a security risk, though there was no evidence that this was so. On the contrary, Armstrong said later that Oldfield's patriotism and loyalty were beyond question.[19]

This cautious, some might say intolerant and crude, approach towards 'character defects' is accompanied by an increasingly aggressive attitude towards 'political' views. The original concern – that officials might be tempted to help a hostile power through espionage – is becoming dangerously confused with the democratic right of any citizen, including civil servants, to question the policies of the government of the day or to be sympathetic to groups which challenge the status quo. Questioning, even free thinking, appears to have become a synonym for disloyalty.

Successive governments, not just the Thatcher administration, have also confused loyalty and the interests of national security with the threat of embarrassing leaks. For example, in 1970 a special Committee on Protective Security under Lord Helsby, a former Head of the Civil Service, warned that 'individual Trotskyists, Maoists, or anarchists might use protected information in such a way that would further their political aims or give such information publicity if they thought that this would embarrass or damage the reputation of the government.' Greater openness and greater trust – and, presumably, greater confidence by the government in its own policies – might have been better advice.

Instead, Whitehall – where, in any case, most leaks are authorised either directly or indirectly by ministers (as in the notorious Westland affair) – is heading in the opposite direction. The expanding and increasingly vague definition of 'subversion' and of views deemed 'political' creates an atmosphere of suppression and fear, unrelated to what should be a clearly defined PV procedure. 'Subversion' is regarded as a prime reason for vetting. But the charge of 'subversion' is made against individuals who have already been vetted, but who question government policy or disclose information they know is being suppressed for political rather than genuine security reasons. Defenders of the system say that when PV investigators ask subjects for their views about current political controversies or personalities, they are interested not in the opinions expressed, but in how they are expressed. The implication is that what matters is not the individual's particular preferences, but how enthusiastically – one way or the other – they are expressed. One cannot help wondering, in the present climate, just how credible this explanation is.

There are three areas where this extension of vetting has become particularly evident: GCHQ, the Ministry of Defence and the nuclear industry where Civil Service practice merges into the private sector. We shall examine these in the next chapter.

2

'Political Views': The Civil Service and the Nuclear Industry

Although evidence is largely anecdotal, and the officials involved do not want to be named, the indications are that a pattern is emerging and that civil servants are increasingly being asked about their attitudes towards specific contemporary political issues – a long way from being asked only about sympathies with extreme, or even 'subversive' groups. In response to a questionnaire sent by the FDA to its members in 1985, one senior civil servant (not in the Ministry of Defence) was asked: 'If Mrs Thatcher told you, would you press the button to launch a nuclear attack on Moscow?' In the course of an interview another was asked his opinion about the coal dispute: the PV investigator described the miners as 'toe rags'.

In 1984 official, classified, instructions to Whitehall officials conducting interviews – not only those responsible for positive vetting – advised that: 'Attitudes to authority can be assessed by asking questions about past relations with others of higher or lower status, and attitudes towards traditionally respected groups and institutions, and towards commonly despised social groups.' They added: 'Some areas need carefully phrased questions to elicit relevant answers; for example, judgement can be assessed from questions about controversial issues with which he is acquainted, e.g. student relations with the police, or the situation in Northern Ireland.' (They also said that 'young women can also be difficult to assess accurately, for example, if they turn the interview into a social occasion.')

Staff at GCHQ, the government's intelligence-gathering centre based in Cheltenham, are being asked overtly political questions during their five-yearly positive vetting interviews. Questions have included what they think of Mrs Thatcher's performance as Prime Minister, and their attitudes towards Arthur Scargill, the miners' leader, the Labour MP Tony Benn, the Greenham Common women and the situation in Northern Ireland.

Asked in the Commons by the Labour MP Tam Dalyell to explain the instructions given to PV investigators, Mrs Thatcher replied that 'they have discretion . . . to discuss and put questions on topics of current political interest with a view to ascertaining whether the subject has, or may be likely to have, extreme views or associations of a kind which might suggest that he or she would not be suitable for employment in a post which required regular and constant access to highly classified information, the improper disclosure of which could be damaging to the security of the state.' Familiar phraseology here. The Prime Minister went on to explain that 'such questions have no other purpose than that, and the expression of views which may not coincide with those of the government of the day has no bearing on or relevance to an investigation unless it appears to the investigator to go beyond the normal expression of dissent in a Parliamentary democracy.'[1] She also said that questions about an official's attitude towards herself were unnecessary and inappropriate and, if they had been asked, had been without her knowledge or consent. She had given instructions for her views to be made clear to PV investigators.

Her lengthy Parliamentary answer raised the question whether a Prime Minister can intervene directly on other matters relating to the PV procedure. It also raises the question of what could be included in the rather loose phrase about the 'normal expression of dissent' in a Parliamentary democracy and what could be excluded by it.

The political climate of the 1980s has been reflected by a series of warnings against civil servants, in their capacity as members of trades unions, criticising government policy. Department of Health and Social Security officials, in a circular issued in 1985, warned managers of local offices 'how thin the dividing line is between sympathy for the claimant's circumstances, which is allowable, and criticism of government policy, which is not.' One official had written to a member of the public who had asked about a heating allowance: 'I regret that this situation has arisen but is entirely due to central government legislation.' That, said the DHSS, overstepped the mark. In October 1983, civil servants working in the Royal Ordnance Factories were told that their campaign against privatisation was in breach of the Ministry of Defence code of conduct, and at the ROF plant in Blackburn, management read out extracts from the Official Secrets Act to Transport and General Workers' Union convenors. Civil servants contributing to union journals in the Inland Revenue, the Manpower Services Commission, the Department of Transport and the Property Services Agency have all been threatened with disciplinary measures for opposing government policy on issues – including privatisation – which directly affect their terms and conditions of employment.

The Thatcher government's broadening of the definition of what is 'political', the vague way in which it describes the term and its limited definition of a trade dispute, notably in the 1982 Employment Act, which describes it as one relating 'wholly or mainly' to issues such as pay and conditions, has for the first time led Civil Service unions, traditionally moderate and apolitical, to set up political funds.[2]

Pressure has also been put on individual civil servants unconnected with union activities. During the 1983 General Election, one civil servant, Anne Marek, was instructed by her department, the Welsh Office, not to give any active support to her husband, the Labour candidate for Wrexham. Initially, she was told she could not attend the count of votes on election night. A year later, a woman who worked in a job centre at Colchester, a garrison town, was warned that she would risk losing her job unless she gave up her role as an official of her local CND branch.[3]

GCHQ and the Unions

Political vetting need not be a formal system like West Germany's *Berufsverbot*, whereby public-sector employees have to pledge absolute loyalty to the state above personal conscience and opinion. It can be done by stealth, through unspoken pressure. Dennis Mitchell, a senior GCHQ official who opted for early retirement after the union ban, has warned that the ban and the resultant divisions in the workforce could lead to staff being 'in a sense political employees'. The workforce has traditionally reflected a cross-section of opinion, but that could change because of the attitude of management, which would mean that new recruits would be forced to 'toe the line'. In future, the only people who will be recruited, or will even want to be candidates, will be those who accept working in an environment where unions have been banned.

At the height of the controversy over the union ban at GCHQ, Mrs Thatcher suggested there was a basic conflict of interest between membership of a national trade union and loyalty to the

State. There was an 'inherent conflict of loyalties', she told union leaders at a meeting in 10 Downing Street on 23 February 1984, between membership of a union and the defence of national security. However, there is no evidence that membership of a trade union has ever caused any damage to GCHQ's operations. The small group of staff who refused to give up their union membership by the government's deadline of 1 March 1984 included those who had worked day and night through the Falklands conflict – and were collectively praised by the Queen for their work – and other crises. (Ironically, Geoffrey Prime resigned his union membership when Russian linguists at GCHQ failed to get the extra allowances they were asking for.)

GCHQ staff are 'indoctrinated' – specially vetted – before having access to signals intelligence which is classified not only Top Secret, but with the added codeword, UMBRA. This will have the desired effect if staff accept that they are working in Britain's national interest against real or potential threats. But if they are asked to pay a price – including giving away the right to free association to a union of their choice, a fundamental right in a society whose relative freedom they are working to defend – then something must be wrong. 'The government expects absolute total loyalty,' one GCHQ official said after the imposition of the union ban, 'but it doesn't give it back.'

A disturbing and unprecedented example of how positive vetting could be used as a political weapon occurred in November 1987. Mike Grindley, a Mandarin Chinese linguist at GCHQ, was stripped of his security clearance and suspended from his job for having spoken to journalists without authority. In March 1988 he appealed to the Director of GCHQ, Sir Peter Marychurch, but to no avail. Three days after their meeting he was told to inform GCHQ personnel officers if he intended 'to be away from home overnight or longer.'

The charges made against Grindley were that he had publicly referred to there being 7,000 civilian staff at GCHQ, that he had revealed that he was a Chinese language expert, and that he had failed to report immediately to GCHQ security officers the fact – which he himself volunteered – that he had contacts with 'members of communist and Trotskyist organisations.' This was a reference to a casual conversation with a *Morning Star* journalist at the Irish Conference of Trade Unions in Cork in the summer of 1987. He was also charged (and GCHQ management made it clear that, for them, this was the last straw) with disclosing extracts of a classified circular to a journalist. Another charge was added later; that he had contributed to a BBC radio programme without authority.

The figure of 7,000 GCHQ employees and Grindley's area of expertise had already been repeated many times in the media, and the number of staff at GCHQ had been referred to openly by MPS. The circular Grindley had shown to the journalist did no more than echo the scepticism, voiced in a Security Commission report published in 1983, about whether a system of random searches would frustrate a trained and determined spy. In any case, there was a long tradition that individuals like Grindley – one of the GCHQ employees who continued to defy the ban on unions imposed in 1984 – could speak about general staff conditions and that classified documents could be disclosed in a sanitised form. Grindley also made the specific point, in an interview for the BBC Radio 4 series, *My Country Right or Wrong*, banned by the government in 1987, that he was not prepared to discuss his work or GCHQ operations.

All these incidents, with the exception of the radio interview, occurred *before* Grindley was invited to attend a top secret conference in the United States as an official GCHQ representative.

For Mike Grindley, who was 50 when he was suspended, the withdrawal of his PV clearance seemed to be the end of his career. All staff at GCHQ must have this clearance. Grindley was chairman of the GCHQ Trade Union group when the action was taken against him. He was widely respected and had played a prominent part in the campaign to restore trade union rights at the intelligence-gathering centre. He had made significant and innovative contributions to GCHQ's working practices. His activities did not touch on national security – and GCHQ management never gave any evidence, never even argued, that he had endangered national security. But he was told that his superiors could 'no longer rely' on his 'good sense' and 'discretion' on 'security matters'.

GCHQ staff are asked to 'spy' on each other – that is, they are asked to report to their supervisors or personnel officers any strange behaviour or contacts with 'subversives' or 'potential subversives'. They are still threatened by the polygraph, or lie detector – first proposed, albeit tentatively, by the Security Commission's report into the Prime affair published in 1983. Since 1987, they have been asked to give permission to the Civil

Service Medical Adviser to approach their doctors to pass on medical reports considered relevant to their ability to carry out their work (under the initial proposal, blocked by the Civil Service Unions and the British Medical Association, GCHQ staff would have been obliged to grant permission for their doctors to pass on all medical records). Staff will also be asked whether they support alternative medicine.

Vetting in the Civil Service is being extended mechanically – to 'neighbourhood enquiries' and to the investigation of an individual's bank accounts as well as medical records. Since 1987, supervisors at GCHQ have been asked to fill in forms about their staff every year (see opposite). Telephones are sometimes tapped during positive vetting investigations.[4] The withdrawal of PV clearance has also been used as a weapon to force GCHQ staff to fall into line with government policy on issues such as the union ban, which have nothing to do with national security. Without such clearance, they would lose their jobs.

The MoD and CND

In February 1984, Sir Clive Whitmore, then Permanent Secretary at the Ministry of Defence (now Permanent Secretary at the Home Office), chaired a meeting of senior officials to investigate ways of dealing with civil servants and members of the armed forces who were known to disagree strongly with aspects of government policy. Minutes of the meeting record that an agreement was reached that Ewen Broadbent, then Second Permanent Secretary, 'would investigate what guidelines existed for managers on the policy to be adopted towards servicemen and civil servants who belonged to or sympathised with organisations promoting policies fundamentally contrary to those of the government, but which were neither extreme right or left wing.'[5] Ministers said the meeting had been provoked by a scientist at the Royal Signals and Radar Establishment at Malvern, Dr Dennis Longstaff. He had distributed circulars about a meeting protesting against nuclear armaments after permission to stick up posters had been refused. He was an active member of Scientists against Nuclear Arms (SANA) as well as of CND. He said at the time: 'I am employed by the Ministry of Defence and I believe in defence, but I don't believe certain aspects of defence policy are right.' The Ministry said: 'It is axiomatic that civil servants should serve loyally the govern-

Security Appraisal Form

(To be completed annually in respect of all PV postholders)

Details of postholder

Name (Mr/Mrs/Miss/Ms) .... Grade ....

Division/Branch etc ....

How long have you supervised the Postholder in his/her post? From .... To ....

	please tick

1. Are you satisfied with the Postholder's attitude to security?   Yes ☐ No ☐

   If NO, please explain why ....

   ....

   ....

2. To the best of your knowledge, has he/she shown any evidence of

   a. Sympathy or contact with subversive organisations of British or foreign origin   a   Yes ☐ No ☐

   b. Misuse or illegal use of drugs   b   Yes ☐ No ☐

   c. Drinking to excess   c   Yes ☐ No ☐

   d. Unreliability/dishonesty/untrustworthiness/indiscretion   d   Yes ☐ No ☐

   e. Financial difficulties   e   Yes ☐ No ☐

   f. Conduct liable to lead to vulnerability to blackmail (eg sexual or other)   f   Yes ☐ No ☐

   g. Illness, including mental illness, which might cause defective judgement   g   Yes ☐ No ☐

   If YES please give details ....

   ....

   ....

3. How well is the postholder known to you outside working hours?   Well ☐ Slightly ☐ Not at all ☐

4. Are you aware of any other grounds for doubting the postholder's suitability for continued PV clearance?   Yes ☐ No ☐

   If YES, please give details ....

   ....

   ....

   ....

5. Please provide a brief pen picture of the postholder's character ....

   ....

   ....

   ....

   ....

Signed .... Grade .... Location ....

Name in block letters .... Date .... Telephone Extension ....

ment of the day and if a civil servant feels he cannot do that, he should resign.'

Longstaff was disciplined, not for being a member of CND, but for misusing the internal postal system. His case had occurred the previous September, five months before the meeting chaired by Whitmore. That meeting discussed much broader issues, going far beyond CND membership. The top MoD officials were suggesting (though it was later denied) that any civil servant who was a member of the Labour or Alliance parties, or even suspected of being one, could be removed from their jobs since those parties opposed the Trident missile system, for example. Whitmore, according to his spokesmen, decided that it was time to see whether individual managers should be issued with new guidelines. It immediately became clear that this meant giving management and senior armed forces officers more discretion. Two days after details of the meeting inside the MoD had been made public, it was disclosed that servicemen and women would in future be prohibited from actively participating in political demonstrations in or out of uniform, in subtle, but significant, changes to the Queen's Regulations which had just been agreed by the government. An amendment to paragraph J5,581 of the regulations says that in future 'regular service personnel are not to take an active part in the affairs of any political organisation, party or movement' – this last phrase was new, and reflected concern about the growth of such groups as CND and Greenpeace, which do not fit neatly into the description of 'political organisation or party'. It should be said that these restrictions should apply equally to right-wing, as to left-wing, political groups. The question remains whether single-issue pressure groups like Greenpeace are 'political' in the sense traditionally applied to restrictions on public servants. The Ministry of Defence suggested that the word 'movement' should be deliberately left ill-defined. 'You will know it when you see it,' is how one spokesman put it.

There was evidence that servicemen were becoming increasingly concerned about the discretion given their commanding officers over whether they had the right to join organisations or attend meetings when off duty. Mrs Gwyn Gwynthoper, of the voluntary organisation At Ease, which was set up in 1974 to counsel servicemen, said that the situation seemed to be approaching the point where servicemen 'may not hold a political opinion or associate in any form, or allow any form of expression.' She said that off-duty sailors at the nuclear submarine base at Faslane on the Clyde and soldiers at Greenham Common had been arrested by military police simply for talking to peace campers. They had neither expressed support for the demonstrators nor argued with them, but had asked about their views and how long they were going to remain in the camps.

The First Division Association, representing about 8,000 top officials, had already expressed concern that CND membership was an automatic bar to positive vetting clearance. The Cabinet Office told the FDA in July 1983:

'One of the objectives of the movement (i.e. CND) has remained over the years the abandonment by this country of all nuclear weapons, irrespective of what disarmament measures are or are not being taken by any other country. Given that we have a nuclear deterrent policy in the United Kingdom, it is clear that a possible conflict of interest and/or conscience could arise, which could put a considerable strain upon the loyalties of persons with access to classified information and particularly those who are employed in nuclear-related areas.'[6]

Significantly, perhaps, this letter was written just a month before the then Home Secretary, Leon Brittan, sanctioned MI5 telephone tapping of a leading CND activist.[7]

The FDA made the point that this 'conflict of interest and/or conscience' was surely not confined to members of CND. Most civil servants in the course of their careers would find themselves advising on and assisting with policies which conflict with their personal views. It gave as examples supporters of Shelter working on housing policy, of the National Council for Civil Liberties working in the Home Office, of the Child Poverty Action Group working on social security. The way to avoid this, the FDA suggested was by 'sensitive personnel management', including, if appropriate, transfer between departments, rather than using PV procedures.

'Positive vetting (like the Official Secrets Act) is designed to protect the security of the realm and not to prevent unsuitable postings. Departments should be able to avoid putting square pegs into round holes without having to blight the career prospects of individuals, whose loyalty to the state is in no way in question, by denying them positive vetting.'[8]

Two episodes highlight a problem where there should not have been one. Firstly, Clive Ponting, the Ministry of Defence official acquitted of Official Secrets Act charges in February 1985, had

earlier asked to leave his department. Secondly, a number of
FDA members had reported that they had been asked by PV
investigators about their attitudes towards CND even though
their jobs had nothing to do with defence-related work. One
official at the Department of Health and Social Security said that
he left his interview with 'an uneasy feeling that CND is bracketed
with subversive groups.' This was after the Cabinet Office official
responsible for vetting and security matters, Rex Davie, had
given the impression to Civil Service union leaders that Whitehall
'definitely does not regard CND as a subversive organisation.'
They were told that CND membership was not 'in itself' a bar to
PV clearance, but that much would depend upon 'the nature of
the post and the degree of commitment which the individual
shows towards CND.'

Another experienced civil servant working in a 'home' department reported after his third PV review in eighteen years that he
'came away with the firm impression that had I declared
membership of or an interest in CND's activities, I would not have
got the job envisaged.' He said that there appeared to be a new
emphasis on politics – he was uneasy about the way he had been
drawn into disclosing how he voted.

The Nuclear Industry and Public Criticism

Richard Shackleton joined the UK Atomic Energy Authority as an
Administrative Trainee in 1981 after studying politics at the
London School of Economics. He was positively vetted. During
the interview, the PV investigator went through the ritual
questions, including whether he had studied Marx, whether he
believed what he had read there, and what he thought of the
government's nuclear policy.

In February 1983, Shackleton was put in charge of the Archives
and Documentation Department at the UKAEA's plant at
Dounreay, on the north Scottish coast, where the authority has
built a prototype fast-breeder reactor and plans to install a large
reprocessing facility. Browsing through some papers, he discovered a document which, he says, disclosed how an MI5 officer
from London had organised a 'security exercise' which dealt with
the potential threat of terrorist attacks on nuclear installations.
Local military personnel and police officers attended the exercise.
But early in May 1983, just before the General Election,
Shackleton says he found a set of contemporary files. They were

stored in taped-up boxes in a special section of the archives room. One of the documents was a memorandum from MI5 (complete with the agency's famous postal box No 500) with the question: 'Is there anyone in your establishment working for the UKAEA who is hostile to the government's policy on nuclear weapons?' (This was at a time when the government was seriously concerned about the degree of support CND was attracting. The Ministry of Defence had set up a special unit, DS19, which obtained information about CND collected by MI5.) According to Shackleton, virtually the entire workforce at Dounreay was enthusiastic about the development of nuclear power, though many were hostile to the government's nuclear weapons policy.

The research and development of nuclear power – and Anglo-American co-operation in this sensitive, secretive area – provided the first impetus, and was the first focus, for the introduction of vetting and purge procedures in Britain during the Cold War. American concern, and British embarrassment, about the atom spies Nunn May, Fuchs and Pontecorvo, and Donald Maclean, the Foreign Office diplomat – were important factors.

The significance of the Anglo-American partnership was explicitly recognised by the Security Commission in its 1982 Report: 'The threat in the case of UKAEA and BNFL [now British Nuclear Fuels plc] is not only from the intelligence services of the Soviet bloc but also from nations anxious to acquire know-how to enable them to enter the nuclear weapons field.'

It goes on: 'In accord with an undertaking given to the United States, all employees of UKAEA . . . and BNFL are subject to a form of vetting known as full record check under which the employee has to fill in a written questionnaire; but although they are concerned with the peaceful uses of nuclear energy and have but little access to TOP SECRET information, an agreement with the United States requires that persons with actual or potential access to SECRET ATOMIC information must hold PV clearances: any reduction in the extent of PV would therefore need to be negotiated with the United States Government.'[9]

All 50,000 employees in the nuclear industry – indeed, in the electricity supply industry as a whole – are vetted. Checks are also made on contractors working on nuclear sites, including Sellafield, where about 4,500 contractors are employed. Staff directly involved in civil nuclear research, in senior managerial posts and who work with nuclear fuel, including plutonium –

estimated to be about 10 per cent of the total – are also subject to full-scale PV clearance. All Ministry of Defence staff working in the nuclear area also have to have PV clearance '[In] the nuclear area . . . everybody is PV-ed on recruitment. That means, of course, quite a lot of young people, young apprentices and so on, are being considered for PV and the rejection rate in that area at least is probably rather above average.'[10] The expansion of the Atomic Weapons Research Establishment at Aldermaston to accommodate the government's new nuclear weapons programme (including the Trident missile system), where about 7,000 staff are employed, has put severe pressure on the MoD's Personnel Security Investigating Unit. What the United States Atomic Energy Commission calls 'plutonium workers' are also subjected to special checks.

The development of nuclear power, sometimes described as the plutonium economy, has special implications for civil liberties, beyond the vetting of the staff employed in the field. 'Plutonium,' one American writer has said, 'provides the first rational justification for widespread intelligence gathering against the civilian population.'[11]

This is not the place to consider the wider aspects of the threat to civil rights posed by nuclear power. But the issues were summed up in the Report by the Royal Commission on Environmental Pollution on 'Nuclear Power and the Environment.' In the context of the possible threat to nuclear materials from blackmail or terrorism, it expressed concern about the role of the police and the Security Service, what it called 'the secret surveillance of members of the public and possibly of employees who may make "undesirable" contacts. Activities,' it said, 'might include the use of informers, infiltrators, wiretapping, checking on bank accounts and the opening of mail' of members or suspected members of extremist or terrorist groups. These activities, it went on, would be 'highly likely and indeed inevitable.' It added: 'What is most to be feared is an insidious growth in surveillance in response to a growing threat as the amount of plutonium in existence, and familiarity with its properties, increases; and the possibility that a single serious incident in future might bring a realisation of the need to increase security measures and surveillance to a degree that would be regarded as wholly unacceptable, but which could not then be avoided because of the extent of our dependence for energy supplies.'[12] Or simply because of the sheer quantities of plutonium produced, stored and transported in Britain. 'We have at this moment,' the Energy Secretary, Cecil Parkinson, said in 1987, '500 years' supply of plutonium in this country.'[13]

The UK Atomic Energy Authority police were given new powers in 1976. Under legislation passed that year, they can carry arms at all times, enter premises at will, and have the power to arrest on suspicion. They are used by BNFL – the only company with a police force established by legislation – and are not directly accountable to an elected body or a Minister.

The nuclear industry is unique because of the physical threat which it represents. There are other ways in which it has been treated, and treats itself, as special. The excuse for secrecy (employees of the Central Electricity Generating Board, British Nuclear Fuels plc, and the UK Atomic Energy Authority are asked to sign a declaration warning them of the provisions of the Official Secrets Act) has turned the industry in on itself. It has shielded itself from criticism and public concern. An internal staff rulebook circulated to Sellafield workers not only reminds them of the Official Secrets Act but advises them 'to report immediately any incident wherever which appears to indicate a breach of fidelity.'[14]

A dangerous habit to which many governments and bureaucracies succumb, but which is particularly prevalent in the nuclear industry, is that of regarding criticism as hostility, and hostility as subversion. And 'subversion' often means no more than 'leaking', or disclosing information which conscientious scientists regard as a matter for public concern. A number of cases illustrate this point.

Trevor Brown, a scientist who worked on the production of Britain's H-bomb in the 1950s, was brought in to Aldermaston in 1961 to improve safety conditions there. Twelve years later, he was elected a Liberal Councillor for Berkshire. Encouraged by his colleagues at Aldermaston, he spoke out about contamination, but the management at Aldermaston applied pressure to try and silence him, and he was accused (wrongly) of using office equipment for his council work. Eventually, after a decade of public questioning about the safety facilities at Aldermaston, especially on the plutonium line, the government agreed to set up an official inquiry, under Sir Edward Pochin. The inquiry largely upheld Brown's argument that safety precautions were not adequate. In 1981, three years after the inquiry, Brown publicly criticised safety conditions on a BBC *Newsnight* pro-

gramme. It was then made clear to him that he had no future at
Aldermaston, and he was offered a job in Scotland. He resigned,
saying: 'I wonder whether I would not have done better had I
been an upper-class spy rather than a working-class patriotic
scientist.'

John Taylor, a chemist at Sellafield, now owned by British
Nuclear Fuels plc, wrote a study in 1980 suggesting that it was not
necessary to discharge so much radioactive effluent into the Irish
Sea, and other reports proposing changes to reduce the contamination of workers and improve safety conditions. A year
later, his reports were criticised by management on the grounds
that they were 'difficult to understand' and that he had misinter-
preted data. In 1982 he was transferred to a different job. When
he threatened to go public, he was transferred to a post
responsible for records which required security clearance. He
then resigned, saying: 'I am forced to conclude that honestly
seeking to perform an honest job is not required.'[15] He applied
unsuccessfully for fifty jobs.

Other people have lost their jobs because they have spoken out
openly about the risks of nuclear power.

Dr Ross Hesketh, a physicist at the Central Electricity Generating Board's research laboratories in Berkeley, Gloucestershire,
wrote to *The Times* in 1981 drawing attention to the (1958) Anglo-
American Mutual Defence Agreement, which enabled Britain to
export plutonium from its civil reactors for use in American
nuclear weapons in exchange for US material, including enriched
uranium. He said that the British government was misleading the
public by saying that British plutonium was not being used, or
intended to be used, for US weapons. Hesketh was told that he
had breached his contract, which stated that CEGB staff must
conduct themselves 'in a manner consistent with the proper
performance of their duties and the maintenance of good
working relationships.' He was dismissed, according to the
CEGB, after refusing to be transferred to a new job, which
Hesketh described as appropriate for a first-year research student. A few months later, in October 1983, he was reinstated after
the intervention of his union, the Electrical Power Engineers'
Association. Under the terms of the agreement, he was prevented from making any further comment in public. He left the
CEGB and is now teaching physics at the University of Bayero in
Nigeria.

This is vetting of an open and crude kind. It certainly has

nothing to do with politics, or with threats to national security. But, as far as the government and the nuclear industry are concerned, these scientists are the kind who are embarrassing – who 'leak' – and who should be weeded out, if possible, by the prior vetting procedures.

There is, indeed, a thin and blurred line between vetting to protect genuine operational secrets and promote trust and efficiency, and political vetting, which is intended to bully or weed out people who have different values or views to those of the government. The line is even more blurred in a climate of political intolerance, of populist ideology, with a weak Parliament and a strong executive, when no clear distinction is made between the State – the wider interest of the community – and the narrower interest of the government of the day. Mr Justice McCowan told the jury in the Ponting secrets case in 1985 that 'the interests of the State' were the same as 'the policies of the organs of government'. In his statement on 'the duties and responsibilities of civil servants in relation to ministers' issued shortly after Ponting's acquittal in February 1985 and repeated shortly before he retired in December 1987, Sir Robert Armstrong, the Cabinet Secretary, said that the civil servant's 'first duty is to his or her Minister.' Traditionally, the broader concept of 'the public good' has been held to be more important. In 1950, Sir Edward Bridges, then head of the Civil Service, argued that officials were concerned with the 'continued well-being of the State' – an implied distinction between the State and the government of the day. Later, Sir William Armstrong, Edward Heath's Civil Service head, spoke of the officials' concern for 'the common good'. The code of conduct for American federal officials still asks them to expose corruption wherever it appears and 'to put loyalty to the highest moral principals and to country above loyalty to persons, party or government department.'

In January 1988, Mrs Thatcher imposed a three-line whip which killed an attempt by Richard Shepherd, a Conservative backbencher, in a private member's bill, to reform the Official Secrets Act. Neither she nor the Home Secretary, Douglas Hurd, explained why they so disliked the measure. It was clear that one of the reasons was that a civil servant, charged with disclosing official information, would have been able to mount a 'public interest defence' – that the disclosure would reveal crime, or 'abuse of authority'.

The history of the positive vetting system has been marked, as most security scandals have demonstrated, by bureaucratic incompetence. Because the criteria of the investigations are so vague, and there are no clear guidelines, the personal and political views of the PV investigators – former middle-ranking armed forces officers, policemen, and colonial officials – become important, especially when they are shared by senior management. There is evidence that this is now happening. Positive vetting is a system, ostensibly with a specific and rational purpose, which is wide open to abuse.

It is impossible to judge how many potential misfits or unreliable people have been prevented by vetting from holding positions of trust which they might have betrayed. What one can say is that the PV system has often failed: Prime slipped through the net; Bettaney, a very different case, passed the tests. But there have been other victims of PV and the climate of which it was both a symptom and a cause. One was Alan Turing, the brilliant mathematician whose work at the government Code and Cypher School at Bletchley Park helped to save many thousands of lives during the Second World War. His eccentricities – and his homosexuality – were accepted because of the special circumstances which prevail in wartime. But in 1954 – two years after PV was introduced in Britain – he committed suicide after being hounded by a bureaucracy which paid no attention to his unique contribution to the war effort or his special gifts.

PV has produced a breed of investigators with a view of the world and a set of values which do not reflect the reality and diversity of British society. This can lead to almost farcical decision-making processes. For example, there was recently a lengthy debate within the Ministry of Agriculture's Personnel Branch about whether to give PV clearance to a woman who had just been promoted. She had a baby, but was not married. This was considered to be a potential security risk, but only a minor one since her marital and parental status was not publicly known.

It can also lead to unhealthy, unacceptable, and ultimately dangerous situations. The system's original objective was openly declared and was fairly uncontroversial. PV was a crude filter, but one, nevertheless, with a defined purpose. Now it is becoming a different kind of weapon, developing, it seems, by stealth, in a particularly British way. The criteria are becoming vaguer. Management or security officials, as in the Mike Grindley case at

GCHQ, can assert that an employee is 'unreliable' in matters of 'security'. Such claims are open to broad and subjective interpretations.

The system must become more open, and it must be subjected to outside scrutiny. PV investigators, and those who appoint them, should be ultimately accountable to a Parliamentary Select Committee, made up perhaps of members of both the Commons and the Lords. The question 'Who Vets the Vetters?' is more than a rhetorical cliché: it is a serious question that has not been adequately addressed.

3

Defence Companies: Reconciling Security and Justice

'You say Ministry of Defence vetting takes place in the private sector, but I have no knowledge of it.'
John Higgins, Personnel Director of MEL,
a division of Philips Electronics Ltd,
Computer Talk, 23 June 1986.

Iwan Graves has always wanted to be a skilled printer. Before leaving school in the summer of 1985 his best subjects were art and design, and he spent much of his spare time working at technical drawing. When he was offered an interview for the job of print room assistant at Scicon Ltd, a computer company based in his home town of Milton Keynes, he was delighted. But at the interview he was rather surprised to be asked whether he had any 'hang-ups' about nuclear disarmament, if he had any political views or was a member of any political party. Graves was not remotely interested in politics so he replied 'no' to all three questions.

That afternoon, 9 September 1985, he received a phone call from Hazel Smith, a Scicon Personnel Officer. She offered him the job. Graves was ecstatic. It was his first full-time job. He was 17 years old. His main work in the print room involved collating, binding and glueing technical catalogues and booklets about the company. It was a training job at the low salary of £3,500. But Graves saw it as vital experience which he could use to move up to higher skilled, better-paid work in the future.

For the first three months Graves was quite happy in his new job. Then one day in December 1985 Jeff Arnold, his print room supervisor, approached him and said: 'We've got a problem with your clearance under the Official Secrets Act.' Graves asked what he meant, but Arnold seemed unconcerned: 'I've just got to supply more information about you, but don't worry about it.' Graves didn't give it another thought.

It was not until 2.40 pm on Wednesday 5 February 1986 that the question of his 'clearance' was again raised. This time Arnold was more secretive. He merely told Graves that Mike Sheridan, the Divisional Manager, wanted to see him. At first Arnold refused to talk about the reason for the meeting. 'Don't worry, it's not important,' he said as they walked along the corridor towards Sheridan's office. Graves again asked if he knew why he had been summoned. 'Yes, but I'm not going to tell you,' replied Arnold.

Sheridan began by saying he had something very difficult to tell him. Then came the thunderbolt: 'As from Friday your contract will be terminated. I can't tell you why, but there is nothing wrong with your work and you have done nothing wrong.' He added, however, that the company was prepared to offer him alternative work but it couldn't be in the print room. Sheridan was apologetic but commented: 'There is nothing we can do about it.'

Graves managed to ask a series of questions about the reasons for his dismissal. But Sheridan refused to give answers and would only restate the company's satisfaction with him as an employee. He told Graves he had until the next day to accept the new job. If he did not, he would be given a month's salary, any outstanding holiday pay and a 'first-class' reference. Within ten minutes Graves was escorted by Arnold to see his new manager Keith Moulden, who explained the proposed new job. It was in the maintenance department, carrying boxes and moving equipment around the building. Graves didn't take much notice, as he was still shell-shocked by the decision. 'It was like they had cut my throat and now they were half-way through my stitches,' he recalled.

Later that afternoon Graves went to see Hazel Smith, the Personnel Officer who had originally recruited him.

'Why have I been sacked?' he asked her.

'I'm sorry but I can't tell you,' Smith replied apologetically.

'Well, who could I see who will be able to tell me?'

'Nobody will be able to tell you.'

Graves went back to the print room and telephoned Ian Townsend, Scicon's Senior Personnel Officer, to ask for a meeting. Townsend agreed and Graves went to his office. By this time Graves was tired of vague apologies. He wanted a reason for his sacking. But Townsend also said he couldn't tell him: 'I know it's an awful situation but there is nothing the company can do about it.'

Graves then asked if he could be given a clue as to why it had happened. Townsend answered: 'What do you have in the print room that you won't have in the other job we have offered you.' Graves replied: 'The only thing that I can think of is classified documents.' Townsend said nothing – he just looked at Graves.

Graves had indeed been handling some classified documents. Scicon Ltd, the UK operating company of Scicon International Ltd, which is a wholly-owned subsidiary of British Petroleum, is a major contractor with the Ministry of Defence. The company specialises in designing computer software programmes and then recommending how best they can be operated. About a third of Scicon's £161 million annual business comes from contracts with the Defence Ministry (MoD), GEC and Marconi Avionics. Despite being a private company, Scicon, like other defence contractors, are obliged to submit their new employees for security clearance with the MoD. The vetting is carried out by MI5. Graves should have been positively vetted, like civil servants. Instead, he was the subject of 'normal vetting' (in reality secret vetting), which explains the reluctance of Scicon's management to disclose the reason for the termination of his contract.

The day after his dismissal, Graves returned to Scicon to see Mike Sheridan. He asked for a copy of the Staff Employment Handbook to show his parents. Sheridan refused to give him one, saying that the document contained 'confidential information' and could not leave the company premises. This was not consistent with the official explanation given by Ian Townsend, who told new employees 'It is not practical, primarily for reasons of size, to send you a copy.'[1] Graves protested, and was allowed to read through the document's contents.

By now, however, he had reluctantly decided to accept the new job in the maintenance department. That afternoon he went to see Hazel Smith for details of the new contract. Smith expressed sympathy for Graves's situation but said: 'If you try to find out the reason [for his dismissal] you will probably end up worse off. There is nothing you can do. There is nothing any of us can do.'

The two chatted for a while, and Smith became increasingly relaxed. Graves was startled to hear her say: 'It is unfortunate how things other people do rub off on you. Only you can figure out what it is.' Suddenly it all made sense. 'I think I have, I think I know what it is now,' said Graves. As he left her office Smith told him to 'Work hard, keep your head down and hope that in time you will be judged as a person in your own right and not by others around you.'

Smith's advice was of little comfort to Graves – he was still sacked. But at least he had some idea of what was going on. He had been refused security clearance because of the political views and activities of one of his relatives or friends.

That weekend Graves discussed the situation with his step-father Vic and his mother Kim. It was obvious that his mother wasn't the 'security risk'. Both her parents had been staunch Conservatives. She had voted Tory at every election until 1979, when she switched to Plaid Cymru, and then became an inactive Labour Party member for two years. She currently works as a freelance market research interviewer and is neither a member of a trade union nor a political party. 'I wouldn't say I'm a political person at all,' she said. 'The things I feel strongly about are social issues. In fact, I'm a bit right wing on things like law and order.'

Iwan Graves's brothers are even less political. None has ever belonged to any political party, although one is currently a member of the building workers' union UCATT. Iwan himself has also never been a member of any political party nor of any trade union. According to his family and friends, he is completely non-political. 'I can't ever remember saying anything about politics either at home or with friends – even after all this has happened,' he said. When he was asked political questions at his interview with Scicon, he was surprised but not concerned: 'I wasn't worried because I knew I wasn't involved.' He does recall handling MoD documents in the print room. But he had little idea what they meant, and did not take any notice of their content. He only remembered them because some had very long titles with their code number on the cardboard cover. 'They meant nothing to me,' he said. 'I was an assistant and we were just trying to get as much work done as possible. I just wanted to learn all aspects of the printing industry.'

Yet the Ministry of Defence has confirmed that Iwan Graves was refused security clearance. Archie Hamilton, the Parliamentary Under-Secretary of State for Defence Procurement, said: 'In the case of Mr Graves, it was not possible to allow such access. Scicon was notified of the Ministry of Defence decision to move him to another part of the company, as classified documents were handled in the print room.'[2]

The comments made by Scicon Personnel Officer Hazel Smith make it clear why Iwan Graves was blacklisted by MI5. His stepfather Vic, a life-long trade unionist, had become actively involved in setting up centres for the unemployed in the south-east. Since 1985 he has been based at the TUC's Congress House as an assistant regional organiser helping to run these centres. Vic Graves is also active in local trades councils.

But it was his political views that would have caught MI5's eye. In 1975, aged 21, he became a supporter of the Militant Tendency, the Trotskyist grouping inside the Labour Party. For three years he sold their newspaper and took the Militant line at meetings. But by early 1979 he was no longer involved with the organisation. He remains a Labour Party member but firmly believes that 'any changes [to the system of government] must be made through the democratic process.' He also says that he has never sought to influence his family politically, although he does put his views across in rare family discussions.

There is a belief in MI5 circles that 'the sins of the fathers are visited on the sons.' It was with this belief that Vic Graves accompanied his stepson to see Scicon's Personnel Manager Ian Townsend on Monday 10 February 1986. In a small interview room Townsend told them that when Iwan was appointed it was on the basis that his references were satisfactory. 'This is where the problem was,' said Townsend. 'There had been a problem with one of his references.' This was untrue. We have copies of Iwan's two references – from his school, Stantonbury Campus, and the supermarket Waitrose Ltd. Both are very favourable.

It was clear that the company was not going to admit that MI5 had been the real reference for their decision. So the three discussed how to prevent further damage to Iwan's future career. He wanted to be a skilled printer. His stepfather asked how Iwan was supposed to explain the reason for his contract being terminated by Scicon. Townsend reassured him, saying that the company would 'ensure Iwan was seen in a favourable light.' But if Iwan Graves was to have any chance of getting a printer's job he needed to show he had direct work experience. How could he explain his dismissal from the print room to prospective employers? He could not give the real reason because Scicon would not tell him. And if he neglected to say that he worked in the print room he wouldn't get the job because of his lack of experience. He was trapped in a Catch-22 situation.

The only solution was for the company to provide a false or misleading reference. In the summer of 1986 Iwan Graves approached Townsend and explained his predicament. 'We'll get round it by giving you an excellent reference,' the Personnel Manager replied. On 4 August 1986 the reference was provided. It stated that Graves 'was transferred to the Office Management Division as an Administrative Assistant as a reorganisation of staff was necessary.'

This reference was completely untrue, of course, not least in its description of the new job. Graves now has the most menial job of all the company's 500 employees. Based in the maintenance department, he spends most of his time delivering stationery, fixing lights, sweeping up leaves and moving furniture and equipment. He earns £4,600 a year on grade five – the lowest salary in the company.

Iwan Graves is now increasingly anxious to obtain a proper job or training. Two years after being vetted out of the print room, he applied for a Trainee Operator's post. A manager replied: 'As soon as we feel there is a job suitable for you within the company we'll let you know.' He has applied for jobs with GEC Avionics and other defence companies. But despite being interviewed, he has always been rejected. 'I've given up now,' he said. 'Everything is stacked against me. It's a waste of time.' At 20 years of age he is too old for training and apprentice jobs. And yet he can't apply for more senior positions because he doesn't have the qualifications. In desperation he has gone back to college to get some A levels.

In the meantime, his stepfather believes that the source of the problem – his own security file – remains the key to Iwan Graves's future. His is also concerned it could affect other members of his family: 'Somebody, somewhere, has got a record on me that is preventing my family from taking up employment in certain spheres. I don't know what that information is. I don't know if it's accurate. I just do not know what it is and I've got a right to know.'

Vetting Procedures for Defence Companies

Although Scicon asked the MoD to double-check their decision to refuse Iwan Graves his security clearance, they did not press the issue. This was hardly surprising. It was not in their interests, for, like up to ten thousand British companies, they depend for much of their business on contracts with the Ministry of Defence, and it has not been unusual for the MoD to discreetly inform companies that, if they persisted in questioning or resisting security vetting decisions, their contracts would be withdrawn. This explains why many companies have been so secretive about their vetting procedures. Some personnel officers have been relatively open about it at interviews. Others, like John Higgins of the electronics firm MEL, even deny that it takes place at all!

In fact, prospective employees of defence contractors have been vetted by MI5 since the purge procedures were introduced in 1948. Companies with access to classified information are placed on a document called 'List X', containing 2000 firms, and their security, both physical and personnel, is controlled by MI5. Each firm is provided with a manual which gives guidance on security procedures. Their own security officers (known as 'controllers') and management personnel are encouraged to take part in special training courses run by MI5 officers from C Branch. But most important is the 'secret aspects letter' which is sent by MI5 to companies before a contract is signed. This details the security provisions stipulated by MI5, including their right to security check new employees. Defence firms are keen to co-operate with MI5, as 'failure to carry out these security obligations gives the Department [the MoD] the right to terminate the contract.[3]

To ensure that the vetting procedures are implemented MI5 employs a select team of officers from C Branch who act as special advisors to the company. These MI5 special advisors, whose numbers have been substantially increased in recent years,[4] often visit the firm's premises to brief their Security Officer and to inspect their vetting arrangements.

In theory, defence company employees are positively vetted, like civil servants. This should involve an open and detailed investigation of the individual's personal and political background by MoD vetting officers. But in reality most applicants are vetted 'normally' (i.e. secretly) by MI5 and the MoD.

The system works like this. The contractor is required to supply the MoD with full particulars of its new employees. The names are then passed onto a section of MI5 called C3. The officer on that desk then writes the name of the person on a request form and hands it to the Registry on the ground floor, where all of MI5's files are kept. Once located, the file is passed to F2, a section of MI5 on the first floor which deals with domestic subversion, and particularly with trade unionists. The F branch officer then makes an assessment and records it on the person's file. This is then written on a memo sheet and handed back to the C Branch officer responsible. That officer also checks with the Criminal Records Office through its links with the Special Branch. The C3 branch officer then makes a recommendation based on four categories. This ranges from 'A' grade, which allows complete security clearance, down to 'D' grade, which means that the employee is 'not recommended for sensitive work' and is refused clearance. But if there are any doubts at all the security services will give a negative report (if a trace is requested on an employee more than once, a file is automatically opened).

MI5's recommendation is then passed to the Ministry of Defence's Security Division, which has about 150 vetting officers, although they also do work for other government departments. The MoD then decides whether the employee should be allowed to work for the contractor.

The MoD says the final decision is up to the company. 'I think our task finishes at telling the company that the man cannot have clearance,' says Mr Ewen Broadbent, a Deputy Under-Secretary. 'The company then has to decide whether it can put him on civil work or redeploy him into some other post.'[5] But, as the MoD retains the power to terminate their contracts, there is rarely much resistance from the company concerned.

'In the Care of Reasonable Men'

A good illustration of how defence contractors have been forced into accepting security vetting decisions since the war is the case of John Lang, an able young lawyer for Imperial Chemical Industries (ICI). In May 1951, after working for ICI for ten years, Lang was promoted to be the company's second most senior legal advisor. As the new job involved handling some secret papers regarding contracts with the Ministry of Supply (later incorporated into the MoD), ICI asked for security clearance. Two months later ICI were told that clearance could not be granted and that Lang should be denied access to confidential government documents. MI5 had told the Ministry that Lang had just married a woman who was a Communist Party member. This was untrue. Mrs Lang had resigned from the Communist Party in

1950 – a year before their marriage – and had since severed all links with it.

As a major part of Lang's job involved handling secret government papers, ICI had no choice but to dismiss him. He protested that this was unfair, and that as an experienced solicitor he was used to dealing with information on a confidential basis. During the Second World War he had served as an NCO and as an officer in the Intelligence Corps. Besides, as a lawyer with no scientific background, the documentation would have been unintelligible to him.

At first ICI resisted the instruction, saying that Lang was a valued employee, and he was promoted to Assistant Solicitor. But it was clear that it was impossible for Lang to do his new job without seeing secret government papers. The Ministry of Supply claimed that they tried to reconcile Lang being 'a security risk' with his continued employment with ICI. But on 4 January 1956 the Ministry took drastic action. The Treasury Solicitor wrote to ICI criticising their handling of the case. The letter stated that if Lang continued to have access to secret information the Ministry of Supply would withdraw from negotiating future contracts with ICI. Lang was swiftly, if politely, sacked.

He decided to fight the decision. Instead of appealing to the 'Three Security Advisers' tribunal, he chose to see Sir Cyril Musgrave, the Ministry of Supply's Deputy Under-Secretary. Musgrave confirmed that Lang's wife's past association with the Communist Party was the only substantial matter the Ministry held against him. But Lang failed to convince Musgrave that he was not a security risk. So Mrs Lang went to see Musgrave, and offered a drastic solution. 'I do not want to ruin my husband's career, as this is going to do,' she told him. 'I will go away, leave him and live in a different part of the country altogether, so that he may go on with his career at ICI.' Musgrave was unmoved: 'It is no good your offering to do that, because it would not make a penny-worth of difference.' Lang remained sacked; the stress affected his health, he had a serious operation, and entered a nursing home. He never worked for ICI again.

Lang's supporters included Lord Chorley, a former Labour Minister who had liaised with MI5 during the war, while he was working at the Home Office. He argued that Lang's case should have been put before an independent judicial tribunal. Lord Chorley also said that security would not be breached if MI5's evidence against Lang was produced – as had been shown in cases in the US Federal Courts. The government rejected this, but the Lord Chancellor's response was revealing: 'This is not a question of guilt or innocence of a particular charge which can be proved or disproved in a court of law. A person is denied access to secret defence information because in the careful and considered opinion of reasonable men there is doubt as to his reliability. This is a matter of judgement which must be made in the light of the available evidence. It must be realised that some of this evidence comes from highly secret sources which have been built up over a long period and which must not be jeopardised.'[6]

It is this 'available evidence', however questionable its degree of accuracy and relevance, that has disrupted many careers in the defence industry.

In the autumn of 1970 Mike Lewis, a freelance technical author, applied for a job with Elliot Automation, a defence contractor based at Rochester, Kent. The company needed a writer for MoD maintenance manuals on electronic weapon-aiming and navigational equipment for the Tornado, Jaguar and Nimrod aircraft. Four people, including Lewis, were interviewed for the post. The company told them that they would be informed of the outcome of the interviews as soon as their MoD security clearance was received.

'Having worked for Elliots before, I had a certain advantage, but qualification-wise one man was far more suited,' said Lewis. Five days later, much to his surprise, Lewis was offered the job.

Soon after joining the company he went to see the Chief Security Officer at their building overlooking Chatham harbour. He asked why he had been chosen over the more highly qualified applicant. Lewis recalls: 'I was told he had not received security clearance. I asked why not. I was told that he had been photographed sitting on the steps of St Martin-in-the-Fields in Trafalgar Square during a CND demonstration, even though he had not been taking part. I was told that he might never know that this had been the reason that he had been turned down.'[7]

Lewis was told that the main reason he had been appointed was that his security clearance had come through fastest, not necessarily because of his ability to do the job. Lewis, who had previously worked in Air Ministry Intelligence, was amazed that a person could be refused a job purely because of Special Branch photographs of him sitting in Trafalgar Square during a demonstration: 'I thought it was most unfair . . . That man was damned as far as the MoD was concerned.'

Ken Richardson has been another victim, although he suffered in rather unusual circumstances. In October 1976 he joined a leading electronics firm as a Design Engineer. Based in the West Country, the company has contracts with the MoD in radar equipment. In the spring of 1980, Richardson went to Botswana for several months as a lecturer. In late 1980 he returned to Britain. In January 1981 he began applying for jobs as a stress and design engineer, mainly with defence companies in the south-west and Bristol area. After five months and applications to several aerospace firms he was still unemployed, despite being interviewed for every vacancy for which he had applied.

For the first time in his life Richardson could not get a job. Yet he had worked continuously for thirty-five years in five different countries, chiefly as an engineer in the aircraft industry but also as a lecturer. He could not understand it, particularly as he knew that stress engineers were in demand at that time.

As the weeks went by he began to suspect that the reason might have something to do with security. On the afternoon of Thursday 14 May 1981, he decided to try a little test. He telephoned his old company's Personnel Manager at their head office and pretended to be a Canadian employer (he had worked in Canada in the early 1960s). In an assumed Canadian accent he said he was 'Mr Blackwell from Stress and Allied Engineering Ltd, Toronto,' and that he wanted to employ an engineer called Ken Richardson. 'Can you give me your views on him?' he asked. According to his diary entry for that day, the Personnel Manager replied: 'He's OK, he's a stress engineer. He did a bit of drawing for us. He's competent, but you should check with the security people because he did tend to gossip about his job with other people. He's a good worker but was a security risk.'

Richardson was dumbstruck. In his thirty-five-year career he had never been spoken to about any security lapses. Two weeks later, on 27 May 1981, he rang the Personnel Manager again, and asked him why he had branded him a security risk to 'Mr Blackwell'. The Personnel Manager admitted having had the conversation about his work record, but denied having said that he was a 'security risk'.

Richardson believes he has been blacklisted because of his interest in the Russian language and the Soviet Union. While lecturing in Zambia in the mid-1970s he made occasional social visits to the Soviet embassy. And in April 1979, while still at the company, he booked a two-week holiday in Moscow. In the preceding weeks he began learning Russian, and one day he left some translation notes on his desk. A few days later, on returning to his office the company's Security Officer was waiting for him. He expressed concern and asked him why he was learning Russian. Richardson told him it was for his holiday in Moscow, about which he had already told him. Since leaving the company he has joined the British-Soviet Friendship Society, a cultural organisation which spends most of its time escorting Russian visitors around London.

Richardson has now been unemployed since 1981, and exists on £36 a week supplementary benefit. At fifty-eight he is unlikely to get another job in his chosen profession. 'When I first realised I was being blacked in 1981,' he said, 'I did have good chances of getting a job back in "stressing" because there were vacancies then. But now, frankly, I don't think I would be asked to go for an interview.' He also resents being labelled a security risk: 'I am not a security risk. I'm not a communist and never have been. I've been to the Soviet Union and there is no way I want to see my country run like that . . . I do have slight left-wing leanings and joined the Labour Party in 1982. But that doesn't make me a red or a commie.'

In the defence industry it is much more difficult to blacklist employees once they are established and qualified. So it proved with Tony Wilson, a Reliability Engineer and independent consultant in the defence industry since 1972. For eight years he worked on a series of major military contracts, including the nuclear Chevaline project, as a specialist engineer. But in 1980 Wilson became a supporter of the peace movement, and opposed what he saw as the militarisation of the defence industry. 'I underwent a change in consciousness and became politically and socially aware for the first time,' says Wilson. 'While still firmly believing in an adequate defence, I abhorred the enormous waste of resources in our archaic military procurement system, the vast overkill in weapons provision and, most of all, the devastating effects on the Third World of our armaments policies.'

It was not long before he had turned down a long-term offer to work on the Trident programme and become a freelance. In 1982 he set up 'Electronics For Peace', a research and campaigning organisation designed, among other things, to 'reduce the involvement of industry in arms manufacture, research and development.' Wilson also became increasingly public in stating his views of the defence industry, being interviewed by newspapers and television.

Wilson was skating on thin ice, as he was still working for defence firms as a Reliability Engineer. But he believed, perhaps naively, that the right to freedom of speech would prevail.

By the autumn of 1985, however, the patience of the Ministry of Defence and of one of their contractors had finally run out. In October Wilson's 'Electronics For Peace' group was featured prominently in the magazine *Electronics Times* under the headline 'Concerned Engineers Draft Plans for Conscience Forum'. The article outlined the organisation's criticisms of the defence industry and mentioned that it intended strengthening its links with CND.[8]

At the time the article was published, Wilson was working as a Reliability Engineer for a hydraulics company in Hampshire. The firm was doing subcontracting work for British Aerospace on the anti-aircraft Rapier project. One afternoon Wilson received a phone call from his Manager: 'I have been told to sack you by the MoD and British Aerospace,' he said. British Aerospace objected to Wilson's association with CND and demanded his security clearance be withdrawn.

The subcontractor refused, saying that Wilson could not be dismissed for holding certain opinions. He wrote to British Aerospace: 'We agree that some aspects of the article could be of concern, particularly those references to connections with CND . . . However, it must not be assumed that someone who talks to CND necessarily agrees with all or any of their views . . . We do not believe that anyone as overt as Tony Wilson can be a real threat, as even were we to have "controversial" documents we would be able to ensure that he was not privy to them.'[9]

Wilson was suspended while discussions about his position continued. The MoD agreed to back down. But British Aerospace was adamant that Wilson was not even to be allowed on their premises, although he continued to work for the hydraulics company.

Wilson was always treading a thin line, and he was well known for his criticism of the defence industry: his dismissal was open and the reasons for it were clear. But most vetting of private defence contractors is, by contrast, carried out secretly. This was shown by the case of a young accountant. He has asked us not to disclose his identity as he fears this could jeopardise his future employment prospects. So we will use a pseudonym – 'John Simpson'.

In May 1985 Simpson had qualified as an accountant while

working for an electronics firm, and became a member of the Institute of Cost and Management Accountants. He was interested in working for defence companies, as his background was in electronics, and these firms had a decentralised structure which enabled accountants to work on a variety of different projects. That summer he began applying for such jobs through an accountants' recruitment agency based in Brighton.

One position for which he applied was as a financial analyst for MEL, a division of Philips Electronic and Associated Industries Ltd. At 3 pm on Friday 6 September 1985, Simpson attended an interview at MEL's head office in Crawley, West Sussex. He realised the defence nature of the job while filling out the long and detailed application form. The work involved providing a full management accounting service to the Electronic Warfare Division and assessing costs in the Research and Development Department. Simpson then spoke to Colin Gills, MEL's Senior Personnel Officer, and Brian Chester, Financial Controller. The interview went extremely well. After the standard questions, Gills told Simpson he was impressed with his application and remarked how disappointed they had been with the other candidates. 'They were hack accountants,' he confided. Gills then asked whether he wanted to work in the Electronics Warfare Division or in the Communications Department. Simpson said he preferred the Warfare Division because it was a more dynamic professional environment. It was now quite clear to Simpson that he had an excellent chance of being offered the job. But he needed to know the company's decision quickly because he wanted to buy a house in another part of the country. So he asked Gills how long MEL would take before making their choice. Gills was guarded but relatively relaxed: 'You are going to be working within the defence industry. Can you think of any reason why you shouldn't be offered the job unconditionally?'

'Presumably I will have to go through some sort of vetting procedure,' replied Simpson.

'Yes, that is correct.'

Simpson went home confident. His optimism was increased on the Monday when he was telephoned by the Manager of his employment agency, who told him that MEL had just rung to say how impressed they were with Simpson's application. Four days later, on the afternoon of Friday 13 September, Simpson was summoned for a second interview, where he met a Mr Wright, General Manager of the Electronic Warfare Division. He also met

Mr A. G. Tween, a Personnel Officer, who offered him the job of Financial Analyst. After a brief discussion over salaries and benefits, Simpson verbally accepted. Tween then told him that security clearance with the MoD usually took two weeks – the usual interval between the first and second interview. But, as Simpson had needed to know the company's decision quickly, the security clearance was delayed until after they offered him the position.

Simpson had not provided any references, as he had not been asked to, and believed the security clearance would be a formality. The next day he received a letter from MEL confirming the offer: 'We are very pleased to offer you the position of Financial Analyst, subject to our obtaining satisfactory references.'[10] Simpson was delighted and wrote back formally accepting the job.

During the following week he waited to be told by phone about his security clearance. But by Friday 27 September he had heard nothing. So he rang Tween at MEL, who told him there had been no response from the MoD. As the days went by Simpson became increasingly anxious, as he could not understand why he had not been cleared. He continued to ring Tween, who acknowledged that it did seem to be taking a long time. Tween also said that the company had asked the MoD to make Simpson's clearance a priority. But, he added, they had to be careful because the MoD could be obstructive, and if they pressurised too much it might be counter-productive.

Eventually, on 22 October 1985, over six weeks after having been formally offered the job, Simpson received a five-line letter from MEL. It stated: 'I very much regret to inform you that references have not proved satisfactory. We shall not therefore be proceeding with an unconditional offer of employment.'[11]

Simpson was shocked and angry at the decision, particularly as the company did not give any reason. Nor did they acknowledge that it was because of his security status. He wrote to MEL asking them to confirm that it was the MoD reference that had 'proved unsatisfactory'.[12] Colin Gills, the Personnel Officer, replied: 'It is not the policy of this company to reveal the source or substance of references.'[13]

Simpson was completely baffled as to why he had been blacklisted. He was aware that his political past might be relevant, but could not believe it would affect his security clearance. His father had been vetted and cleared in 1979 when he joined the defence industry after thirty years in the Royal Navy. Both his parents have been life-long Liberal Party members. But neither his sister nor his brother are or ever have been politically inclined in any way. He himself had not been politically active for several years. During his final year at Birmingham Polytechnic in 1982 he spoke at student union meetings, and once called for the occupation of the college's administration building in protest at education cuts. He also attended meetings arranged by the Socialist Workers' Student Organisation. But he was never a member of any political party. His only other political activity was attending demonstrations against racism and education cuts. In July 1983 he had joined the Labour Party, but he left it the following year.

The incident which almost certainly caused M I5 to brand him a security risk occurred in 1984, during the miners' strike. He was interested in what various left-wing groups were saying about the dispute, so he took out short-term subscriptions to a number of newspapers. One of these was to *The Next Step*, journal of the Revolutionary Communist Party (R C P), which he cancelled by the end of the year. But that summer he also went to an R C P meeting, during which he signed an attendance note. That was the only R C P meeting he ever attended. By 1985 his political interests and activities had evaporated. But that brief flirtation with the R C P had found its way into his M I5 file.

The result of being refused security clearance was that Simpson's chosen career in the defence industry was ruined. It took him over a year to get a job suited to his qualifications, interests and ability.

What Simpson's case reveals is the covert nature of most defence company vetting. He was not positively vetted. Neither his college tutor nor his parents were approached by MoD investigating officers as, officially, they should have been. Everything was left to M I5.

This obsession with secrecy is also illustrated by the response of M E L when asked about Simpson's case. At first a company spokesman said he was sure the whole story was fabricated and that MoD vetting does not take place! John Higgins, M E L's Personnel Director, commented: 'I have no knowledge of this. You say MoD vetting takes place in the private sector, but I have no knowledge of it.' When asked if the company would be prepared to see Simpson, as the MoD had advised, Higgins replied: 'I would not recommend that the man in question comes here. Definitely not. We would have nothing to say to him.'[14]

The American Influence

The existence of American companies in Britain with defence contracts has given an extra dimension to security vetting. Many of them allow their prospective employees to be vetted not only by MI5, but also by US intelligence agencies. This is in line with American government policy of controlling the movement of technological products and information from US companies with sites abroad. The procedure has been implemented even when it contravenes the law of the country concerned.

One corporation which runs such American security checks is Dec Inc, a digital equipment company based in Ayr, Scotland. It is allowed to trade by the US Department of Commerce Licence Department, which is controlled by the CIA.[15] 'We like to get all the names of people who are going to visit the site [of the company],' says Jim Manderson, Dec's Personnel Services Manager in Ayr. 'They're checked against a list of names and nationalities and if we find someone we're uncertain about we make an application to the States to check them. We send off the application and then wait for it to come back with clearance. The whole thing usually takes about a month.'

Manderson confirmed that the policy extended to people who applied for jobs with the company, particularly foreign nationals: 'The people who would concern us most would be those with Russian or Eastern bloc nationalities.'[16]

Dec Inc is the biggest supplier of computer systems to the Ministry of Defence, and sets the standard for computers used in UK defence establishments. It is now the second largest and fastest growing computer company in the world, with about 7,500 employees in Britain.

The US intelligence agency most likely to process these security checks is the National Security Agency (NSA), based at Fort Meade, Maryland. Their computer has been receiving the names and details of British citizens who have been seen or questioned near American nuclear bases in the UK or have been involved in anti-nuclear protests. None of them have been charged with any offence. But their names have been supplied by MoD police and servicemen to GCHQ, the government's spy centre, and then passed on to the American agency. The NSA then places them on a computer programme – which is supposed to help trace terrorists – under the classification 'C Group Three', which covers intelligence operations in Europe. The names on file are then classified as 'Hostile' or 'Non-Hostile' and are then placed on security files for vetting purposes.[17]

All this was discovered by Ellis Plaice, Defence Correspondent of the *Today* newspaper, who was given a list of British names from the US computer intelligence network COMSEC. They were collected during eighteen incidents following anti-nuclear protests in Britain. On one occasion five British people were placed on the blacklist after a nuclear weapons carrier crash in Wiltshire in January 1987. It turned out they had just happened to be in the area at the time. Plaice obtained hard evidence of the American blacklist when he got access to the NSA computer at Fort Meade. He chose a random month – January 1985 – and the computer came up with twenty-seven 'hostile' British citizens after an 'incident'. That month twenty-seven demonstrators had been arrested outside the American airbase at Sculthorpe in Norfolk.

Secrecy for Secrecy's Sake

There cannot be many people working for defence companies who would argue that some security vetting should not take place. It is clearly necessary for firms who handle sensitive and classified information and documents in connection with their MoD contracts to apply stringent security checks.

But the ways in which vetting procedures have been implemented for defence contractors by the MoD and MI5 have been inconsistent and unnecessarily secretive. Employees working on classified contracts are supposed to be positively vetted. This means an open investigation by MoD officers into their personal and political background. Relatives, friends, former teachers and professional colleagues should all be interviewed as well as the applicant himself. Other inquiries are made by MI5 and the police. But it seems that many, if not most, defence firms do their vetting secretly, and some, like MEL, even deny it takes place. Iwan Graves and John Simpson were not positively vetted. The companies concerned simply relied on MI5's recommendation and then refused to tell the individuals why they had been sacked. This leads us to the second problem. The political criteria used by the Security Services are both too wide and too speculative. 'Stepfather who used to be a member of Militant' (Graves) and 'was a subscriber to a communist newspaper' (Simpson) are hardly grounds for denying security clearance.

This secrecy and inconsistency also give rise to unnecessary anxiety among defence workers, according to Tony Wilson, who worked for a number of contractors as an engineer. He accepts that vetting is needed, but the way it is done creates an authoritarian atmosphere inside the company. He didn't feel free even to join such non-political organisations as Amnesty International, and was afraid of visiting the Greenham Common Peace Camp, as he thought these activities would be held against him and could affect his future employment in the defence industry. 'People who work in defence companies never talk about politics,' said Wilson. 'If they do, it's usually only in disparaging terms. They're afraid that if they do then they might be seen as unreliable.'

The major problem remains the absence of an independent judicial body which could hear appeals by employees who believe they have been refused security clearance unfairly. At the moment the MoD retains the right to be prosecutor, judge and jury.

4

British Telecom: A Question of Secrecy

'Any enquiries you make should be made discreetly and should
not come to the subject's knowledge.'
                    Confidential instructions on vetting procedures by
                        British Telecom Personnel Office to Terry Carlin,
                        BT Divisional Manager in City of London District,
                                                            13 May 1985.

Since October 1984 Michael Dolan has worked for British Telecom
as a filing clerk in one of their telephone sales offices on London
Bridge Street, just across the Thames from the City. His job
involves taking orders for new domestic phones and dealing with
customers' enquiries about additional sockets and extensions. It
is a poorly paid, mundane office post which, like thousands of
other BT jobs, doesn't involve handling any sensitive or confidential information.

Yet during his probationary period BT secretly kept a 'Security
Questionnaire' on him which included comments on his political
activities. The document, headed 'Confidential', was drafted by
BT's Personnel Department at their headquarters in Newgate
Street. It consisted of seven questions. These included a job
description and whether or not the employee needed security
clearance or required access to classified or confidential information. The questionnaire then asked: 'Are you aware of any
circumstances which might cast doubt on his/her reliability for
employment on work giving access to information classified or
confidential?'

This was followed by: 'Indicate any known interests or
activities outside his/her normal duty which might have a bearing
on attitudes towards security matters.'

It concluded with enquiries about the name and address of
his/her previous employer.

The document was attached to a memo from the Personnel
Department and was addressed to Dolan's Divisional Manager

Terry Carlin, Head of BT's Business and Consumer Services in the City area. The memo stated:

'I should be grateful if you would personally complete questions 1–7. Any enquiries you make should be made discreetly and should not come to the subject's knowledge . . . Your reply should be double enveloped and clearly marked on inner envelope CONFIDENTIAL in red ink.'

Carlin completed the questionnaire and made it clear that Dolan's job as a Clerical Assistant was not connected with government secrets or national security, that Dolan did not need security clearance and did not require access to information which was classified or confidential. He added, significantly, that Dolan would not need access to classified information in the future either. However, in response to the question on 'outside activities or interests', Carlin wrote: 'Nothing specific, but is felt to have hard left interests.' Dolan has been a member of the Socialist Workers' Party since June 1981. But he was not particularly active in the National Communications Union (NCU) in the City District, although he did attend the 1985 NCU National Conference as an observer.

When asked about his involvement in BT's vetting procedures, Carlin, now General Manager of the Westminster Area, said: 'I myself find it perfectly acceptable . . . The business that British Telecom conducts is sometimes involved in security and so occasionally that type of question will be asked.' The BT Personnel Officer who had sent him the questionnaire, Shirley Williams, said: 'I'm not prepared to comment on this.' Neither official was able to explain why the questionnaire should ask about the political views of employees who were not engaged on classified work.

More senior BT executives also had difficulty in explaining why they compiled data about an employee's political views when he was not involved in sensitive or security work. When the questionnaire was disclosed publicly in the autumn of 1985, BT refused to comment on Dolan's case. In correspondence with the NCU, Malcolm Argent, the Company Secretary, denied that there was a political motivation: 'For all normal purposes an employee's private life, including his political views, is of no concern to BT.'[1]

It was not until Monday 16 June 1986 that Dolan's case and the vetting document were discussed by BT security officials. That afternoon in the Rosewood Room on the 8th floor of BT's London headquarters Malcolm Argent chaired a meeting on security procedures. He said that use of the questionnaire was rare and not part of 'general procedures' used by the Security Division (known as s05). Its purpose, he added, was to establish certain facts about an individual's duties and location with particular reference to any work on classified work. He admitted that the questions which went beyond this were 'unjustified and superfluous'. BT accepted that 'they served no useful purpose,' he said. 'Information based purely on opinions was of no value and would not be, and never had been, used to the detriment of any employee.'

Argent also disclosed that the specific questions asking for information on 'outside activities' had been removed from the vetting form in late 1985. He concluded, however, that it might still be necessary for BT to compile details of an individual's employment. But, he said, 'all such enquiries would be purely factual.'[2]

Inside BT Centre

Whatever BT's justification, the contents of the 'Security Questionnaire' provide a clear insight into the company's vetting procedures. But they also give an indication of its complex and highly secretive structure.

Vetting of BT employees is nothing new, of course. Before privatisation in 1983, when the company was part of the Post Office, many members of staff were positively vetted, like their fellow civil servants. On one occasion in the 1950s the Post Office refused to negotiate with a full-time trade union official because he was a Communist Party member. The ban was only lifted after the unions refused to meet management until he was reinstated. Now that BT is like any other private defence contractor, the situation is more intricate and secret. This is primarily because the company refuses to discuss vetting publicly. 'It is not our policy to discuss staff matters with third parties,' is now the standard response from BT spokespersons when asked about vetting. Even in private Malcolm Argent told the unions he was 'limited to what he could say.'[3]

The trades unions argue that BT's 250,000 employees are entitled to know whether or not they are being vetted by the company – if only in general terms. BT has always refused to tell them. It has, however, been possible to piece together the general structure of their security procedures. The company maintains that only personnel involved in classified work are vetted before they are formally appointed. Argent maintains that the number of such posts is 'very small'. At a meeting to discuss security procedures in June 1986, he said that BT ensured that if individuals were found 'unsuitable', then alternative appointments would be arranged. But he refused to accept that it was 'in the interests of security to make public the identity of posts' subject to vetting. Argent later commented that this would only 'draw attention to the very work areas which those people who wish to undermine security are seeking as targets . . . It is essentially State information that we are protecting and for that reason it is not for BT to determine what may or may not be disclosed.'[4]

However, it is known that staff working on 'Government Services', which deals with planning government and defence private circuits, are positively vetted. These employees include those working on communications links between defence installations and government departments. Also vetted are staff working on the 'Regional Seats of Government' (the underground nuclear bunkers).

An indication of the political criteria used by MI5 and vetting officers in this area is provided by what happened to Arthur Simper. In 1975 he sat on the Post Office Engineering Union's Establishment Committee, which looked at the working conditions of their members in the nuclear installations and underground bunkers. During that year the eight members of the Committee, including Simper, were due to visit the regional bunkers for inspection. But when the time came Simper was refused access. He had failed the security clearance. At the time he was a Labour Party parliamentary candidate. But the real reason, he was later told, was that he had previously had close friends and associates who had been Communist Party members in the 1950s. Simper himself had never been a party member.

A more recent insight into BT's vetting procedures was given to the authors by one of the company's senior executives. He joined BT in the early 1970s after working for an electronics company which had government defence contracts. So he was used to security measures. But he found the atmosphere at BT far more paranoid. 'Everything was treated as security sensitive,' he said, 'and everyone was expected to be silent about their work.'

At first the executive (who has asked not to be identified) noticed little vetting. He wasn't security checked himself when he joined BT. But in 1977, while working on the classification of files and documents, he discovered that the practice was being extended. He was about to be promoted to a potentially sensitive job when he was asked to be positively vetted. But he regarded it as 'a bureaucratic waste of time' and 'refused on principle'. He also confirmed that staff working on maintaining private telephone exchanges, including high security government buildings, are positively vetted. One employee told him how his neighbours had been approached and asked if there was 'anything suspicious' about him.

In 1986 the executive had direct experience of the positive vetting procedures when he was asked to act as a referee for an employee who was being transferred to a 'top secret' department. One day he received a phone call from a man calling himself 'Commander' (our source declined to give his name). The man said he did not work for BT but was from 'Government Security', and wanted to meet him to discuss the employee in question. The 'Commander' told the executive that he could check his credentials with a senior security manager at BT's headquarters. The executive recognised 'Government Security' as a euphemism for MI5. He spoke to the Senior Security Manager at Newgate House who confirmed this and verified the Commander's credentials. A meeting was then arranged.

When the MI5 officer turned up the first thing the BT executive noticed was that the name of the person being vetted was spelt incorrectly on his notepad. The officer began by asking whether the person in question had 'any political affiliations', and later asked: 'Does he have any links with any other organisations?' The MI5 officer also revealed that he knew a lot of detailed information about various activities of the executive himself. It was a rather disconcerting experience.

As well as 'Government Services', many employees based in network management are also positively vetted. Network management deals with rerouting circuits if there is a breakdown in the system. When this happens the staff have to give priority to certain circuits, so they need to know precise details of the circuit structure. We know of at least two cases in recent years where staff were unable to take up posts with network management for several months while, they were told, vetting investigations were being carried out. They were both eventually appointed.

Although BT have substantially reduced the number of staff requiring positive vetting since privatisation in 1983, their security procedures are still intact. Ultimate responsibility for security vetting lies with Malcolm Argent, BT's Company Secretary, who is also on the board of directors. He answers for the company. But the official who oversees and directly co-ordinates vetting procedures, as well as all security matters, is Major Gordon Oehlers. He actually became Director of BT's Security and Investigation Department in May 1987, although this was not publicly disclosed until August. Oehlers joined BT from the Ministry of Defence, where he was Assistant Chief of the Defence Staff, responsible for Command Control Communications and Information Systems. Before that he managed the British worldwide Defence Communications Network. Major Oehlers also spent thirty years in the army and served on several defence and government committees.

Oehlers's department – Security and Investigation – is split into two separate divisions. One is the Investigation Division (BTID), headed by C. R. Ward, a Territorial Army officer. This section deals with criminal offences by staff and the public – sabotage, theft of equipment, payphone offences, computer fraud – and general crime prevention. It liaises with the police and Special Branch as well as making its own enquiries. The BTID is not responsible for vetting, although it is in a position to provide information on individuals through its police and Special Branch contacts. It is the Security Division (Sec D), headed by Ken England, which deals with vetting and liaises with MI5 during the positive and secret vetting of employees. England and fourteen other security advisors and officers control the operation in Room A138, a large network of offices on the first floor of BT headquarters in the City. The key official who co-ordinates the vetting procedures is Peter N. Jones, the Personnel Security Advisor. Jones is a former RAF officer who was commissioned in 1967. He became a Flight Lieutenant in 1973 before retiring from the RAF's engineering branch in April 1982. Another official deals with 'travel to Communist countries'.

Jones reports directly to England, head of Sec D. Both men accompanied Malcolm Argent to a meeting with the BT unions in June 1986 to discuss security vetting. England said little, and Jones spent most of the time taking copious notes, attitudes consistent with England's policy of total secrecy on the vetting issue. The trades unions argue that this secrecy is dangerous because it does not provide enough safeguards for the individual. 'Our concern is that individuals subjected to the secret, "negative" vetting procedures employed by BT may innocently, and without means of redress, have their careers prejudiced, without their knowledge, on the basis of inaccurate information,' said Alan Chamberlain, secretary of the BT Unions Committee, in November 1986.[5]

England argues that the individual is protected because BT places constraints on its own vetting procedures: 'These lie in the balancing need for us to give very careful protection to any information to which we become privy and to ensure that it is never used in any context other than that of national security.'[6] He says that information in an employee's security file is protected by a 'cordon sanitaire' – a buffer line which is restricted to only a handful of officials. Hence, claims England: 'It cannot affect career prospects, line management attitudes or interpersonal relationships. We firmly believe that it affords the best form of protection for the individual employee whose interests would not be well served by any form of open procedure.'[7]

The unions responded that BT *already* has positive vetting procedures for employees in security-sensitive jobs. They therefore saw no reason why other positions should be vetted secretly rather than openly. This brought an interesting reply from Malcolm Argent. In his letter he appeared to confirm that secret security checking did take place, mainly in low-grade jobs: 'Most of the posts in this category are in every other sense standard jobs. Appointment to them rarely involves promotion and confers no special status or career advantage. If there is a security doubt in any particular case which cannot be resolved . . . it makes sense to employ that person on duties where the issue need never surface.'[8]

One problem with secret vetting is that inaccurate and misleading information can accumulate on an individual's security file, because material is collected from second-hand sources rather than from the person concerned or from close relatives and friends. The data is thus often based on assumptions, speculation and gossip rather than fact. This is why the BT unions have demanded that any adverse information kept on individuals should be included in their personal files and should be open to inspection, and that the employee should have the opportunity of refuting or confirming such information.[9]

BT has completely rejected these requests. Argent said at a

private meeting that the information was 'subject to the most careful protection'. He said that only a small number of people have access to an employee's security file – the Security Division (about fourteen officials), Argent himself, the Company Chairman Sir George Jefferson, and 'one or two others'. He added that it was the company's policy to ensure that 'information acquired only for national security purposes could not be used in a way which could be detrimental to an individual's employment generally. Present arrangements, based on a strict "need-to-know", provided the individual with the best safeguards possible.'[10]

In other words, BT's Security Division should have control over their own vetting procedures, although they would be answerable to a case before the 'Three Security Advisers'.

The new executive responsible for vetting, Major Gordon Oehlers, has been quick to review BT's security procedures. Soon after entering office he read all the files on the issue and held a meeting with top union officials, along with his predecessor Laurie Heatherington. Oehlers made it clear that vetting should continue to be done secretly, with access to information on file restricted to a few management officials – the 'cordon sanitaire' model. 'I am totally convinced,' he said, 'that the "cordon sanitaire" provides the very best protection for the individual.'[11]

BT have maintained that this 'tight' security procedure ensures that the political views of individual employees are not taken into consideration when they apply for jobs. But a new recruitment vetting document shows this not to be the case. The form, marked 'Staff-In-Confidence', is compiled at BT's head office and is used throughout the company. It is a detailed, four-page application form containing twenty-three questions. Among them are the following:

Q.16: Have you at any time visited or resided in a country having, at the time of the visit or residence, a communist government? Answer YES or NO. Where the answer is YES give particulars.

Q.20: Have you any relative by blood or marriage who is living or has lived in a country having, at the time of residence, a communist government? Answer YES or NO. Where the answer is YES give such particulars.

Q.22: Have you ever been a member of a communist or fascist party or any organisation controlled by or connected with such parties? Answer YES or NO. Where the answer is YES give particulars.

The questionnaire is clearly used for positive vetting purposes. This was confirmed by Malcolm Argent, who disclosed that it has been used since the mid-1960s. He said: 'It is a form used in the Civil Service and BT's use of it stems from provisions in the 1984 Telecommunications Act.'[12] Argent did not explain which clause in the Act is used by BT to justify the existence of this document. But he did agree to review security procedures when asked about the form. The danger of this vetting questionnaire is that it will inevitably be made available to managers involved in appointing new staff. It could also result in 'hit lists' being compiled and the information being used against employees applying for non-sensitive jobs within the company.

Meanwhile, the BT trades unions remain far from militant on the vetting issue. 'We do accept the need for security vetting, however distasteful it is on civil liberties grounds,' said Ben Marshall, Assistant Secretary of the Society of Telecom Executives. 'BT does carry out work of a security sensitive nature, and we have no wish to see that work go elsewhere, even if it could. We also accept that it is as much in the interests of BT staff as of national security that those employed on this work are not a risk to security.' But, Marshall argued: 'What we cannot accept is that this vetting should be carried out in secret. Any individual vetted in this way has no way of challenging the findings of the exercise.'[13]

BTI and the Cable Ship Cover-up

A vivid illustration of the secrecy of BT's vetting procedures occurred on one of their cable ships in the summer of 1986.

British Telecom International (BTI), a division of BT plc, operates a fleet of three cable ships – CS *Monarch*, CS *Iris* and CS *Alert*. Based in the marine depot at Southampton, the ships are used to maintain the network of submarine cables linking Britain with Europe and the rest of the world. These cables, expanded by satellite links, are the principal means of carrying telephone, telex and data calls between Britain and other countries.

CS *Monarch*'s main job is to repair any damage to these cables as quickly as possible. The ship is also used for military work, including the maintenance of Britain's anti-submarine defences. But BTI also has contracts with the US Navy and sub-contract work with private American telecommunications for the Americans in the North Atlantic.

In May 1986, BTI was commissioned by the US Navy to do such defence work on cable communications in the Atlantic. Some of the work was given to Western Electric, the manufacturing subsidiary of the American multi-national AT & T, who then sub-contracted it to BTI. The contract was worth £2 million, which is about 20 per cent of the BTI Maritime Division's total income. The *Monarch* was immediately made ready to sail from Southampton. But what the sixty crew were not told was that the American customers had written a specific requirement into the contract – that they had the right to accept or reject individual crewmen. This provision for vetting by US intelligence agencies was accepted by BTI management.

The power of these secret vetting procedures was felt on the morning of Friday 30 May 1986, when three seamen and cable-hands were summoned to the Captain's quarters. There they were met by the Captain and Mr A. B. Lewis, Personnel Manager of BTI Marine Division. The men were told they were 'not acceptable' as part of the crew for this contract, because they had not obtained security clearance. 'It's not our decision. It's the contractor's,' said the Captain. He told them he did not know why they had been singled out and was unhappy with the decision. The BTI management were not prepared to disclose the reasons for it.

Within a few hours six more crewmen had been refused security clearance. They included caterers and engine room crew as well as cable-hands. One of the victims said: 'I was so indignant. If it was my own company I could accept that, but the fact that it was the Americans who wanted me off was another matter.' The men were particularly surprised as cable ship workers are renowned throughout the industry for their lack of militancy and their reluctance to take strike action. There was little sign of political activity on the *Monarch*. As one of the vetted seamen said: 'Only my membership of Amnesty International could have raised an eyebrow.'

The ship's crew were also bemused because they had all already been vetted by British Telecom. They argued that to pose any risk to security they would need to have access to the charts on the bridge and to be experts on satellite navigation. This was virtually impossible, as they were not allowed on the bridge, and even tighter restrictions were imposed when they did sensitive work for the British government.

So it was with a mixture of shock and disbelief that the nine crewmen met with union shop stewards to discuss their situation. They were each asked if they had been politically active. None of them had ever even been members of political parties. They demanded that BTI give them reasons for their rejection. The management steadfastly refused. This provoked a mass walk-out by the sixty crew on the *Monarch*. Many of them had fought for their country during the Falklands War, they said. They were not going to allow their patriotism to be questioned by a foreign intelligence agency.

The strike brought national union officers into the fray. On Tuesday 3 June 1986, Len Gillard, Secretary of the National Communications Union (NCU) Networks Committee, travelled down to Southampton to meet his members. They told him they wanted to know why they had been refused security clearance. Later that day Gillard had a meeting with two BTI executives – Operations Manager P. J. Rogers and Personnel Manager A. B. Lewis – to discuss the dispute. Two days later, on 5 June, a deal was agreed which allowed the *Monarch* to sail but without the nine crewmen.

The agreement ensured that the nine would remain security risks and would 'remain at home on enforced leave'.[14] However, they would be on full pay and 'regarded as available for work' on CS *Iris*, one of the other cable ships. If the *Iris* was not being used then the vetted crewmen would receive ex-gratia payments to make up for lost earnings while their own ship was at sea. But, on the basic principle of secret vetting, management had won the day. The contractor, not the employer or the union, would retain the right to decide who would crew the ship. In an internal NCU memorandum Len Gillard 'accepted that such a provision cannot be rejected.'[15]

After the deal was negotiated the ship's crew accepted the package and the *Monarch* left Southampton for the Atlantic. But there was then a concerted effort by the union and management to cover up the dispute which, according to national NCU officer John Starmer, was 'very serious indeed, with far reaching implications.'[16]

On the day the agreement was signed, Thursday 5 June 1986, Starmer told the *Monarch*'s shop steward: 'We believe it is in the interests of our members to maintain confidentiality about this case.'[17] Although the dispute occurred during the union's national annual conference in Blackpool, the delegates were not told about the incident – privately or publicly. There has also been enormous pressure on the vetted crewmen and their shop steward to keep quiet. One frightened union official was threatened with the Official Secrets Act by BTI management if he disclosed any information to the authors. Len Gillard, the NCU officer responsible for the cable ships, also refused to provide any information on the case during our enquiries.

Vetting by the Personnel Department

The common characteristic of BT's vetting policies is its secrecy. But it is clear that there are two distinct procedures adopted by two different sectors of the company. Firstly, there is security vetting, implemented by the Security Division, which is often secret but includes open positive vetting for many employees. Secondly, there are operations run by the Corporate Personnel Services Department, which are even more clandestine.

There are some links between the Security Division and the Personnel Department. BT's nominated security officers in each part of the company – such as the International Division or UK Communications – are invariably personnel managers with other responsibilities. But their vetting methods remain separate. The personnel department is much more involved in vetting employees *after* they have joined BT. They are also more concerned with political and industrial factors than with security implications. Some of their information comes from confidential 'Security Questionnaires', which are distributed to the various BT divisions. These are filled in by local managers, who provide data about their employees' political views and return them to the Personnel Department – as in the Michael Dolan case.

For some years this operation was supervised by Michael Bett, now Managing Director of BT's UK Communications Division and the company's chief negotiator with the unions. Before joining BT in 1981, Bett was the BBC's Director of Personnel for four years, and controlled the corporation's vetting arrangements with MI5. An abrasive right winger, Bett was BT's Director of Personnel and Industrial Relations until 1984. He then became Director of Corporate Personnel Services until his promotion in May 1986.

Apart from its Corporate Director, the Personnel Department also has a battery of advisors and managers, including a separate unit known as CP7. This section has five officials, including Mr A. Gullett, responsible for 'Industrial Relations Research and

Briefing'. According to several union sources, BT executives appear to be supplied with complete dossiers of information on their trade union counterparts, including their political affiliations, during negotiations.

A notable victim of the Personnel Department's vetting policies was John Deason. In February 1984 he had joined the company as a technician, fitting private telephone wires in BT's City of London District. For two years he was not active in the union, although he did represent a small group of fitters. Then, in early 1986, he led a number of workers out of Rupert Murdoch's Wapping plant during the printworkers' dispute. This forced BT to use junior managers to do the work. Later that year, in October, Deason scored a notable victory over BT's City management. The company wanted to move the seventy-five fitters some distance from their original place of work. Deason argued that this would be 'a waste of time' as well as an inconvenience to the employees. Tony Linsall, the District Sales Manager, did not believe Deason was representing his members. So he called for a staff meeting on the issue. But, to the management's embarrassment, the workers voted unanimously to back Deason and to stay at their original headquarters.

It was not until the national strike by BT workers over pay in January 1987 that Deason really came to the notice of management. At first the industrial action had little success, as it did not include the City Branch. When the NCU City members joined the strike it had a major impact on the dispute. The City Branch was not only the largest in the union, it was also the most strategically important. For it services the City of London's 'Big Bang'. BT's lucrative contracts with merchant banks and institutions depended on the certainty that the City's telecommunications network would not break down. One communications expert says: 'City computer users do rely heavily on BT lines, especially the big land lines linking London to Manchester. They form the spine of big national networks. Industrial action could effectively break their backs.' Another analyst commented: 'The City's prestige position as the centre of the international financial community largely rests on its advanced communications. Good and uninterrupted communications are unquestionably the City's most precious commodity.'[18]

Any strike in that area would clearly be very damaging and effective. So when the City Branch workers joined the national dispute it was a major blow to the BT management. Deason was an enthusiastic backer of the action. He was on the City Branch Strike Committee, responsible for fund-raising (which mainly involved ensuring that pickets were paid their expenses). He also spoke at mass meetings in support of the strike.

After two weeks the NCU leadership recommended an end to the dispute and their members voted to return to work, but the City was one of the branches which voted to continue the strike. On the first day back at work, 12 February 1987, there was chaos. Many employees walked out again, accusing BT of breaking local agreements. The management, however, had laid careful plans for Deason and the other strikers. On that first morning Deason was transferred out, with two other union activists, to Piece Park depot on Marshalsea Road on the southernmost edge of the City area. This was a residential location used by BT for their disabled and handicapped workers, whose job was to clean and refurbish old telephones. Deason and the other two activists, also skilled workers, were issued with a can of Pledge and a toothbrush each. They were there for a month without doing a scrap of work. There was none to do.

BT's explanation for this transfer was that the three men were deployed 'in order to meet the requirements of the business.'[19] In fact, this was untrue. Deason had been co-ordinating a major contract with the bankers Samuel Montagu and Co. Ltd, based at 114 Old Broad Street in the City. The manager there specifically asked for Deason's return after his transfer because of staff shortages. BT refused.

Deason's transfer came at a time when he had just been nominated for one of the City Branch's senior positions – Financial Secretary. But being based at the Piece Park depot (known as 'the Penal Colony') made it almost impossible for him to canvass for the position. On 12 March 1987, Deason was again transferred, this time outside the City District to Pentonville Road to recover unused telephones, making it even more difficult for him to win support.

On 16 March, the day before the branch elections, a curious three-page letter was circulated to union members and managers. It was a blistering attack on the political views and activities of some branch members: 'During the past three years or more extremist elements of the Branch membership have continuously put their political self-interest BEFORE the interests of the Union.' The letter named seven activists, including Deason, as the 'extremists' and called on union members to oppose them.

This letter was given much credence as its author was Jock Campbell, the Branch's long-time Secretary until his resignation in October 1986. But Campbell was, in fact, a BT District Manager in the City Area when he wrote the letter. Combined with the transfers, the document was clearly designed to influence the internal union election. And it worked. Deason lost the election for Financial Secretary.

Deason had never made a secret of his political views and activities. He has been a member of the Socialist Workers' Party (SWP) since 1968 and its Industrial Organiser since 1975. Before joining BT he was also Secretary of the 'Right-To-Work' campaign. But it was only after the strike that the company took action against him and other activists in the City District. One of them, John Treadaway, was sacked for 'unacceptable behaviour whilst picketing' – he had called a working engineer a 'scab'. On Tuesday 12 May 1987, a week before Deason again stood for Financial Secretary in new branch elections, he was summoned to discuss 'a personal matter'. He was told it was to help him with his domestic problems (his wife had post-natal depression, worsened by the fire-bombing of a neighbour's flat). When he arrived in Room 410 at BT's Riverside House that afternoon he was surprised to be greeted by Maureen Dresser, a senior Personnel Officer. Normally the matter would have been dealt with by a Welfare Officer.

Dresser promptly closed the door and said she knew nothing of his personal problems. She then told him: 'It has come to my attention that there may have been a number of irregularities in the application form you completed when you applied for employment.' Deason was stunned. He had filled out the application forms in October 1983 – nearly four years previously. Dresser then passed him a letter outlining the allegations and stating that he had until 4 pm the next day to reply. Deason was asked to give 'a written confirmation that the information on the application form was complete and accurate'. Later that day he replied: 'At the time of writing, I did not enter any details that I believed to be false.'[20]

The following morning, on Thursday 14 May, Deason was again summoned for an interview with Maureen Dresser. She was accompanied by Shirley Williams, another Personnel Officer, who took detailed notes of what was said. Dresser began the meeting by saying that the central charge was that Deason had failed to provide full details of his past criminal convictions.

'Your application shows that you declared one unspent conviction for a motoring offence,' said Dresser. 'Was that the only unspent conviction you had at the time of your application?'

'I do not want to say anything more,' replied Deason, 'because you have not allowed me time to consult my solicitor.'

'It is not BT policy to allow solicitors to become involved in matters which are purely internal.'

Deason refused to answer any questions until he could see his solicitor: 'I'm being put under duress. I need to spend time with my wife who has got problems . . . I demand the right to see my solicitor.'

But Dresser was persistent: 'Are you telling me that you are not prepared to give me answers today and now?'

'Yes,' responded Deason.

The meeting ended inconclusively. But Dresser then sat down to draft a memorandum to Deason. It was his letter of dismissal: 'I believe that you have deceived British Telecom into giving you employment by deliberately concealing facts that should have been included in your application form.' At 4 pm he was handed the letter by his Manager at the Pentonville Road depot and told that 'under no circumstances' should he enter any BT building in the future. At 4.30 pm he was escorted from the premises.

Deason's sacking provoked an immediate outcry of protest from many of his colleagues. But they were also wary of management's tactics. For instance, they suspected that the Branch's union office telephone was being tapped. So they used the phone to make several calls, pretending to organise a rally in support of Deason outside Riverside House the next day, 15 May. Sure enough, an internal BT memo from the personnel office was quickly dispatched to company staff: 'There is likely to be a march on Riverside House at 1 pm today, as a result of City of London dismissing Deason. You are advised not to approach or make contact with any of the marchers. Any of your staff who absent themselves from duty should have their pay stopped.'

The 'march' never took place.

It is also clear from BT documents that management had detailed intelligence about the internal decisions, activities and personalities of the union. One memorandum from City Personnel Manager Richard Hammock to senior BT executives advocated leaking their inside information: 'Media interest is a strong possibility and I will be grateful if Corporate Relations (BT euphemism for Press Office) will discuss the judicious release of

information with me.'[21] This explains previous exclusive leaks to
the *London Standard*.[22] But it is rather inconsistent with BT's
official line. 'We do not discuss staff matters with third parties,'
was the standard public relations response to more sceptical
inquiries about Deason's case.

The real motives behind BT's dismissal of Deason were only
fully revealed when he brought the case before an Industrial
Tribunal. It was true that Deason had not included previous
convictions for three offences incurred during political demonstrations between 1976 and 1982 on his job application form (he
thought they were 'spent' convictions). He had been fined twice
and given a suspended sentence for 'obstruction', 'threatening
behaviour' and 'inciting reckless driving'. But the reality was that
BT had carried out a secret vetting investigation into Deason. The
aim was to prevent him from securing any influence in the City
Branch, using the application form as the pretext.

This was confirmed by an internal memorandum from the
Economic League, Britain's largest vetting agency, dated 9
December 1987. Written by Russell Walters, an Industrial Relations Department worker, and sent to John Udall, the League's
Liaison Director, it stated: 'Claims from several sources are that
BT was using a former senior Scotland Yard detective to
investigate Deason and other activists. The Economic League
provided BT with evidence and there has been no suggestion that
we did so in the press.'

At first BT denied having any links with the Economic League.
'We do not use, nor have we used, the Economic League,' a
spokesperson told *Time Out*.[23] But, a few days later, BT released a
statement:

'As necessary and prudent business practice, BT, in common with most
major national and international companies, provides itself with access
to a wide range of economic and commercial intelligence sources. BT is
not a member of the Economic League but does subscribe to its
information services.'

The company's political vetting of Deason was further corroborated by the Industrial Tribunal hearings. One internal memo BT
was obliged to disclose showed how Deason's initial transfer was
for political rather than professional reasons. Deason's name is
listed with those of the other two activists, and a Personnel
Officer has written alongside them: 'prefer to isolate'. The key
Personnel Officer involved in Deason's case, Maureen Dresser,

did appear at the preliminary hearing. But after it was adjourned she declined to be cross-examined because of 'mental anxiety'.

Just before the full tribunal hearing, in October 1987, BT tried to persuade Deason to accept financial compensation instead of continuing the case. Deason refused. Rather than defend their case in open court and be cross-examined on their political vetting policies, BT caved in. The company openly admitted they had sacked Deason for his trade union activities. They were then ordered by the Tribunal to reinstate him. BT refused, so they were forced to pay him £41,563 in compensation – one of the highest ever awards for unfair dismissal.

It was an embarrassing defeat for BT. But Deason was far from satisfied by the final outcome: 'It seems a complete travesty of natural justice that big powerful employers like BT can sack trade union activists with impunity . . . These are McCarthyite tactics with BT employing secret political vetting techniques to hound out socialists like me.'

BT's admission of guilt in Deason's case was a measure of their anxiety to preserve complete secrecy over the vetting issue, motivated by a desire to undermine active trade unionism in the company. There was also a commercial reason. As a BT spokesman commented, in a rare candid moment: 'We have a number of customers who want to be assured that we employ the right kind of people.'[24]

5

MI5 and the BBC: Stamping the 'Christmas Tree' Files

'One thing I can state quite categorically is that there has never been any victimisation of anyone for their political views at the BBC.'

Sir Hugh Greene, Director-General of the BBC 1960–69, reported in the *Sunday Times*, 20 February 1977.

'On employment, our policy is to appoint the best people we can.'

Sir Ian Trethowan, Director-General of the BBC 1977–82, in a letter to Lord Avebury, 13 November 1980.

If ever there was an example of 'security' factors being used as a pretext for political vetting, it is at the BBC. When their security procedures were revealed in 1985, the corporation said that vetting was restricted to a relatively small number of people who had access to 'sensitive information'. But in reality a large number of BBC employees – ranging from Graduate Trainees and journalists to arts producers and drama directors – were vetted by MI5 via the Personnel Department.

Perhaps the most graphic illustration of this was the attempt to blacklist Roland Joffe, probably Britain's most distinguished film and television director. His track record includes *The Killing Fields*, for which Joffe received an Academy Award nomination, and *The Mission* which won the top prize at the 1986 Cannes Film Festival.

In the spring of 1977 he was commissioned by the BBC to direct *The Spongers*, a new play about the failures of the welfare state and the desperate struggle of one woman caught in the poverty trap. The play's author was Jim Allen and its producer was Tony Garnett. Garnett informed the BBC's Drama Department that he wanted to hire Joffe as the director. But there was an unusually long delay in confirming his appointment. Eventually Garnett was summoned by Shaun Sutton, Head of Drama, to his fifth-floor office at the Television Centre, Wood Lane. Garnett had always had a frosty relationship with the corporation's top executives. He had deliberately chosen an office on top of the East Tower – 'to be as far away from management as possible.' But as he walked into Sutton's office that afternoon he was little prepared for what his Head of Drama was about to tell him.

Sutton looked distinctly uncomfortable. 'There is a problem with Joffe's contract,' he said. 'He hasn't got BH (Broadcasting House) clearance.' Astonished, Garnett asked why. Sutton refused to give a reason except to mutter: 'It was the man in the mac in Broadcasting House.'

Garnett stormed out and went straight to see Alasdair Milne, then Managing Director of BBC TV. Milne confirmed there was a problem and tried to placate Garnett by offering him a glass of whisky. But Garnett was seething, and said he would 'go public' if the veto on Joffe's appointment was not withdrawn: 'If you want all this business to come out then it's in your hands. If you don't hire Joffe then I'm off as well and imagine what it would look like if I walked out in the middle of my contract.' Milne said nothing, so Garnett continued, 'If this continues to happen then I won't be able to hire the people I want, which is my job as a producer.' Milne didn't argue. He picked up the phone and rang Sutton. 'Hire Joffe,' he snapped. Joffe's contract was confirmed and *The Spongers* became a big success, winning that year's prestigious Prix Italia award.

The 'problem' with Joffe's appointment was that the BBC's Personnel Department had, according to Garnett and the then Head of Plays, James Cellan-Jones, branded the director a 'security risk' because of his political views. This accusation was based on the fact that Joffe had attended Workers' Revolutionary Party (WRP) meetings in the early 1970s. Like many dramatists at the time he was briefly interested in the WRP, but he was never a party member, and by 1977 he had long severed his association with it. Joffe describes himself as a left winger, and says, 'I was very interested in politics at that time. But I was interested in what all the political parties were doing, not just the WRP, and I was never actively involved.'

Film producer and SDP supporter David Puttnam says of Joffe's politics: 'Roland would have nothing to do with the ideologies of the hard left. He detests that kind of imposition on the human spirit. He's a member of the Labour Party, and a socialist in the humanist sense. His heart is in sync with his mind.'[1]

The attempt to blacklist Joffe had nothing to do with the BBC's Drama Department. The recommendation had come from the Personnel Office at Broadcasting House on the advice of MI5. It was part of the highly secretive political vetting which the BBC had been practising since 1937, a situation only reformed in 1986, after considerable public and trade union pressure.

The system meant that all news and current affairs journalists, film editors, directors and producers in every department were vetted by the Security Services. Vetting was run from Room 105, a secluded office on the first floor of Broadcasting House – a part of the same network of corridors on which George Orwell modelled his Ministry of Truth in *1984*. There the BBC employed a Security Liaison Officer who received the names of all successful job applicants from the chairmen of interviewing boards. Then the vetting, which in BBC-speak became known as 'colleging' or 'the fomalities', took place.

All BBC employees had a personnel file which included their basic personal details and work record. But there was also a second file. This included 'security information' collected by Special Branch and MI5, who have always kept political surveillance on 'subversives in the media'. If a staff member was shortlisted for a job this second file was handed to the department head, who had to sign for it. The file was a buff folder with a round red sticker, stamped with the legend 'SECRET' and a symbol which looked like a Christmas tree. On the basis of information in this file, the Personnel Office recommended whether the person in question should be given the job or not. A former senior BBC executive recalls seeing one journalist's security file, stamped with a Christmas tree symbol: 'For about twelve years it had recorded notes such as "has subscription to *Daily Worker*" or "our friends say he associates with communists and CND activists." It is fair to say that there were contemporary memos from personnel officials adding they thought this was ridiculous. But it was still on file.'[2]

The names of outside job applicants were submitted directly to C Branch of MI5. They were then passed on to the F Branch 'domestic subversion', whose F7 section looks at political 'extremists', MP's, lawyers, teachers and journalists. After consulting the registry of files, the names were fed into MI5's computer, which contains the identities of about a million 'subversives'.

Once M15 had vetted an applicant their decision was given in writing to the BBC's Personnel Office. M15 never gave reasons for their recommendations. But, quite often, if they said a person was a 'security risk', that was enough to blacklist him or her permanently. Members of board interviews were advised not to ask questions. And it was only when an executive or editor put pressure on the Personnel Department that M15's decision was overruled.

For many years a BBC staff member was used as the Security Liaison Officer. But in 1982 Brigadier Ronald L. Stonham, a retired army officer, moved into Room 105 as 'Special Assistant' to the Director of Personnel, Christopher Martin, himself a former Royal Marine. Stonham began his working life in the Post Office Engineering Department during the Second World War. In 1948 he was commissioned into the Royal Signals Regiment, and by 1963 he had worked his way through the ranks to Major. He also had a spell in the intelligence section of the Chief of General Staff in 1971. Six years later he was promoted to Brigadier of the Signals Regiment.

Stonham saw security vetting as part of his responsibility to co-ordinate BBC's contingency plans for a wartime and emergency broadcasting service. This was the official line taken after the *Observer* revealed the corporation's blacklisting policies in 1985. The BBC stated: 'Only relatively few members of staff go through this [vetting] procedure. They are necessarily involved in sensitive areas or require access to classified information.'

This was untrue. The evidence shows that vetting was used in a much wider context – and for political, not security, reasons.

Vetting – a Reithian Legacy

Security vetting was set up in 1937, at a time when the BBC was almost taken over by the government as a State propaganda outlet. The corporation was under constant political pressure, particularly from the Foreign Office. But Sir John Reith, the BBC's founder and first Director-General, was also keen on including vetting as part of his vision of a wartime BBC. In 1935 Reith was a member of a sub-committee of the Government Committee of Imperial Defence which included military personnel. The sub-committee decided that 'in time of war or when the threat of an emergency was imminent, the government should assume effective control over broadcasting and the BBC'. Two years later, in 1937, the Ullswater Committee on the future of broadcasting recommended that 'in serious or national emergencies . . . full government control over the BBC would be necessary.'

Reith wanted to be actively involved in the government's defence preparations in case of war. On 5 March 1937 he went to the Home Office to see Sir John Simon, the Home Secretary, and Geoffrey Lloyd, the Parliamentary Under-Secretary, and a contract was negotiated between the BBC and the government 'in case of war'.[3] It seems highly likely that the implementation of security vetting was part of this agreement.

By 1937 the security services were certainly geared up for vetting BBC staff. In 1935 the Secret Service budget – including both MI5 and MI6 – was increased by secret vote from £180,000 to £350,000. By 1939 it was £500,000. But early BBC liaison with MI5 was often sluggish and inefficient, as the then Director-General, Frederick Ogilvie, a former Tory MP, revealed in a note written in late 1939. Among the problems he was encountering was 'the failure of MI5 to okay our artists at reasonable speed.'[4] Sir Hugh Greene, later to be Director-General himself, was one of the first to encounter 'security clearance' when he joined the BBC as head of their German Service: 'I was vetted in 1940. MI5 thought I was a communist, but it turned out to be a mistake.'[5] The following year the actor Michael Redgrave encountered more serious problems when he signed the 'People's Convention'. This was a socialist manifesto which called for 'a people's war' and 'a people's peace'. It was not long before Redgrave was summoned to Broadcasting House. On 25 February 1941 he was met by a Mr Streeton and another BBC official. They told him that the 'People's Convention' was 'not in the national interest' and asked him where he stood regarding it. Redgrave replied that since it was not an illegal or seditious document he supported it and it was not for the BBC to censure him. The official thanked him for making his position clear and told him he would no longer be allowed to broadcast for the BBC. Three weeks later, after angry protests from MPs and fellow actors, the ban was lifted.[6]

During the Cold War of the late 1940s and early 1950s, MI5 vetting of BBC staff was expanded, and the secrecy of the operation frequently laid it open to abuse. Sir Hugh Greene recalled one victim in the External Services while he was Controller of Broadcasting in the German Zone: 'He wasn't a security risk at all. It turned out he had worked for M16, the rival secret service, and there had been an internal quarrel.'[7]

Other blacklists were also being compiled by the BBC hierarchy. This was confirmed by General Sir Ian Jacob, former Military Assistant to the War Cabinet, who was appointed Director-General of the BBC by Winston Churchill in 1952 after being Director of the Overseas Services. He recalled: 'I was shown lists of communists in the BBC. It was handled by the Controller of Administration. A relative of mine was actually on the list because he had a communist wife.'

That relative was his second cousin Alaric Jacob, who had joined the BBC Monitoring Service at Caversham in August 1948. In February 1951 he was suddenly refused establishment rights, which meant he would receive no pension. He went to see his relative Sir Ian Jacob at Broadcasting House to complain.

'Are you in the Communist Party?' the Director of Overseas Services asked.

'No,' replied Alaric Jacob.

'What about your wife?'

'You have no business to put that question. The BBC knows perfectly well that I hope to become a Labour MP. I am not prepared to discuss Iris's politics with any BBC official. They have nothing whatever to do with my professional ability which no one at the BBC has ever questioned.'[8]

The 'communist wife' was Iris Morley, the novelist and Marxist historian. She had been the Moscow Correspondent of the *Observer* during the Second World War, and Alaric Jacob did the same job for the *Daily Express*. The discrimination against Jacob was only resolved in 1953 when his wife died from cancer. Just after her obituary appeared in *The Times* he was told by a BBC administrator that he could now receive full establishment and pension rights.

By the 1950s and early 1960s political vetting was so well entrenched that BBC interviews were resembling Civil Service selection boards. At one time, according to former senior BBC executive Stuart Hood, a Civil Service commissioner even attended the interviews. Hood recalls the selection boards using Whitehall euphemisms for vetting during their post-interview discussions. 'Does he play with a straight bat?' or 'Does he have snow on the right foot?' were typical BBC expressions for political suitability.

Hood was a key witness of vetting during this period. He had joined the BBC in 1946 and was head of the World Service throughout the 1950s. He became Controller of Programmes in 1961 before leaving in 1964. He recalls attending BBC Board of Management meetings: 'During those meetings senior administrative officials used to approach me, show me these slips of paper and say, "I think you should know this," and then show me an article in *Peace News*.' Hood also saw the security files: 'The investigative reports produced on staff and performers by the security services are testimony to the amount of petty espionage and surveillance to which citizens of our society are subjected.'[9]

Although Sir Hugh Greene's Director-Generalship of the 1960s led to a liberalisation of the rather stuffy BBC, vetting continued. A notable subject was the distinguished documentary director Stephen Peet. In 1965 he was appointed to a senior position in the BBC's Documentary and Features Department after several years of successful freelance work. According to Hallam Tennyson, a BBC Careers Officer, and Stuart Hood, the offer was suddenly withdrawn because of an adverse security report.

MI5 had told the BBC that Peet could not be allowed on the staff because he continued to contact and meet his communist brother John, who lived and worked in East Germany. In 1950, fifteen years before Stephen Peet's job application, his brother had left his post as Reuters' West Berlin Correspondent and defected to East Germany, where he still lives. Stephen Peet was not and never has been a communist or politically active in any way. Yet he was consistently rejected for full-time BBC jobs. Eventually, when some BBC executives told him informally about the blacklisting, he appealed to his MP, Kenneth Robinson, then Minister for Health in Harold Wilson's Labour government. Robinson lobbied the Home Office: 'I went to see a Minister and I made representations on Peet's behalf.' About four months later Peet received a letter from Robinson, which told him he could now join the BBC staff: 'There is now no barrier.' Sure enough, Peet was soon recruited, and he went on to make the highly praised series *Yesterday's Witness*, winner of a Royal Television Society special award.

By the early 1970s many BBC executives were taking the view that the secret vetting procedures had little to do with security. Politics were much more relevant. John Laird, a former External Services producer who worked in the Appointments Department, was one such executive. He was also chairman of many interview boards. He points to one conversation he had with Sir

Ian Trethowan, then Managing Director of BBC Radio and later Director-General, as indicative of the situation. Trethowan, a Conservative and a close friend of the then Prime Minister Edward Heath, asked Laird why he had appointed so many 'reds' and 'commies' as general trainees.

'They're not communists,' replied Laird. 'They're independent socialists and dissidents. Besides, all the bright young people are left wing these days.'

'Oh, they're all the same to me,' said Trethowan. 'They're all commies. I can't believe that there weren't some bright right wing people.'[10]

One of the bright young people Laird appointed as a Graduate Trainee at the time was Michael Rosen. He had been a student activist and well-known actor and dramatist at Oxford University in the late 1960s. During his interviews with the BBC Rosen made no secret of his Marxist views. And during his training he was equally uncompromising, making a radio documentary about the French Marxist Regis Debray.

In 1972 Rosen was sacked and told that no department would offer him a job. He was offered a £330 ex-gratia payment by Owen Reed, head of Staff Training, and told: 'We think it would be better if you went freelance.' In fact, at least two departments, Arts Features and Further Education, wanted to employ him but were prevented from doing so because there was a 'security problem'. According to John Laird, who was in charge of Graduate Trainees, 'I was called by the chairman of one board who said: "You'll be glad to know we've appointed Rosen." Then he called again, embarrassed, and said it had been "blocked".' Fortunately for Rosen he was sufficiently talented to overcome being blacklisted. He has since become a successful writer of plays and children's poetry books, and frequently appears on television.

Targetting Journalists

In 1975 a special desk was set up within MI5 to look at 'subversives in the media'. Based in F Branch, one of the desk's first tasks was to compile a report on 'bias in the media'. This was inspired by the notion that Trotskyists had infiltrated the press and broadcasting. The strategy was to recruit journalists as agents for MI5 and to persuade them to spy on their left-wing colleagues. MI5 officers were told to list possible recruits in the monthly 'Resources Index' and pass the names on to FX Division.

One reporter who was approached was Tim Jones, a labour correspondent on *The Times*. In 1975 he was taken out to lunch at Simpsons in the Strand by an MI5 officer and told that the security services were worried about 'Soviet penetration of the industrial correspondents group'. Jones was asked to provide 'intelligence' about certain journalists, but he refused.[11]

MI5 tried harder the following year with Jon Snow, a senior ITN correspondent. He was approached as a possible agent because his background as the son of the Bishop of Whitby was thought promising. At first he was asked to give information about the Communist Party. But he was then asked to spy on certain 'left-wing people' working in television. In return MI5 would make secret monthly tax-free payments into his bank account. Snow rejected the approach.[12]

It was clear that this intelligence-gathering operation was for blacklisting purposes. Evidence for this was revealed by MI5's attempts to block the career of Anna Ford, the former ITN news reader and darling of the popular press. In 1974 she had joined Granada Television and became a journalist for their daily news programme *Granada Reports*. There she met fellow-journalist Trevor Hyett, and they soon began living together. It was then that the Security Services began their operation against her. Although she had been an outspoken student politician at Manchester University in the late 1960s, Ford was not politically active. Yet she was logged in intelligence records as 'an associate of a subversive'. For Trevor Hyett was a former member of the Communist Party. He had joined the Young Communist League in 1962, and three years later was appointed Editor of the YCL newspaper *Challenge*. Under Hyett's editorship it was the first Western communist publication to criticise the Soviet Union over its treatment of artists and writers. And in 1968 Hyett led a YCL delegation to Moscow to protest at the Russian invasion of Czechoslovakia. He was becoming increasingly disillusioned by the British Communist Party's refusal to change its internal structure and its unwillingness to criticise Soviet policy. In 1972 Hyett resigned and returned his party card.

Despite his resignation, Special Branch officers in Manchester kept a file on Hyett, details of which were relayed to MI5 in London. The file showed that he was living with Anna Ford. In 1975, in an attempt to discover more information about the couple, particularly Hyett, Special Branch tried to recruit Granada journalists as office spies. One such reporter was

Geoffrey Seed, who was then working with Ford and Hyett on *Granada Reports*. He was approached by a Special Branch officer, Constable Kevin Moore.

'I had met Moore two or three times,' Seed recalls. 'To me he was just another contact, a police contact. Then one evening, when I was having a drink with him, he started saying that he could help me with information if I would help him. He said he was interested in some people who worked for Granada – "lefties and communists". And he specifically mentioned Trevor Hyett, who was sharing a house with Anna. He wanted me to give him information. I had a feeling of revulsion. It had nothing to do with national security. This was pure Eastern Europe. I simply refused and finished my drink.'

The following year, in September 1976, Anna Ford was offered a job on *Man Alive*, the BBC 2 documentary programme. But soon after putting forward her contract for approval, Michael Latham, *Man Alive*'s editor, received a phone call from the BBC Personnel Secretariat. 'We don't think you should give this woman a contract,' said the caller. He refused to give a reason. Latham then approached his superior, Desmond Wilcox, then Head of Features, who took up the matter. 'When I approached the Personnel Department,' said Wilcox, 'they told me their opposition was because she had been living with a former communist. I was outraged.' Wilcox then protested to his boss, Aubrey Singer, Controller of BBC 2, who told him: 'Don't worry. Take no notice of them.' But Wilcox was indignant: 'At that time I, and 99 per cent of the BBC staff, had no idea that MI5 vetting was taking place. Anna Ford was an excellent journalist and presenter whom we wanted to take on. I could not care less who she used to live with and I could not understand why any opposition had been raised against her.'[13]

Eventually MI5's objections were overruled and Ford was able to join *Man Alive* in January 1977. By that time she and Hyett had separated. In 1978 she became ITN's first female newscaster. Hyett went on to become a successful freelance TV producer. He reflects ruefully on the criteria MI5 used for trying to wreck Ford's career – that she had once had a boyfriend who used to be in the Communist Party. 'Along with Sir Alfred Sherman, Lord Chapple and Denis Healey, I belong to the biggest party in the world – the ex-communists,' said Hyett. 'Taxpayers didn't get much for their money from this surveillance and activity.'

Another young journalist, who applied for a BBC job in the same month as Anna Ford, was not so lucky. In September 1976 Isabel Hilton was interviewed for a reporter's job on BBC Scotland's current affairs programme *Current Account*. The board agreed unanimously that she was the best candidate and appointed her. The decision was then relayed to the London Personnel Office.

About a week later Alastair Hetherington, then Controller of BBC Scotland, received a phone call from the BBC's Security Liaison Officer in London. Hilton could not be appointed, he said. When asked why, the official replied 'procedures'. Hetherington couldn't believe it. 'I knew she couldn't have been a security risk,' he recalls. He told the Security Officer that he was not prepared to accept the blacklisting of Hilton without reasons. The Security Officer said this was unprecedented. But Hetherington insisted. So the Security Officer visited Hetherington at his BBC Scotland office in Glasgow. The cautious BBC mandarin said 'it was not done' for Personnel to give reasons why an individual had failed 'procedures'. Hetherington replied that he had been dealing with security people for over twenty years, as a defence correspondent from 1953 to 1956 and later as editor of the *Guardian*. He said he was not satisfied and wanted to know the reasons for their decision. The Security Officer said he was shocked by his attitude. It was the first time a BBC executive had challenged a security assessment, he added. Nothing was resolved by the meeting. But about two weeks later the Security Officer rang Hetherington and agreed to give the reason. He said Hilton had been rejected because she had been Secretary of the Scottish-China Association. 'It is regarded as suspect and so she cannot be appointed,' he added. 'There is a risk of subversive influences in the organisation.' According to government sources, MI5 had advised the BBC that while Hilton remained Secretary of that Association she should not be appointed – unless the BBC had very good reasons otherwise.

Hetherington was not happy with these reasons. He telephoned Kay Carmichael, a fellow member of the Broadcasting Council for Scotland who was then an advisor to 10 Downing Street on social policy. She was also a member of the Scottish-China Association. He told her what had happened and asked her whether the Association was a subversive organisation. Carmichael couldn't believe it. She told Hetherington that the idea of the Scottish-China Association being subversive was so ludicrous that M15 must have mixed it up with another organisation . . . the Society for Anglo-Chinese Understanding, perhaps.

In fact, M15 had got the 'right' organisation. But in no way was it subversive. The Scottish-China Association was a small cultural group based at Edinburgh University. Its main activity was being addressed by eminent Chinese scholars, and Hilton spent most of her time organising conferences on issues like population control. The Association never took any political position on events in China. Nor did it discuss politics.

Hetherington continued to protest. But it was not until January 1977 that he was finally told by the BBC Security Liaison Officer that Hilton could now be employed. Meanwhile, Hilton had been waiting in Edinburgh for four months and had not even received a rejection letter from the BBC, so she accepted a job as a feature writer on the *Daily Express* in London.

Before leaving Scotland Hilton threw a farewell party and rang Hetherington, a personal friend, to invite him. Hetherington was puzzled as to why she was leaving. 'Why didn't you accept the BBC job?' he asked. 'I haven't been offered it,' she replied. Hetherington was upset: 'I'll make some enquiries.' Ten minutes later Hilton was telephoned by a BBC Personnel Officer who offered her the job and apologised for the delay. But it was too late. She was already committed to the *Daily Express* job.

Hilton was unable to pursue her chosen career as a television journalist, and she had not wanted to leave Edinburgh, particularly as her future husband Neal Ascherson was then working there for the *Scotsman*. She is now Latin America Editor of the *Independent*, but she remains resentful about her experience: 'I was extremely distressed to discover that a citizen can be maligned and damaged by the security services without his or her knowledge and without any means of redress. It is a squalid system and greatly to the discredit of the BBC that they should have been party to it.'

Another young journalist to be targetted was given a three-month contract as a Researcher for *Nationwide*, the now defunct daily magazine programme, in February 1982. One of the incidents he reported concerned a rape by a Saudi Arabian army officer being concealed by Manchester police because of diplomatic pressure.

A few days after the item was broadcast he received a memo from his editor congratulating him on 'an excellent story' and a fine start to his career at the BBC. But a week before his contract expired, he received a letter from the Personnel Department informing him that it would not be renewed. His editor, who had planned to retain him, protested to Personnel, who eventually conceded there were 'security reasons'. The journalist had been a student activist at Manchester University, and then, briefly, a member of the small Maoist group, Communist Party of Britain (Marxist-Leninist).

Eventually the Personnel Department agreed to compromise. He could work at the BBC – but not on politically sensitive current affairs programmes. He was then offered an eight-month contract on the consumer series *That's Life*. He refused. Fortunately, his editor felt so aggrieved about his treatment that he continued to employ him privately for four months, but he then had to leave the BBC.

Perhaps the most bizarre case of journalist blacklisting was that of Richard Gott, who had applied to be Editor of the *Listener*, the BBC's weekly magazine. According to Sir Hugh Greene, Director-General from 1960 to 1969, MI5 vetting of this position was introduced in the mid-1970s.

In 1981 Gott was interviewed by a BBC Board and was chosen for the post. But MI5 vetoed the appointment. According to a senior executive who was on the Board, 'His file went off for "colleging" and it was blocked. They said he was an ultra-leftist and that "he digs with the wrong foot".' This was confirmed by Alasdair Milne, then Deputy Director-General and Managing Director of BBC TV, who also sat on the Board. 'That was a classic case,' he said. 'I don't feel very happy.'[14]

After a ten-day delay during which Gott was vetted, Russell Twisk was appointed Editor. MI5's specific objection to Gott was his support for revolutionary movements in Latin America and South-East Asia. In 1966 he had resigned from the Labour Party to stand as an independent candidate in the Hull by-election in protest at the British government's support for American involvement in Vietnam. He had also openly supported Che Guevara and his guerrillas in Bolivia, which resulted in his imprisonment by the Bolivian government for 'communist' activities. In addition, he had caused ripples among the establishment while broadcasting on the Foreign Office-funded BBC World Service for supporting trade unionists in the then British colony of Aden. Gott is now Features Editor of the *Guardian*.

Open Space – Closed Door

The BBC has always been proud of its Community Programmes Unit. Based in Hammersmith Grove, west London, some distance from the main Television Centre, the unit has always seen itself as having considerable autonomy within the vast BBC corporate structure. But even this independence did not exempt it from the BBC's vetting procedures.

Paul Turner is one person who found his way blocked to the BBC's 'access' programmes department. He had joined BBC Wales in 1971, as an assistant film editor, while an active member of the Young Liberals. Soon afterwards he joined the Communist Party, and it was then that his troubles began. He began applying for jobs elsewhere in the BBC but was consistently rejected.

One of his applications in 1975 was as a film editor on a six-month attachment to the Community Programmes Unit. Again he was unsuccessful. A senior executive, who sat on one of his interview boards, explained why: 'He was interviewed, but as soon as he left the room, the Appointments Officer said there had been a mistake. His file had a Christmas tree (i.e. a security file was held) and he should not have even been allowed an interview. He was a "security risk" because of something to do with Welsh nationalism.'[15]

His Communist Party membership was also a problem; although Turner had left the party in 1973 because of its apologetic attitude towards the Soviet Union, he remained blacklisted. This became obvious when he was asked by a BBC Wales executive at one board in 1980: 'Do you feel being in the Communist Party would interfere with your work?' Turner told him he had stopped being a communist in 1973 – seven years earlier. He didn't get the job.

His Welsh nationalist activities amounted to learning the Welsh language because he was working on programmes of Welsh interest. He does now vote Plaid Cymru, but this hardly qualifies him as a 'security risk'.

Turner, who now runs a successful independent production company, was actually relieved when he was told of the blacklisting: 'For years I had worried my career at the BBC never blossomed because I was somehow second rate, applying for those jobs and not getting them.'[16]

The door to BBC's 'access' programmes was similarly closed to Yvette Vanson. In 1979 she applied for a job at the Community

Programmes Unit and was offered the position of Production Assistant on *Open Space*. She was delighted, as she had only just left college. But five days before she was due to start an executive was told by a Personnel Officer: 'We can't give her a contract. She was an active member of the WRP (Workers' Revolutionary Party) and so we cannot employ her.' The executive then rang Vanson: 'I'm sorry, I don't know what to say. The Personnel Department have said I can't employ you.'

Vanson was distraught, as she had just turned down other job offers and places at the University of Kent and the Central London Polytechnic. She appealed against the decision, and went to see Christopher Storey, a Personnel Officer at Television Centre. Storey told her there had been a 'misunderstanding'. He agreed that she had been offered a job, but added that the editor 'was not aware that there was a suitably qualified person already on the staff who was available to do the work. I am very sorry that that meant we were not in a position to offer you a formal contract.'[17]

This official line was nonsense, according to the executive concerned. He was told he couldn't hire her because she had been a 'WRP organiser'. Although she had been active in the WRP in the early 1970s while working as an actress, Vanson had left the party in 1975 – four years before applying for the BBC job.

Eventually the BBC agreed to give her £500 as an ex-gratia payment. Vanson accepted the money, as by then she was penniless. But the blacklisting had a severe impact on her life: she was unemployed for the next five months, despite applying for nearly 200 jobs, and was forced to return to college. 'It was a very traumatic experience for me,' she recalls. 'I was on the crest of a wave about getting a job at the BBC so soon after leaving college . . . The WRP is not an illegal or proscribed organisation. It's ridiculous that just because you're politically active you are victimised in this way.'

Five years later, in July 1984, Vanson again approached the BBC and was again interviewed for *Open Space*, this time as an Assistant Producer. Once again she was appointed, and once again Personnel objected because of her past political affiliations. 'Wasn't she in the WRP?' an executive was asked. But this time the executive angrily stood his ground and she was able to join *Open Space*. Vanson has since become a successful freelance director.

Moves Against the Arts and Drama

When the BBC acknowledged the existence of MI5 vetting, after its public disclosure in 1985, much was made of the claim that it was restricted to a relatively small number of staff. Alasdair Milne, then Director-General, said: 'It may sometimes look foolish, but it is another source of information when you are trying to work out whether people are up to certain jobs. Clearly we are involved, a number of us, in very sensitive areas of material and the process of establishing that people can handle that sort of material is important, even in a democratic society.'[18]

But many of the victims of the BBC blacklist were working in areas which had nothing remotely to do with 'handling sensitive material', for instance the Arts and Drama Departments.

One arts programme affected was *Omnibus*, whose editor from 1975 to 1982 was Barrie Gavin. In February 1976, he received a detailed and well-presented proposal for a documentary from the young director Jeff Perks. Gavin, who remembered his work as a graduate director at the British Film Institute, found Perks's proposal – about the poster maker Ken Sprague – interesting and exciting. He agreed to make the programme, and a three-month contract was passed to the Personnel Office for approval.

A week later, in his office at Kensington House, Gavin received a telephone call from Christopher Storey, Senior Personnel Officer for BBC TV, who was based at Threshold House, Shepherds Bush Green.

'There may be a problem about employing Jeff Perks,' said Storey.

'Why?' asked Gavin.

'He may not be acceptable.'

'What do you mean by not acceptable?'

'Not acceptable.'

Gavin then asked for a reason. But Storey refused to give him one. 'I presume Leslie Page [Head of Personnel] will tell me why,' said Gavin impatiently.

'Not necessarily,' replied Storey.

'Well, if you don't tell me, I'm going to do two things. One, I'm going straight to the head of my department and two, I'm going public and will make sure that every newspaper and television station knows about this.'

'I would strongly advise you not to do that.'

As editor of a major programme with a large budget, Gavin resented being prevented from choosing his own staff. As soon as he put the phone down, he went to see Humphrey Burton, head of the Arts Department. At first Burton's attitude was flippant: 'Perhaps it's because he's a communist or maybe he has a foreign background or name.' Gavin told Burton he wanted to take the matter further. Two weeks later he saw Sir Ian Trethowan, then Managing Director of BBC TV. It was a strange conversation – rather like two civil servants discussing a sensitive issue, but without specifically referring to the heart of the matter. Trethowan wrung his hands and was clearly uncomfortable. 'Yes, well, these kind of cases are very difficult,' he said.

'I don't see what's so difficult about this,' replied Gavin. 'I am asking him [Perks] to make a film about a poster maker in the middle of Exmoor. I'm not sending him out on a Poseidon nuclear submarine.'

Trethowan agreed to look into the matter. Three weeks later Perks was given a contract, and his film went on to secure the highest ratings of any *Omnibus* programme that year. Humphrey Burton also liked it. 'That was a very good film,' he remarked to Gavin. 'I think you should pursue this combination further.' So, in December 1976, Gavin asked Perks and Sprague to make a series of pilot programmes for *Omnibus*.

But once again MI5 objected. A Personnel Officer told Gavin it was not possible to use him. Now he was outraged. Not only was this unjust, it was also unnecessary and a complete waste of time. Angry memos flew between departments. The matter was referred to Alasdair Milne, then Director of Programmes, who supported the ban. So Burton went higher – to Sir Ian Trethowan. Eventually, three days before Christmas, Gavin got a call at home from Burton, who told him: 'It's OK now, you can use Jeff Perks.'

MI5 objected to Perks for a simple reason. He had been a member of the Communist Party since 1971. But to Gavin this did not make him a legitimate target: 'The Communist Party is not a proscribed or illegal organisation. And anyway, the notion that the modern Communist Party is revolutionary is laughable.' Perks would also have been put on MI5's files in 1973 after making a film with Michael Rosen at the National Film School about the 'Shrewsbury Three', three building workers who had been jailed for picketing offences during a strike. Part of the film was shown on Thames Television's *This Week*, and caused a storm of protest from Tory MPs in the Commons.

It was lucky for Perks that he had an editor of such integrity as Gavin. If he had been turned down by the BBC, it would have been hard for him to find work because at the time the independent sector was very limited for young film makers. Perks left the Communist Party in 1977. Since then he has had no employment problems in the BBC.

As well as vetting directors on BBC arts programmes, MI5 were also keeping a close eye on the corporation's Drama Department. Actors, actresses, producers and directors were all vetted. According to Stuart Hood: 'Actors and performers were blacklisted. I went to one meeting in the early 1960s where slips of paper were being handed out about an actress. They said: "Not to be used on sensitive programmes." I knew the woman. She was not political, but her husband was a pre-war left-wing Austrian refugee. I strongly protested at the time.'

But MI5 reserved their strongest objections to BBC drama producers in the early and mid-1970s. It was a period of great political turmoil and activity. And television drama reflected the new radical mood with plays like *Cathy Come Home*, *Leeds United*, *Law and Order* and others. These were hard-hitting, naturalistic dramas which portrayed working-class people in a sympathetic light. They also sparked off political controversy. As Kenith Trodd recalled: 'There was a general view at the time that drama has a powerful hold on people's hearts and minds and that it was a source of political influence.'

Many of the producers, writers and directors of these plays were also politically active. They included Ken Loach, Roy Battersby, Trevor Griffiths, Kenith Trodd, Roland Joffe and Tony Garnett. As well as being active in their trades unions, they held regular Friday night meetings – either at Tony Garnett's flat in Notting Hill Gate or Roy Battersby's house in Maida Vale. In the early 1970s they also attended meetings of the Socialist Labour League (later the WRP), although only a few actually became members.

The head of BBC Drama during this crucial period – 1969–81 – was Shaun Sutton, a former theatre and television director who had been at the BBC since 1952. He believed that good television drama should be controversial, and was a strong backer of his producers and directors.

On MI5 vetting of his staff he said: 'I suppose it happened because the BBC had the system and we had to apply to it.' But, to his credit, Sutton did stand up to the Personnel Department. 'One needs to be quietly firm with these people,' he remarked to James Cellan-Jones, his Head of Plays, during the attempts to blacklist Roland Joffe.

One of Sutton's first battles occurred in 1970, when he tried to employ Tony Garnett, producer of *Cathy Come Home*. A Personnel Officer objected, 'Isn't he a bit of a left winger?' Sutton then talked to Garnett, and decided that his professional ability was more important than his political views. A more significant episode occurred the following year. In 1971 John Goldschmidt was commissioned to direct a *Play for Today* about school leavers. He was much relieved, as two years previously his contract as a director on *Omnibus* had been abruptly terminated without explanation. He was soon installed in an office in the BBC Drama Department, and began work on the play. But once again he was blacklisted. An embarrassed executive came into his office and told him: 'You're not supposed to be allowed to work here.' A Personnel Officer had said he could not be employed. A major row erupted in the Drama Department and an angry deputation went to see Huw Weldon, then Managing Director of BBC TV. Weldon took the matter up, and Goldschmidt was reinstated.[19] His 'offence' was that he had taken part in an exchange of students between his art college in Hornsey, north London, and a Czech film school, spending a few weeks in Czechoslovakia. He was not, and never had been, a communist.

By the mid-1970s MI5 and the Personnel Department were clearly out to purge the BBC's radical dramatists. Christopher Morahan, a distinguished director who was Head of Plays from 1972 to 1976, said: 'There was an opinion expressed at that particular time by Personnel that a number of people should not be used. But I have to say that I won in every argument I was involved in.'

Apart from Roland Joffe, one of the most notable people the Personnel Department objected to was Kenith Trodd, probably the BBC's most respected and successful drama producer. His credits included Colin Welland's *Leeds United*, *Days of Hope* (about the General Strike) and *Coming Out*. He also produced much of Dennis Potter's work, notably *Pennies from Heaven* and *Brimstone and Treacle* (banned by the BBC for eleven years). Shaun Sutton said of him: 'He is absolutely first class. He has done some damn good work.'

Yet, in September 1976, Trodd's freelance contract as producer on *Play for Today* was terminated, despite having been renewed annually for the previous four years. There was an immediate storm of protest from Trodd's colleagues, who suspected that this act was politically motivated. Director Bryan Gibson drafted a letter with the actor Simon Gray registering 'surprise and dismay that his [Trodd's] contract is not being renewed.' It was signed by Dennis Potter, Colin Welland and Michael Lindsay-Hogg, among others, and dispatched to Alasdair Milne. Milne and Sir Ian Trethowan both strongly denied that there was a plot against Trodd. They claimed that the system of freelance contracts was being reorganised in order to phase out one-year renewable deals. Trodd's contract was simply being renegotiated and he would eventually be invited back as a 'guest producer'.

In fact the Personnel Office and MI5 had branded Trodd a 'security risk' since the early 1970s, when he had attended WRP meetings (although he was never a party member).

In 1976 the management made their move. The key executive involved was James Cellan-Jones, a talented director who had become Head of Plays that autumn. One of his first tasks was to deal with Trodd's contract. Cellan-Jones didn't always agree with Trodd, but he had no intention of sacking him. But one day Trethowan came into his office. Cellan-Jones recalls: 'Ian Trethowan said he wanted to remove Trodd and I was not to renew him because there were "security problems" . . . He said Trodd was a troublemaker and suspected by the security people.'

Cellan-Jones didn't like it. He thought about it for a few days and then went to see Trethowan. He argued against sacking Trodd, and Trethowan backed down. But it was a few weeks before Trodd's contract was renewed. He then went on to make *Pennies from Heaven*, winner of the 1979 British Academy award for most original programme.

Trodd survived one blacklisting attempt, but director Roy Battersby was a marked man for thirteen years. In 1972 he had been invited by Christopher Morahan, head of plays, to direct *The Operation*, a satire about a property speculator. MI5 objected: he was an active member of the WRP. 'Yes, there was an objection to him,' recalls Morahan. 'It was indicated to me that they [the Personnel Department] would be happier if he was not engaged. I said he was the best director for the job and I wasn't prepared to accept it.'

Battersby went on to direct *Leeds United*, a controversial play about a clothing strike in Leeds. He then left television to work full-time for the WRP. It wasn't until the spring of 1985 that he next came up against the BBC blacklist. He had been asked by Kenith Trodd to direct a play based on Stuart Hood's book *Pebbles From My Skull*, an account of Italian resistance fighters during the Second World War. Battersby was invited to Bologna to start work on the project, but before he could leave, Trodd spoke to Peter Goodchild, Head of Plays, and told him he wanted to employ Battersby. 'Come on, Ken,' sighed Goodchild, 'you know there are always some people we can't employ on sensitive subjects.' Battersby was refused a contract.

Within six weeks MI5 again targetted Battersby. In June 1985 he was asked to direct four episodes of the BBC 2 series *King of the Ghetto*. He accepted the offer and went to see the producer, Stephen Gilbert, at his office in Union House, Shepherds Bush Green, to discuss the project. Just as he was about to tell Gilbert to expect problems about his contract because of his political activities, the phone rang, and Gilbert was summoned upstairs to see Ken Riddington, acting Head of Drama while Jonathan Powell was on holiday in Italy. 'There is a problem,' an embarrassed Riddington told him. 'You can't offer him [Battersby] the job.' Gilbert was amazed, and returned to his office to break the news to Battersby: 'They're not prepared to accept you.'

The blacklisting of the director meant that the production, already well behind schedule, was suspended for four days. Eventually the matter was dealt with by Graeme Macdonald, Controller of BBC 2, who overruled the Personnel Department and insisted that Battersby be employed.

For much of the time drama and arts producers and directors like Battersby were able to survive MI5's attempts to blacklist them. This had little to do with the security services' or Personnel Office's magnanimity or flexibility. It was for two reasons. Firstly, some of the victims were sufficiently talented to overcome the blacklist. Secondly, the individualistic, even iconoclastic nature of many arts and drama executives meant that they often refused to accept the recommendations from Room 105 of Broadcasting House.

Not everyone trying to get jobs in the BBC's Arts and Drama Departments was so lucky. They were the victims of a much wider move against radical drama in the mid-1970s.

The Denials

For nearly fifty years the BBC denied that security vetting was taking place. While broadcasting unions constantly raised the issue, particularly at National Joint Council negotiations, senior officials like Michael Bett, Personnel Director from 1977 to 1981 and now a senior British Telecom executive, denied it formally and informally. As recently as February 1985 Alasdair Milne, then Director-General, said, 'I cannot believe this is true.'[20] Seven months later Milne was forced to concede: 'It is one of those things one knew about, felt a bit grubby about – I think most of us did – but didn't tackle as radically as we should have done.'[21]

After public disclosure by the *Observer* in August 1985, the BBC confirmed the vetting system existed but claimed: 'Only the BBC decides who to appoint to any post within the corporation, or whether to invoke the vetting procedure. No external agency has a right to veto the appointment or promotion of any member of staff.'

In fact, unless an executive or department head fought the decision, MI5's recommendation was final. As Alastair Hetherington said: 'If "only" the BBC decides [on vetting], why did one of Brigadier Stonham's predecessors tell me that it was "without precedent" that a ruling should be challenged and "impossible" to give me reasons for the decision?'[22]

The Semi-Independence of the BBC

So why did the BBC shroud the issue of security vetting in such secrecy – even to the extent of not telling their own Chairman, Stuart Young (1983–86) until early 1985? Apart from their own embarrassment at having to admit to clandestine vetting, the answer lies in the peculiar status of the corporation and its employees.

The BBC's relationship with the State was outlined in their memorandum to the 1971 Franks Commission on the Official Secrets Act. The BBC referred to a ruling by the Treasury Solicitor in 1943 which said: 'The official view is that the Governors of the BBC are persons holding office under His Majesty within the meaning of Section 2 of the 1911 Official Secrets Act and that the Director-General and staff are persons employed under persons who hold such offices.' This ruling clearly bound

BBC staff as being employed by 'persons holding office under His Majesty', and therefore legally in possession of secret information. Hence they would have special obligations to the State. It was on this pretext that security vetting was introduced and preserved with such secrecy. But the BBC's view was that this did not make them State servants: 'Their [BBC staff's] legal status would therefore seem to be neither exactly that of civil servants nor that of men and women employed by commercial organisations.'[23]

Stuart Hood believes this interpretation was spurious. He argues that vetting was a natural consequence of the BBC's constitution: 'If the BBC was honest about its role, it would admit that it must support the central political authority by virtue of the State licence-fee system. But the Corporation has always had this fantasy about itself as a totally independent social organisation.'[24]

Given the corporation's close relationship with the State, the Home Office was well aware of MI5 vetting. Giles Shaw, the Home Office Minister of State, said: 'The goverment believes, as have successive governments over a long period, that it is in the national interest for the BBC to apply certain necessary security procedures.' [25] Tory Home Secretaries William Whitelaw (1979–83) and Leon Brittan (1983–85) both knew about it. Indeed, Whitelaw vigorously defended MI5 vetting: 'There is nothing wrong in the BBC as an employer taking proper precautions to ensure that sensitive posts or information are not open to subversion. Indeed, it would be failing in its duty to the public if it did not do so.'[26] The Home Office was also aware of the number of staff being vetted, and as recently as 1982 told the BBC that the figure 'seemed rather high'.[27]

But what the Home Office and BBC management failed to do was to address the central flaw of the vetting system: that it was used against individuals in non-sensitive jobs. The official line in 1985, according to the then Director-General Alasdair Milne, was: 'There are about eight people who are positively vetted, including me. And a number of other people, particularly in Bush House, for reasons to do with information and access to the War Book (which lays down rules for wartime broadcasting) who are vetted negatively.'[28] This was untrue, as actors and producers working in the Drama Department and directors on the arts programme *Omnibus* were hardly 'involved in sensitive areas or require access to classified information'.

Politics Not Security

MI5 vetting of BBC staff has always had more to do with politics
than security. As John le Carré, the best-selling spy novelist and
former MI5 officer, commented: 'I've always assumed that it [MI5
vetting of BBC staff] happened. I wonder what people would
think if the reverse were to occur – if a known or unknown
member of the Militant Tendency turned out to be shaping news
in the newsroom. There has to be some method of obtaining what
we hope will be an objective middle way in reporting. I don't
think it's irresponsible either to require of a national broadcasting
service that, at times at least, it should be ready to fall in with
government policy and not alarm people.'[29]

MI5 clearly saw the political objective as the major issue in their
role. This was confirmed by the *Observer*'s disclosure that, as well
as vetting, the security services also provided 'background briefs'
to the BBC on industrial disputes. These secret reports included
the alleged involvement of subversives in trade union activity.
They were delivered every three months to a small number of
senior BBC executives, including the head of news and current
affairs. The 'briefs' included the activities of radical and subversive political groups and traced their involvement in strikes and
campaigns. The BBC confirmed the reports' existence, but said
they had stopped receiving them by 1985.

It is not known whether information from these 'background
briefs' ever reached the security files of BBC staff in the Personnel
Department of Broadcasting House. But perhaps it did not have
to. Christopher Martin, Director of Personnel since 1981, and
Brigadier Stonham, Security Liaison Officer since 1982, both had
their own political criteria for vetting. According to BBC officials
who used to work with both of them, they objected to people
most strongly if they had a continuing commitment to the
'extremes' of the political spectrum. Martin and Stonham took
the view that being a member of the Communist Party or CND
would be less of a handicap.

Brigadier Stonham has retained his duties as the BBC's Security
Officer, although public disclosure and pressure from the broadcasting unions has drastically reduced the number of jobs vetted
(to about 120). In October 1985, the BBC agreed to stop all security
vetting except in two areas. Firstly, members of staff involved in
the planning and operation of the wartime broadcasting service,
as they have access to classified information. Secondly, the

External Services. According to Martin, this was due to the threat of infiltration and intimidation of staff by foreign intelligence services. Overseas broadcasters also had access to information from embassies which could be sensitive.[30] In addition, staff would no longer be asked to sign the Official Secrets Act.

In April 1986 the BBC agreed that employees would have access to their personal files, and an independent ombudsman would be appointed to make general inspections of the vetting procedures. It was also disclosed that staff in the Personnel Department had begun to shred the security files and other papers that were kept on BBC employees. Past victims of the blacklist, like Michael Rosen and Isabel Hilton, who asked to see their files, were told they had been destroyed.

But even survivors of vetting remain bitter that information about their political views was secretly kept on file and used against them. And that this data was unchecked, inaccurate and based on second-hand sources because the person concerned was never consulted. As Paddy Leach, a broadcasting union official, commented: 'What is quite frightening is the degree of incompetence and irresponsibility of political vetting. People could have their careers blotted out on the basis of a wrong coding, or wrong initials, or because of a fortnight's membership of the Workers' Revolutionary Party ten years ago.'[31]

Many cases of blacklisting were due to out-of-date information. Take the case of John Dekker. He worked at the BBC from 1962 to 1984. Yet for every job he applied for within the corporation there were long delays, which caused him much distress. MI5 objected every time, particularly when he was appointed Editor of *The Money Programme* in 1972. The Personnel Department told Brian Wenham, then Head of Current Affairs, that Dekker should not be appointed as he was a member of the Communist Party. In fact, Dekker had resigned from the Communist Party sixteen years earlier, in 1956, in protest at the Soviet Union's invasion of Hungary. That was six years before he even joined the BBC. Wenham refused to accept the decision and persuaded the BBC Chairman Lord Charles Hill to overrule it. Dekker went on to become a successful editor of the programme. Not everyone was so lucky.

6

MI5 and the Special Branch: Britain's Political Police

'The Special Branch collects information on those whom I think cause problems for the State.'

Merlyn Rees, Home Secretary 1976–79,
House of Commons, 2 March 1978.

Lord Hugh Scanlon and Jack Jones were for many years the twin pillars of the Labour establishment. Although known as the 'Terrible Twins' for their militant pasts, they became the bedrock of the 1974–79 Labour government. As leaders of the two largest trades unions, the AUEW and the TGWU, their support for Labour's pay policy (the Social Contract) was crucial to that administration's survival. And, despite the opposition of their left wing, Scanlon and Jones delivered.

The Labour establishment was duly grateful. Jones, General Secretary of the transport workers' union the TGWU, was twice offered a peerage by prime ministers Harold Wilson and James Callaghan. Jones refused, but Scanlon entered the House of Lords in 1979.

The Security Service, however, was not impressed. For over a decade, from 1966 to 1977, MI5 ran a secret blacklisting operation against the two trade union leaders. This included sending 'security' reports on their political activities and views to 10 Downing Street, tapping their telephones[1] and four attempts to block their appointment to top jobs in Labour governments. The campaign began in 1967, just before Scanlon became President of the AUEW and while Jones was a TGWU national officer and member of the TUC General Council. MI5 tried hard to find evidence that Jones had direct links with the Communist Party. Their 'justification' for their subsequent surveillance operations was his friendship with Burt Ramelson, the Communist Party's Industrial Organiser.

Neither Jones nor Scanlon were Communist Party members (Scanlon had resigned from the Party in 1954), but that did not stop MI5. Their security files were collated by MI5's F Branch, who were responsible for monitoring domestic subversion, occasionally in collaboration with the Special Branch. The reports were then distributed among selected Labour ministers during the 1964–70 government.

One Junior Minister who saw these files in 1968 said that much of the material was irrelevant trivia, details of trips to Eastern Europe and attendances at meetings where Communists were present.[2] Another who received these dossiers was the then Employment Secretary Barbara Castle. On 6 May 1968 she recorded in her diary: 'One of my discoveries in my new job is that the Minister of Labour has always been furnished with security reports on the Trade Unions.'[3]

Castle was more explicit the following year, on 22 March 1969: 'Another Security Service report on the Ford dispute. The more I read these reports the less confidence I have in our intelligence. To begin with the material is always mighty thin and most of it would be obvious anyway to an informed politician . . . Take Jack Jones: I don't need a Security Service to tell me that he succeeded in giving the impression that he was more militant than Scanlon or that he hadn't been in touch with the Communist Party during the dispute.'[4]

Over the years MI5 compiled forty volumes of material on Jones and about the same on Scanlon. Both were considered 'serious subversives', hostile to the established political order. Hence they were branded security risks whenever government jobs became vacant.

In 1967 Tony Benn, Technology Minister in Harold Wilson's Cabinet, wanted to appoint Jones to his Advisory Council on Technology. But MI5 refused security clearance, telling Benn that Jones was 'a secret member of the Communist Party.' Benn was shocked to discover this surveillance, as Jones was then a member of Labour's National Executive Committee. But there was nothing he could do about it.

When the Conservatives came to power in 1970 under Edward Heath, MI5's security reports continued to pour into 10 Downing Street. Scanlon and Jones were now leaders of their respective unions, but MI5 still saw them as a 'serious threat', particularly when they led the opposition to the government's 1971 industrial relations legislation. By 1972 the dossiers were being sent direct to Prime Minister Edward Heath – bypassing the Home Office command structure.

When Labour was returned to office in 1974, MI5 continued to send reports on Scanlon and Jones to 10 Downing Street. Their distribution during the 1974–76 administration was restricted on a 'need-to-know' basis. In theory, this meant that only ministers with a discreet interest received them. In reality, however, the reports were only circulated to Harold Wilson and Home Secretary Roy Jenkins. The Employment Secretary, Michael Foot, who was responsible for liaison with the trades unions, never received them – unlike his predecessor Barbara Castle in the previous Labour government.

The information in MI5's 'fact-sheets' may have been flimsy and insubstantial, according to Heath's advisor Victor Rothschild (a former MI5 officer), but they had a direct impact inside Wilson's Cabinet Office. In late 1974 Tony Benn, then Industry Secretary, wanted to appoint Jack Jones as Chairman of the new National Enterprise Board. He was told by 10 Downing Street that there was 'a security problem'. MI5 had put in a 'negative report' on Jones, describing him as 'subversive'. Benn complained, and said he wanted to see Jones's security report. MI5's objections were suddenly withdrawn. As it happened, Jones turned the job down anyway and Lord Ryder, then Chairman of Reed International, was appointed instead.

The following year, in December 1975, MI5 tried to blacklist Hugh Scanlon from a top government post. Benn, then Energy Secretary, wanted to make him a Director of the British Gas Corporation, but Sir Arthur Hetherington, then Chairman of British Gas, objected to Scanlon's appointment. 'Well, as far as Scanlon is concerned, I want to be sure the man we have is loyal to the country,' said Hetherington. This confirmed what Benn had been told by MI5: that Scanlon was 'subversive'. In effect, this made him a security risk, and he could not join the Board. Benn refused to agree to MI5's recommendation and asked to see Scanlon's security file. Once again the veto was withdrawn and Scanlon was appointed.

MI5 was more successful a year later, in 1977. Scanlon was proposed as the new Chairman of British Shipbuilding. But according to a former senior civil servant, Scanlon's appointment was blocked by the Security Service. The civil servant was told that Scanlon was not allowed to have access to documents marked 'Confidential' or above, and so could not be appointed.

The job went instead to Sir Anthony Griffin, an Admiral in the Royal Navy.

Within two years both Scanlon and Jones had retired. Scanlon left the trade union movement for the House of Lords in 1979. He says he was 'not surprised' by MI5's actions but adds: 'I can assure you that at no time did any Minister or MP give me any indication of enquiries about myself by MI5.' Jones, who has remained active in the Labour movement as a leading campaigner for Britain's nine million pensioners, was more forthright: 'I think the whole business is outrageous. The most worrying feature is that statements and reports are made without the knowledge of the people concerned and there are no means to question and seek redress.'

Both Scanlon and Jones were baffled as to why they should have been branded as security risks. The answer lies in the willingness of the Security Service to accept speculation and second-hand information as evidence. The original allegations against the two trade unionists were made by the Czech defector Josef Frolik in the late 1960s. Frolik told the CIA that Scanlon and Jones were 'targets' for Czech intelligence and claimed they had been 'approached' by Eastern bloc agents. These allegations soon found their way into MI5's files and were used as criteria for security vetting purposes.

In 1976 Chapman Pincher, the veteran spy author, passed Frolik's claims on to Stephen Hastings, a Tory MP and a former MI6 officer.[5] Hastings informed the Home Office. But it was not until December 1977 that the MP published the charges, under the protection of Parliamentary privilege. They appeared to show cause for MI5's actions. Yet the allegations against Scanlon and Jones were completely unfounded, and even Pincher, a long-time defender of MI5, said: 'I learned later that the Intelligence authorities were not much impressed by Frolik's allegations against the trade union leaders whom he named.'[6]

The attempts to blacklist Scanlon and Jones were highly significant. They clearly illustrated MI5's move away from monitoring Soviet bloc spies in the early 1970s to watching British trade unionists and left wing activists. A series of strikes in the early 1970s had had a profound effect on the thinking of the Heath government, and intelligence on domestic subversion became the new priority.

From 1973 onwards MI5 set about their task. The new Director-General, Sir Michael Hanley, began to pour resources and officers into F Branch (domestic subversion) and away from K Branch (counter-espionage). The Industrial desk of F Branch which studied trades unions – F2(N) – was given extra staff, while sections which looked at hostile foreign powers were cut back.

It was in this climate that MI5's plans to blacklist Scanlon and Jones should be seen. And they were far from isolated cases. Dame Judith Hart, Labour MP from 1959 to 1987, was refused security clearance by MI5 when Harold Wilson wanted to reappoint her Minister for Overseas Development in October 1974. The Security Service told the Prime Minister that they had 'documentary evidence' that Hart had attended a communist meeting in Poland. This 'evidence' was a newspaper cutting from the *Daily Worker* in 1950. The article was about a British communist delegation and was accompanied by a blurred photograph of a young woman laying 'a wreath for peace'. Alongside, the caption named the person as Mrs TUDOR Hart. Yet this cutting was placed in JUDITH Hart's security file and remained there for over twenty years.[7] It was on this 'information' that MI5 recommended that Dame Judith Hart could not be returned to Ministerial office. At first Wilson accepted MI5's veto, and told Hart she could not be appointed. She was only reinstated after he abruptly changed his mind.

MI5's moves against Scanlon, Jones and Hart in the mid-1970s were not just a temporary aberration. They represented a fundamental shift in priorities and resources, highlighting how the surveillance of individuals deemed to be domestic 'subversives' was taking precedence over countering terrorists in Northern Ireland or watching foreign spies. This attitude has had serious consequences, since MI5 remains the most important vetting agency for all government employees. It has also affected staff in defence companies, British Telecom and the BBC.

The Files in Curzon Street

The essence of all personnel vetting is information – how it is compiled, where it is stored and how it is used. MI5's data comes from a variety of sources – tapping telephones, opening mail, bugging rooms and breaking and entering offices and houses. Another favoured MI5 tactic is to send an undercover agent into political organisations and companies to gather information on 'subversive' individuals. Such infiltration is made possible by the Security Service's special relationship with many companies.

Usually, a firm's security officer contacts the police or local Special Branch with information about 'troublemakers'. But the Special Branch has close links with the Security Service. MI5 divides the country into nine regions, each of which has a senior officer who collaborates with a police liaison officer, normally a retired local Assistant Commissioner.

These regional MI5 and Special Branch officers have informal meetings to co-ordinate their intelligence, which then goes to the filing systems in London. Occasionally, MI5 also asks a company's Personnel Director for information about 'subversives'. In return, the Security Service will provide background material on 'dangerous employees'.

In recent years the range of people under such surveillance has expanded considerably. Under pressure from both Labour and Conservative governments since the early 1970s, MI5 has collected information not just on communists and fascists, but on a much larger group – notably trade unionists, peace protesters and environmental dissenters. The consequence is that the dividing line between 'security' and politics has become increasingly thin.

MI5 has files on about one million individuals. They are kept in the Registry, based in a vast hall on the first floor of their headquarters in Curzon Street, Mayfair. Since its foundation in 1909, MI5 has used card indexes and buff-coloured folders for their permanent security files. But since 1971 it has steadily computerised its records. The files are now linked to an alphabetical index which is held on computer. This index contains the individual's name, date of birth, 'recording category' (i.e. political affiliation) and PF number, which refers to their personal file in the Registry. This vast ICL computer databank is connected to a network of about 200 access terminals and smaller computers. Based on the ground floor of the Curzon Street office, the computer has the capacity to record basic data on over 20 million people.[8]

Information stored in these files and computers forms the basis of MI5's vetting procedures. Ostensibly, security vetting is done by C Branch – defence company employees by the C2 desk and civil servants by C3. In practice, however, C Branch officers, usually ex-Army officers who join MI5 late in life because of the military's early retirement policy, only play a liaison role. The real work is done by F Branch, responsible for domestic subversion, which has been greatly expanded in the last decade.

It is F Branch officers who make the decisions on whether an individual should be given security clearance. And for the ordinary employee being vetted the political views of that officer could be vital to the person's whole future. As the former MI5 officer Miranda Ingram said: 'Your vetting assessment may ruin somebody's career.'[9]

The evidence indicates that most members of the Security Service are probably Conservative. Edward Heath, the Conservative Prime Minister from 1970 to 1974, said: 'I met people in the Security Services who talked the most ridiculous nonsense and whose whole philosophy was ridiculous nonsense. If some of them were on a tube and saw someone reading the *Daily Mirror* they would say: "Get after him, that is dangerous. We must find out where he bought it".'[10] Clive Ponting found senior MI5 officers far to the right: 'They're utterly reactionary, tucked away in their little world of their own.'[11] Miranda Ingram, an MI5 officer from 1981 to 1983, agreed:

'Some of them thought that people who wore jeans were potentially subversive, whereas I don't even think the present Communist Party constitutes a threat to the state . . . Some officers live a very sheltered life and never work in the real world and it often means they become conservative . . . The overall tone is right wing. (This may be endemic in the nature of the work, although there is no reason why the protection of democracy, any more than patriotism, should be a right wing concern.) . . . A large majority are content just to "do their job" and not think any further. But the politically uninterested are – again maybe inevitably – conservative, and probably Conservative.'[12]

Who Vets the Vetters?

The Security Service has no legal status and successive governments have persistently refused to answer questions from MPs about its activities. The Labour MP Robin Cook put it this way when he introduced his Security Service Bill in the wake of the Anthony Blunt affair: 'The debate on Mr Blunt concentrated on the question whether the Security Service is properly accountable to Ministers. That missed the point. It does not matter very much whether the Security Services are answerable to a Minister when that Minister is not answerable to the House.'[13]

The Director-General of MI5, currently Patrick Walker, is officially responsible to the Home Secretary, and has the right of direct access to the Prime Minister. But in practice it is an arm's length relationship. MI5 officers are not civil servants, and while they have close links with the Ministry of Defence (which was originally responsible for the Security Service) and the Home Office, they are not part of either department.

James Callaghan gave a remarkably frank answer when asked by the Commons Civil Service Committee whether he was satisfied that the Security Services were sufficiently accountable to Ministers and Parliament. He replied:

'I am not sure what its accountability is to Parliament, I am not sure about Ministers. I find it a difficult question to answer, I really do. They are run – the Security Services and MI5 and MI6 – as separate departments . . . Some Ministers do not want to know a lot: Home Secretary or Foreign Secretary, Prime Minister, others want to know a great deal about what is going on. I am going to give you a very unsatisfactory answer, I do not know. I am certain there must be a very high degree of responsibility among those who serve in MI5 or MI6 because they have very great powers, considerable powers, and I think the ethos of those particular services is probably as important as the degrees of accountability that you can visit upon them. I am very, very mixed up about this, I do not think I can help you with this.'[14]

In his report on the Profumo Affair, Lord Denning noted:

'The Security Service in this country is not established by Statute nor is it recognised by Common Law. Even the Official Secrets Acts do not acknowledge its existence. The members of the Security Service are, in the eye of the law, ordinary citizens with no powers greater than anyone else. They have no special powers of arrest such as the police have . . . They cannot enter premises without the consent of the householder, even though they may suspect a spy is there . . .'[15]

The absence of any legal sanction of the MI5 operations alleged by the former MI5 officer Peter Wright caused problems for Lord Donaldson, Master of the Rolls. During the *Spycatcher* case Lord Donaldson said: 'It is silly for us, to sit here and say that the Security Service is obliged to follow the letter of the law, it isn't real.' In an attempt to get around the difficulty, he added: 'The missing link is possibly this. Of course, there has to be some control; probably the best yet devised is to say the Security Service is bound by a strict rule of the law, but to always bear in mind a prerogative power not to pursue criminal proceedings and a statutory power in the Director of Public Prosecutions to stop criminal prosecutions.' That procedure, Lord Donaldson said, could be perfectly properly used in appropriate cases. It was essential in the public interest for M15 officers to break the law in some ways and for such breaches not to be prosecuted. There would be limits; 'Murder,' he added, 'is an entirely different matter.'

However, Donaldson did concede that the time may have come when Parliament should 'regularise' the status of M15. The public was entitled to demand, and the public interest required, that the security service did not step outside its legitimate role, namely the defence of the realm. 'It would be a sad day for democracy and the rule of law if the service were ever to be considered above or exempt from the law of the land. And it is not.' But he went on: 'It is absurd to contend that *any* [his emphasis] breach of the law, whatever its character, will constitute such "wrongdoing" as to deprive the service of the secrecy without which it cannot possibly operate.'

The distinction emphasised here was not between lawful and unlawful activities, but between the law and secrecy. This was a clear let-out: the judiciary pronounces that the Security Service should not break the law, but we – the public – will not know whether it has done so or not.

The only guidelines covering M15 are those laid down in 1952 by the then Home Secretary, Sir David Maxwell-Fyfe. They state:

'It is essential that the security service should be kept absolutely free from any political bias or influence and nothing should be done that might lend colour to any suggestion that it is concerned with the interests of any particular section of the community, or with any other matter than the Defence of the Realm as a whole.'

No enquiry, it adds, 'is to be carried out on behalf of any government department unless you are satisfied that an important public interest bearing on the Defence of the Realm, as defined in Paragraph 2, is at stake.' But Paragraph 2 says its task is 'Defence of the Realm' not only from espionage or sabotage but also from 'actions of persons and organisations whether directed from within or without the country, which may be judged to be subversive of the State.'

It is only too easy to confuse legitimate targets posing a threat to the country ('the Defence of the Realm as a whole') with other groups or individuals deemed 'subversive', whose definition, as we have seen, is vague. There is no crime called 'subversion'. There is no law defining what is meant by it. Subversion, under the 1985 purge procedures, is what a Minister says it is. No one doubts that MI5 operations have been 'political'. As the former Labour Home Secretary, Roy (now Lord) Jenkins, told the Commons in a debate prompted by allegations of a plot by a group of MI5 officers to undermine the Wilson government in the mid-1970s: 'I took the view before these recent events emerged that it was advisable that MI5 should be pulled out of its political surveillance role. I had been doubtful of the value of that role for some time. I am convinced now that an organisation of people who lived in the fevered world of espionage and counter-espionage is entirely unfitted to judge between what is subversion and what is legitimate dissent.'[16]

The New Targets

In recent years there has been a trend to compile security files on individuals who cannot officially be classified as 'subversive' (i.e. members of communist, Trotskyist or fascist groups). This has been 'justified' by F Branch on the grounds that the individual belongs to an organisation which *includes* a subversive as a leading member. Hence, senior officials of the Scottish area of the National Union of Mineworkers could be deemed subversive while their president was Mick McGahey, a Communist Party activist. MI5 also open files on the leading members of political pressure groups if they are bracketed as a 'subversive front' or 'subversive dominated'.

This practice was revealed by Cathy Massiter, an MI5 officer from 1970 to 1984 who worked in F Branch for many of those years. She disclosed how the National Council for Civil Liberties (NCCL) and the Campaign for Nuclear Disarmament (CND) were targetted by MI5 as subversive organisations. Massiter said that MI5 had been interested in the NCCL, a non-party group of moderate left wing views, since the 1940s. But in the mid-1970s its status was reassessed and it was classified as 'subversive'. Massiter told the Channel 4 programme *20/20 Vision*:

'Anyone who was on the National Executive of the NCCL, who worked for NCCL, or who was an active member to the degree of being, say, a Branch Secretary of NCCL, would be placed on permanent record. Routine enquiries would be instituted to identify such people and police inquiries were sought . . . The police were actually asked to identify branch secretaries in their area and report on the activities of the NCCL.'[17]

Massiter revealed how MI5 opened security files on Patricia Hewitt, the NCCL's General Secretary from 1974 to 1983, and Harriet Harman, Legal Officer from 1978 to 1982. Neither was a member of any communist or Trotskyist party. Harman is now a Labour MP. An MI5 dossier was compiled on Hewitt, now Press Secretary to the Labour Party leader Neil Kinnock, because she was also a close friend of Bill Birtles, a left wing barrister who was then a Communist Party member. The NCCL was not taken off MI5's list of subversive organisations until 1981.

The decision to target the NCCL was taken by Charles J. L. Elwell, a veteran MI5 officer who was then an Assistant Director. He had worked for the Security Service since the early 1950s, when he was based in K Branch, responsible for counter-espionage.

It was while he was in K Branch that he met and married Anne Last, who had compiled a detailed dossier which alleged that MI5 had been deeply penetrated by communists. Elwell left counter-espionage to join F Branch, where he was head of F1 Division, which investigated the Communist Party. It was in his capacity as an Assistant Director that he classified the NCCL as subversive. This action breached official guidelines, but he justified it by arguing that their strong criticisms of the police and MI5 mirrored the views of extreme left wing groups.

Elwell left the Security Service in 1982. He told the MI5 hierarchy that he was going to join Common Cause, the right wing organisation that monitors subversion in industry. Senior officers were unhappy about this and warned him not to use his former colleagues who remained in MI5. Common Cause deny that Elwell worked for them. 'I understood he went to work for Brian Crozier [a right wing propagandist with CIA links],' said a spokesperson.

Another pressure group targeted by MI5 was CND,[18] even though it was not classified as a subversive organisation. MI5 infiltrated its headquarters and tapped the telephone of one of its leading officials, John Cox. Cathy Massiter has described how, after being asked to take over MI5's investigation of alleged left wing 'subversive influence' within CND, increasing political pressure meant she ended up studying the organisation as a whole, with the Security Service breaking its own rules. Surveillance of the organisation became more intense when CND was off the subversive list than it had been during the 1960s, when it was on it. This was because of political pressure – nuclear disarmament became a politically sensitive issue, and an increasingly popular one.

In February 1983, Michael Heseltine, then Defence Secretary, set up a special unit, Defence Secretariat (DS) 19, to counter the CND message. Senior Ministry of Defence officials contacted MI5 and requested information about the political affiliations of CND leaders. 'It did begin to seem,' Massiter said, 'that what the security service was being asked to do was to provide information on a party political issue.' In August 1983 MI5 was asked to tap the phone of a 'suitable' CND target – John Cox, a member of the Communist Party who lived in Wales (an advantage, since he used the telephone a lot to talk to other senior CND activists including Joan Ruddock, now Labour MP for Deptford, and Bruce Kent). The tap, agreed by the Home Secretary, Leon Brittan, began in August – after the General Election. 'It was deferred,' Massiter recalled, 'because of the election, as it was felt that it was too sensitive a matter' to go ahead before. The motivation for the tap, had it been revealed, might have been questioned.

After these revelations, CND took the Home Secretary to court. In an affidavit to the court, Massiter said that at the time the telephone tap warrant was obtained against Cox, MI5 knew from their own work and from other sources within the Communist Party that Cox was *not* 'manipulating CND in a clandestine way,' the sole ground on which the warrant was sought.

One of the criteria for telephone interception by MI5 is that other sources of information – such as informers – have been tried and failed. This was not the case with Cox. MI5's sources were good, and Cox was recorded as a subversive simply because of his membership of the Communist Party. That in itself would not justify the issue of a warrant had MI5 kept to its guidelines. The Home Secretary – the only potentially accountable figure in the whole operation – usually only sees what MI5 describes as the 'short reason' for a warrant. This 'short reason', or summary, is detached from the file and forwarded to the Permanent Secretary at the Home Office, who in turn passes it to his Minister. The file containing the full circumstances of any case will never leave MI5 unless the Home Secretary asks for more details. Experience has shown that Home Secretaries want to have as little as possible to do with what some of them have regarded as a 'grubby' business.[19]

Orders From Box 500

Some victims of MI5 vetting, such as Jack Jones and Hugh Scanlon, have been in jobs which are powerful enough to resist such actions. But not everyone is so lucky. Edward Best, a young scholar working on Central American affairs, was secretly blacklisted by MI5. Best had applied for a job with the Civil Service, but was rejected for unspecified 'security reasons'. It later transpired that he had been refused security clearance because of his marriage to Argentina, a Salvadorean citizen. She had been a member of a musical group whose songs were critical of the military regime of Colonel Sanchez, who ruled El Salvador in the early 1970s.

Best was blacklisted because his name appeared on a confidential Suspects Index document held by immigration officers at ports of entry into Britain. Individuals are placed on the list by the Immigration Intelligence Unit, largely on information from the security service. The movements of the people listed on the Index are monitored by the immigration authorities, and those with high security codes, such as Best, are reported to MI5.

The Index contains over 200 names and aliases with dates of birth and the government department to be alerted if the 'target' attempts to leave the country. Many of the more well-known names on the list are on a lower security classification, such as 'A', which means that MI5 should be informed of the individual's movements as a matter of routine rather than urgency. This grade includes Gerry Lawless, chair of the Labour group of Hackney Borough Council, Tariq Ali, journalist Duncan Campbell, actress Vanessa Redgrave and Professor Victor Allen, a Leeds University lecturer and informal advisor to miners' leader Arthur Scargill. It also lists a number of right wing extremists, Sikh militants and IRA members.

Best, who has never been a member of any political party, is classified on the Suspects Index as 'J', the highest security code, which involves immigration officers communicating directly with MI5. In the same category as Best, according to the *Observer*, which obtained the list, is a suspected Soviet agent and an arms dealer accused of selling military equipment to Libya.

The danger of this secret Index is that innocent people like

Edward Best can be put on it and the information used against them during vetting procedures without their knowledge.

The inclusion of Best on the Index was greeted with amazement by his professional colleagues. Dr Robert O'Neill, Professor of the History of War at Oxford University and a former Director of the International Institute for Strategic Studies, where Best worked, said: 'I think very highly of Edward. He is perceptive, sensitive and a balanced scholar. He showed himself capable of understanding the points of view of the principal sides in the Central American conflict.'[20]

In MI5's eyes, however, Best was seen as a 'potential subversive'. But the Suspects Index is not the only list compiled by the intelligence authorities. Information about journalists is considered particularly important. This became apparent during EEC Ministerial meetings in 1977. Journalists covering a meeting of European agricultural ministers in Lancaster House were asked to supply two photographs of themselves. One was attached to their passes, the other was kept by the authorities. A few days after the meeting, Whitehall press officers were asked to mark boxes next to a list of named journalists with either a tick or a cross. Those deemed, in the view of the press officers, to have taken a 'pro-EEC' stance were given a tick. Those regarded as 'anti-EEC' were marked with a cross. The completed lists were sent to a department of the Foreign Office, based in Vauxhall Bridge Road, involved in intelligence-gathering activities.

It is not clear whether such information is transferred to MI5 files for future vetting purposes. What is known is that permanent security files are compiled on a wide range of people, notably active trade unionists. This was revealed by a police report sent to MI5's headquarters in London in 1980. It was a memorandum about the political and trade union activites of James Hogg, a young TGWU shop steward at the Carnation Food factory in Dumfries, Scotland. The document was written by Detective Constable Gordon Hunter of Dumfries CID, and countersigned by Detective Chief Inspector David Kirkwood, on behalf of the Chief Constable of Galloway and Dumfries Police Force. It was addressed to 'The Director-General, Box 500, Parliament Street BO, London SW1P 1XH – MI5's official address. The memo stated:

'Hogg is a shop steward and a member of the factory negotiating team on behalf of the union at the factory. Hogg has been described by a management contact as being more than usually active in union debates within the factory and is thought of as very left wing. Hogg is thought to be connected with the Socialist Workers' Party also, although this cannot be verified at present . . . Hogg cannot proceed any further within the Carnation Foods factory either in a work capacity or within the union structure at the factory and it is thought by management that he may well leave some time in the near future to take up some kind of full-time employment with the TGWU. This situation will obviously be monitored and any further development will be reported . . . The text of communication has been noted in respect of Hogg's involvement with the Communist Party of Great Britain and this will of course be watched for any subsequent developments.'[21]

Hogg, a Quality-Control Inspector, was not a member of either the Socialist Workers' Party or the Communist Party. 'Anything I have done at the factory has been part of my union activities,' he says. 'I'm just a shop steward, just an ordinary worker doing my job to try and improve the conditions of my fellow workers.' Yet MI5 kept a permanent security file on him (PF 886214), and he was put under surveillance by the F1C desk, which deals with district branches of the Communist Party. Hogg had no criminal record and was not a member of any subversive organisation, yet Detective Constable Hunter, a Special Branch officer, was feeding information about his trade union activities into MI5 files.

The Special Branch – MI5's 'Footsoldiers'

Founded in 1883 to counter the activities of Irish Republicans, the Special Branch was for many years controlled by the Metropolitan Police. But since 1958 all provincial police forces have set up their own Special Branches. In the 1950s there were about 200 Special Branch (SB) officers. During the late 1960s and early 1970s – a time of much political protest – there was a massive increase in SB staff, and by 1975 every local force had its own Special Branch. There are now about 2000 Special Branch officers, including 200 civilian staff, with a total annual budget amounting to about £19.5 million.

Special Branch forces are initially answerable to the head of the local CID and through him to an Assistant Chief Constable, and ultimately to the Chief Constable. They are linked nationally through Scotland Yard, where the Special Branch's computerised index of two million personal files is installed.

According to Sir Harold Scott, former Commissioner of the Metropolitan Police: 'The Special Branch is a part of CID and is primarily an intelligence department. Its business is to keep a watch on any body of people, of whatever political complexion, *whose activities seem likely to result sooner or later* in open acts of sedition or disorder.'[22] (our emphasis)

New guidelines issued by the Home Office in 1984 state that 'a Special Branch gathers information about threats to public order.' They continue: 'A Special Branch assists the security service in carrying out its tasks of defending the Realm against attempts at espionage and sabotage or from the actions of persons and organisations whether directed from within or without the country which may be judged subversive to the State.' Subversion is defined in the same terms as those in the government's purge procedure announced in 1985.

Special Branches also have responsibility for investigating and countering terrorism. They are more active, and probably do more relevant work, in this area than MI5. The threat of Irish-based terrorism and the activities of extremist Irish Republican groups is the responsibility of the Metropolitan Police Special Branch. A National Joint Unit at Scotland Yard co-ordinates information and enquiries when a local Special Branch arrests or questions an individual under the Prevention of Terrorism Act.

Terrorism is one thing. 'Subversives' or political dissenters are quite another. The Special Branch guidelines say that 'data on individuals or organisations should not under any circumstances be collected or held solely on the basis that such a person or organisation supports unpopular causes . . . Care should be taken to ensure that only necessary and relevant information is recorded and retained.'

In January 1985, a month after the new guidelines were published, Leon Brittan, the Home Secretary, told Labour MP John Prescott that he did not accept that the broad definition of subversion allowed Special Branches to make 'political judgements'. There was a clear distinction, he said, 'between subversion and opposition to the policies of the government of the day or peaceful campaigning to bring about changes in those policies or to influence public opinion generally . . . Special Branches,' he continued, were not interested in trade unionists 'as such', but 'only in such activities of individuals within trade unions (as within any other group or section in society) as are relevant to the tasks laid upon them by the guidelines.'

But Brittan also acknowledged: 'The definition [of subversion] is not limited to possible acts of a criminal nature. In an open society such as ours it is all too easy to use tactics which are not themselves unlawful for subversive ends.' He continued, in a reference to Special Branch officers: 'Those who are entrusted with safeguarding our democratic institutions from subversive attack must not be prevented from looking into the activities of those whose real aim is to harm our democracy but who, *for tactical or other reasons choose to keep (either in the long or the short term) within the letter of the law in what they do.*'[23] (our emphasis)

The responsibilities and terms of reference of the SB are vague. The guidelines say that its work arises from the Chief Constable's responsibility for 'the preservation of the Queen's Peace'. They refer to actions which 'may be judged to be subversive to the State' and to gathering information 'about threats to public order.'

The difficulty involved in defining subversion was well illustrated by William (now Lord) Whitelaw, Brittan's predecessor as Home Secretary. The preservation of public order, he told the Labour MP Robin Cook, 'may require information to be kept on individuals who are active in a political movement, not because of the views they hold, but because the activities of the group could be such as to encourage public disorder.'[24] Asked about the extent and nature of the SB's political records, James (now Lord) Callaghan, when Labour's Home Secretary, replied: 'The security of the State necessarily requires that I should be in possession of certain information about political affiliations, which it would not be in the public interest to disclose.'[25]

These criteria are so broad they can only be subjectively evaluated, and are inevitably political in character. John Alderson, the former Chief Constable of Devon and Cornwall who helped to get the SB guidelines published in 1984, warned that the term 'subversive' could mean anything the SB wanted. The whole system was 'anti-democratic', he said – people could be banned from becoming magistrates simply because the SB had something on them in their records. He cautiously described SB officers as 'establishment-minded people', with those at the top having considerable independent influence and authority of their own. 'If the chap at the top gets more and more information, the SB will get it . . . Police want two things: more power and more information.' Of their thirst for information, 'they can't get enough of it.' For example, activists involved in the campaign against the South African rugby tour during the winter of 1969/70 were investigated. Ten years later, their movements were still being recorded.

Alderson actually took the initiative of weeding out superfluous SB files. 'When I looked at my records, I came to the
conclusion that there were items of intelligence in there that
should never be in: I mean, one could make a case out for
including a file on everyone who protests, because of one kind or
another. I mean, some people will go so far as to say that the
League Against Cruel Sports is a threat to liberties . . . the anti-
nuclear movement has very great difficulties in this connection in
expressing its views without being regarded as subversive. So,
looking at my records, I came to the conclusion that getting on for
50 per cent of them should never have been in there, either
because they were a waste of time and clogging up the machine,
or they were records of activities which shouldn't be in those
banks of information.'[26]

This figure of 50 per cent also happens to represent the
proportion of SB officers who are concerned not with terrorism or
watching ports, but with 'politics', including industrial action in
private industry.[27]

Alderson did not get things all his own way, even though he
was constitutionally in charge of his Special Branch. Faced with
his new policy of weeding files, SB officers sent them to MI5 in
London.

One national Special Branch file which was not closed was that
of Hugh Geach, a former social worker and Oxfam employee,
and an SDP candidate in local elections. The file on Geach was
opened when, as a student at Reading University he was one of
the leaders of the 1970 campaign against the tour by South
African rugby players. Though no new information had
appeared in his file since 1972, it still hadn't been weeded out ten
years later.[28]

In another case, West Midlands Special Branch began to
investigate four anti-nuclear campaigners from Sutton Coldfield
who wrote to their local newspaper in 1981. The letter protested
at the failure of the government to give Parliament information
about nuclear weapons policy. Soon afterwards, the women
began to be harassed, mainly by telephone calls. A man visited the
home of one of them, Madeleine Haigh, saying he was investigating a fraud on a mail-order company. She was told by her local
police station that her visitor was not a policeman. After repeated
unsuccessful attempts to find out what was going on, Haigh
approached her MP, the Conservative Cabinet Minister Norman
Fowler. It was discovered that her visitor was a Special Branch

Inspector. He was neither publicly identified nor disciplined. The West Midlands Chief Constable at the time, Sir Philip Knights, defended the Special Branch involvement because, he said, the case 'fell within the terms of reference of the Special Branch.' In a report to his Police Committee, he stated: 'Mrs Haigh had written to a newspaper in terms which were interpreted as indicating that she might be a person prepared to support or get involved in public protests . . . the responsibility of Special Branch (is) analysing and assessing information of that kind.'[29]

Special Branch and the 'need-to-know'

The Home Office guidelines on the conduct of the Special Branch state: 'Access to information held by the Special Branch should be strictly limited to those who have a particular need to know. Under no circumstances should information be passed to commercial firms or to employers' organisations.'

However, evidence from recent years indicates that these rules have been regularly ignored, particularly in relation to the screening of employees by private companies. In 1977 it was revealed that the Branch had supplied information on employees to Reinforcement Steel Services at Greenwich, part of the State-owned British Steel Corporation. Documents reveal that Mr Meynard, a Scotland Yard Special Branch officer, visited Mr Roebuck, the works manager, after the company had asked the police to check out two workers suspected of 'sabotage'. Meynard told Roebuck that one of the employees, Charlie Duffin, had been bound over for two years for breaking and entering in 1954 – when he was 17 years old. By handing over such information Meynard was breaking the 1974 Rehabilitation of Offenders Act. As for the other worker, Paul Lutener, Meynard handed over details of his Special Branch file. According to a memo written by Roebuck: 'The Special Branch have a file on this man for his political activities. 1) Distributing National Socialist literature (a reference to the *International* Socialists). 2) Disturbing the peace during demonstrations. 3) Taking part in illegal demonstrations.'

In fact, Lutener, a union representative, has never been arrested and there is no such thing as an 'illegal demonstration' in Britain. Later that year he was sacked along with five others for taking part in a one-day demonstration against local hospital cuts.

A disturbing case of Special Branch vetting involved Jan Martin, an industrial film-maker. She worked for a private film company run by the television broadcaster Michael Barratt. In September 1978 Barratt was contracted to make promotional films for Taylor Woodrow, the large building company. After submitting the names of all his employees, he was told that Martin was 'a security risk' and 'will not be welcome on our premises'. When asked for a reason, a Taylor Woodrow representative said: 'Well, there is a connection with terrorists in Europe, Baader-Meinhof. We can absolutely confirm this if you tell us her National Insurance number.'[30] Barratt supplied the number and was later rung back and told: 'She is the person who has that connection.'

Barratt suggested that Martin speak to her father, John Robertson, who had been a Detective Superintendent at Scotland Yard and a policeman for thirty-seven years. Robertson contacted Scotland Yard, who disclosed that the information on his daughter was held by the Special Branch and was given to Taylor Woodrow during their vetting procedures.

The real story was revealed when Martin and her father were visited by Detective Superintendent Peter Phelan, a senior Special Branch Officer. He revealed that the 'information' had been supplied by the Dutch Police to the Special Branch. Martin and her husband had been driving through Holland on the day after a shooting by the Baader-Meinhof gang in Amsterdam. They stopped at a café, the owner of which thought Martin's husband resembled the terrorist Willi Stoll, whose photograph had just been circulated. He rang the local police with the car registration number, which was in Martin's name. A report was entered into Special Branch and MI5 files that Jan Martin had been seen escorting a known terrorist. The information was not checked, and it was later used against her in the way we have seen. If her father had not been a former policeman, she would have been blacklisted from a number of jobs and her career ruined. 'I could have spent the rest of my life in the shadow,' said Martin. 'If one company could get that information then every other company could get it.'[31] In the decade since that incident, the Special Branch has proved no more efficient at updating its files. Or at gathering information. Just before the 1987 Conservative Party Conference in Blackpool the Special Branch asked a local travel agent specialising in UK-Ireland travel for lists of his clients. He refused. Two weeks before the conference, the

Branch set up an office on the ground floor of Blackpool's Central Post Office. Post Office staff were told to go for interviews during working hours. At first they complied, because postal workers always co-operate in police security arrangements, particularly since the 1984 Brighton bombing. However, after about fifteen workers had been interviewed, it became clear that they were being asked unusual questions. The interviews would start routinely, but then the Special Branch Officers started asking political questions: 'Which way did you vote in the election?' and 'Do you suspect any of your colleagues of leftist political views?'

There was uproar among the postal workers. They were particularly angry about being asked to spy on colleagues and to inform the police about anyone with 'militant or extremist views'. They asked for legal advice on whether they were obliged to co-operate with the Special Branch. The remaining 350-odd workers refused to be interviewed.

One of the fifteen who was interviewed was a counter-staff employee who did not want to be identified for fear of management reprisals. She was questioned for twenty minutes by two Special Branch Officers, who asked her:

'What are your views on Mrs Thatcher?'

'None of your business,' she replied.

'How do you vote yourself?'

'None of your business.'

Understanding 'Subversion'

Former Chief Constable John Alderson has remained highly critical of the way in which such information has been compiled and used by the Branch. In 1984 he told the Commons Home Affairs Committee's inquiry into the Special Branch:

'The terms of reference of the Special Branches leave much to their discretion. Some officers have a much wider understanding of the term "subversive" than others. To some, all activists may be "subversive" and both individuals and groups critical of the established order are marked out for surveillance and recording. Others, including myself, believe that although "subversion" may not be capable of exact definition, if it is to be the subject of police operations, it should have an obvious criminal connection.'

He elaborated when questioned by MPs:

'Policemen put constructions on situations which often may not suit other people's views. I think the difficulty is the interested citizen does not know what the State considers to be subversive. If we could stand up and say to the public in Devon and Cornwall, or anywhere else, "This is what we consider to be subversive and if you start getting into this area of human activities you render yourself liable to surveillance" – but if you cannot tell the public that, it seems to me that people's liberties are likely to be at risk.'[32]

The SB has been variously described as MI5's 'ears' and its 'footsoldiers'. The two agencies co-operate closely, particularly at a regional level. This is another way in which lines of accountability get blurred or lost. In theory, Special Branches are answerable to the local Chief Constable, who is accountable in turn to the police authority (or directly to the Home Secretary, in the case of the Metropolitan Police). But Chief Constables are not accountable for the operations of MI5 in their areas. According to Alderson, a Chief Constable 'can't do anything about MI5, nobody can do anything about it.' Chief Constables can be bullied. The Chief Constable of Strathclyde in the mid-1970s hesitated to go along with an MI5 request for his men to break into the Glasgow offices of the Communist Party. It took a meeting with MI5's Director-General, Sir Michael Hanley, to persuade him.

In some ways, MI5 and the SB share the workload. For example, when the Security Officer of a company wants information on members of its workforce, he would normally get in touch with the Special Branch rather than with MI5. The SB would contact MI5 if it wanted more, or different, information. Sometimes, however, MI5 would ask the Security Officer about 'subversives' in a company and would even send in its own agents, as it did with British Leyland in the early 1980s.

Alderson describes the relationship of MI5 and the Special Branches as 'an informal thing, an old boys' network.' In general, the Special Branches (who regard themselves as something 'special' within their own force) look up to MI5 officers rather, it is said, as other ranks look up to commissioned officers in the armed forces. MI5 officers, too, feel they are special in Whitehall. They have special access to secret information which no one else enjoys. They are a privileged group of 'Crown servants', separate from the rest of Whitehall and, of course, from transient politicians and Ministers.

In 1977, the government of South Australia appointed a judicial commission into that state's Special Branch, which was based on the British model. The investigation showed that records were held on alleged communists, alleged terrorists, all politicians of the Australian Labor Party at state and federal level, half of the judges of the Supreme Court, magistrates, all university personnel regarded as having 'left' or 'radical' views, prominent trade union officials and demonstrators. Much of the information was inaccurate, and surveillance was motivated by political considerations. The Commissioner in charge of the South Australian police was Harold Salisbury, a former Chief Constable of the York, North Riding and East Riding police forces in Britain. When asked by the BBC programme *Panorama* in March 1981 who he would consider a 'subversive', he replied:

'Obviously anyone who shows any affinity towards communism – that's common sense. The IRA, the PLO and I would say anyone who's decrying marriage, family life – trying to break that up – pushing drugs, advocating the acceptance of certain drugs, homosexuality, indiscipline in schools, weak penalties for anti-social crimes, pushing that sort of thing. Oh, a whole gamut of things like that that could be pecking away at the foundations of our society and weakening it.'[33]

This view of the world, which Callaghan in his response to the Commons Civil Service Committee described as 'the ethos', is the key to the understanding of the security services. That ethos is shaped partly by the group culture, as it is in any society. MI5 and Special Branch officers work, by definition, in a closed environment. They see potential threats where there are none – it was only recently that MI5 agreed that not everyone contributing to *Marxism Today* should be regarded as a potential subversive or communist. But 'the ethos' and their activities are also influenced by the political climate. They will do what they can get away with. They are tempted, like any bureaucracy, to expand their empires and build up their workload, thus claiming that they need more money, more manpower and more resources. There is an intelligence bureaucracy, with its own vested interest – and this interest includes unaccountability and secrecy. It has a vested interest in maintaining an awesome mystique about its operations. Given its record and potential for interfering in basic civil rights, this mystique should be penetrated. It would be healthy for the intelligence agencies themselves, as well as for the general public.

7

The Economic League: Power Without Responsibility

'Some companies may be in a moral dilemma about excluding people from employment on political grounds.'
'Companies Under Attack', official Economic League publication, November 1986.

'I would turn all three down. Let's not bugger up the company before it gets on the road.'
Alan Harvey, Economic League official, in response to question about three prospective employees, *World in Action*, 16 February 1987.

Once a month, a clerk from the Warrington firm of solicitors Barnes and Co, based at 25 Bold Street, collects a cheque and an invoice and takes a 100-metre walk into the heart of the town's commercial centre. His destination is 18 Museum Street, a discreet office adjoining a row of terraced houses opposite the library. There is no name-plate on the dark royal-blue door, and no outward sign of its identity. In fact, it is the north-west headquarters of the Economic League, Britain's largest and most important private vetting agency.

The messenger is taking part in one of the organisations's most secretive operations – the payment of their subscriptions by dozens of local companies. Many of these firms are apparently embarrassed by their support for the League, so an elaborate ploy is used to ensure that their membership is never disclosed either to their shareholders or employees.

As the firms are reluctant to see their payments to the Economic League appear in their accounts, the money is 'laundered' through solicitors throughout the country. The member company agrees a set fee with the regional League office for 'information and advisory services' – the euphemism for political vetting of prospective employees. The local law firm then receives a list of the subscribing companies from the League.

The solicitors send each League member an invoice for 'legal services' (i.e. their subscription). In return the company sends the law firm a cheque and a compliments slip but nothing else. The final stage is for the solicitors to add up the total amount of the subscriptions, deduct VAT and their own legal costs, and deliver the cheque to the League office.

These payments are recorded in company annual accounts as 'legal services', while the law firms list them as 'professional services'. The subscribing companies are thus able to keep their support for the League secret. But one former solicitor who operated the laundering system argues that under the 1967 Companies Act the fees should have been declared. He said: 'There is no doubt that it was a political donation. They would say it isn't. But if it's something else, why should they go through this elaborate charade?' When asked about the laundering operation, Michael Noar, the Economic League's Director-General since June 1986, said:

'Some companies are embarrassed by the public association with us because the League has been subject to a lot of attack over the years . . . If this happens, it is a tiny minority because all the subscriptions that come in here are perfectly ordinary cheques direct from the company. Some of the companies do subscribe only locally and so I cannot say hand-on-heart that it never happens. I don't deny that quite a lot of our companies do not wish to go public on their membership of the League . . . But there is no statutory obligation on us to disclose because we are not a political organisation in the sense that we campaign for or against political parties.'

The laundering system is just one measure of the secrecy that has surrounded the Economic League ever since its foundation in 1919. Many of the 2000 companies which subscribe, and so provide the League's £1 million annual income, have always felt uneasy about their association with it. The Legal & General Group, for example, stated in their 1985 Annual Report that 'this subscription does not need to be declared for statutory purposes and no reference will be made to any subscription in future.' The League is happy to acknowledge the wide range of publications it produces on economics and industry, and the courses it runs on management techniques. But it is the political vetting service, co-ordinated by sixty-two staff in seven regional centres, which has caused most companies to keep their membership secret.

A large number of construction and engineering firms use the labour-screening system. Many banks and financial institutions make regular donations, although they deny taking advantage of the vetting facilities (see Appendix for details). The League has also had long-standing support from the Confederation of British Industry (CBI). For many years senior CBI officials were on the League's Central Council, and CBI and League officials spoke at each other's meetings. This close relationship was crystallised in 1976. A confidential internal CBI memo, written by a Deputy Director-General, John Whitehorn, stated that companies should consult the Economic League, among other organisations, to assist 'in the necessary function of identification of and preventive warning about individual wreckers.'[1] This has since been confirmed as official CBI policy.

The League remains the most significant and powerful blacklisting agency in Britain. Officially, its aims are: 'To assist the development of a widespread understanding of the value and importance of profitable industry and commerce within the United Kingdom's mixed economy. To fight subversion and to keep members informed of the activities of those who are hostile to productive enterprise in industry and commerce.'[2] The League's tactics and methods in carrying out these objectives have caused great controversy.

Origins

The League was formed in early 1919, in the wake of widespread industrial unrest after the Russian Revolution and the First World War. Disputes were taking place all over Britain, notably the unprecedented police strike and mutinies in the Army and Navy. Industrial militancy had reached an all-time peak, with 35 million working days lost in 1919, and a phenomenal 85.9 million in 1921.[3] It was a time of expanding influence for the unofficial shop stewards' movement, and trades unions were winning concessions on wages and the working week. There was also considerable sympathy for the new Bolshevik government and communist ideas.

The establishment's concern and its desire for information was reflected in a letter from Winston Churchill to Prime Minister Lloyd George in early 1920: 'With the world in its present condition of extreme unrest and changing friendships and antagonisms, and with our greatly reduced and weak military forces, it is more than ever vital to us to have good and timely information.'

It was in this atmosphere that a group of top employers met in a room at 4 Dean's Yard, Westminster. The meeting was arranged by Admiral Sir Reginald 'Blinker' Hall, who had just retired as Director of Naval Intelligence and had advised the government on the setting up of M16 in 1909. Among those present were Evan Williams, Chairman of the Mining Association, Cuthbert Laws, Director of the Shipping Federation, Tory MP John Gretton, R. C. Kelly, an industrialist in the brewing industry, and Sir Alan Smith, Director of the Engineering Employers' Federation.[4] There was unanimous agreement at the meeting that 'left-wing subversion' was likely to be a serious danger to the stability of industry during the period of post-war adjustment. It was decided to raise funds to set up an organisation to counter this. Originally known as the National Propaganda Committee, its aim was to co-ordinate the activities of a number of groups (Economic Study Clubs). These groups provided speakers and distributed leaflets outside factory gates warning workers about the evils of socialism and the merits of free enterprise.

Tower Hill in London, Bigg Market in Newcastle-upon-Tyne, and the docksides of Merseyside, Hull and Glasgow became the main venues for these lectures. Many of the Economic Study Club speakers had joined straight from the Services. But they were met with bitter hostility from their audiences, mainly angry unemployed workers, who accused them of being 'blacklegs' and 'bosses' men'.

Their early message was heavily pro-capitalist and anti-socialist. There was also a distinct paternalistic tendency. The founding fathers believed that workers needed to be 'educated' about the market economy. But after the British Communist Party was founded in 1920, it was realised that socialism and militant trade unionism were not about to disappear. So in 1925 a permanent organisation was established, retitled The Economic League, with a governing body – the Central Council – and regional committees. Its financial support came mainly from coal, steel, shipbuilding and engineering companies.

The League's first Director-General, appointed in 1926, was John Baker White, who had been an intelligence officer during the First World War. In the early 1920s White worked for Sir George McGill, a friend of Vernon Kell, the first head of M15. McGill had, according to White, set up 'a highly efficient private intelligence service, investigating not only all forms of subversion, including communism, but also the international traffic in drugs.'[5] White, a Territorial Army officer, remained the League's Director until 1945, when he became Conservative MP for Canterbury. During the Second World War he had returned to intelligence work. For the first six weeks of the war he was stationed at the War Office in London, and continued his work for the Economic League. He then joined Section D of MI6 as a Major, and became a psychological warfare expert in military intelligence.

White's security links were highly significant, and laid the foundation for the League's political vetting services. These were being built up as early as 1925, when the League was stressing the importance of an 'intelligence' network:

'One of the first tasks initiated by Sir Auckland Geddes [a Central Council member] was the compilation of a chart and dossier of socialist and subversive organisations and their "interlocking directorates". Arrangements are in hand for a permanent clearing house of information in connection with alien organisations and individuals. A document containing a considerable body of information on "red" ramifications and methods has already been circulated in confidence to District Economic Leagues. Supplements to the documents will be circulated from time to time.'[6]

It was this information which formed the basis for the League's blacklisting operations. Their Annual Reports from the 1920s and 1930s show that an increasing number of subscribing companies were making confidential enquiries about information on employees. This service was expanded after the 1926 General Strike – during which the League sent daily regional reports to Prime Minister Stanley Baldwin. Dossiers were compiled, occasionally in collaboration with the local police, on the political affiliations and activities of 'dangerous subversives'. One target in the early 1930s was the Young Communist League (YCL), which was undertaking a recruitment drive in major industrial areas. In 1931 alone 150 reports on YCL activists were sent to companies.[7]

Trade union activity was also being monitored. By the mid-1930s card indexes of 'subversive' individuals, detailing their movements and activities, were compiled by the League's Central Council and regional offices. The information was then handed over to companies. For example, full dossiers on union activists were handed to Boulton Paul Ltd, a Wolverhampton aircraft firm, warning them of an impending strike in 1935. The following year, and again early in 1937, the Lancashire region provided 'confidential information' on the past and present activities of certain workers employed by A. V. Ros, Fairey Aviation, Metropolitan Vickers, Ferranti and the Churchill Machine Tool Company. Occasionally, firms like the British Aluminium Company, based in Warrington, were simply informed of increasing trade union membership in their factory.

It was not until after World War Two that the League's political vetting system was formally set up. Post-war Britain was again in some industrial turmoil, particularly on the docks. The late 1940s was also the time of the 'Red Scare'. The response of many employers was to use the League's then informal screening operation.

By 1950 requests for information about employees had increased so rapidly that the League decided to establish a formal vetting procedure for subscribing companies. The service was started in the London region, and was based on records supplied by a senior Special Branch officer who had just been recruited. These files were confined to known Communist Party members, but they were expanded to include other political and trade union activists. The blacklist was born.

How the System Works

A prime motivation for companies to use the League's vetting service is to avoid employment laws protecting individuals from unfair dismissal. As the League stated in 1987: 'The Employment Protection, Redundancy Payments, Equal Opportunities and Race Relations Acts can be used as sticks with which to attack employers. An allegation of unfair dismissal or discrimination can be extremely expensive in management time and disruption.'[8]

Companies see the League's labour-screening facilities as a way of sacking 'troublemakers' without being called to account. The key to the continued success of the system is secrecy. For many years senior League executives even denied that vetting took place. The League is now more open, but the procedure remains confidential.

A former Personnel Director for a light engineering company based in the north-west of England has described the vetting procedure to the authors. He said that if more than six names are to be vetted, it is done by post. He was often asked to check 100 employees at a time, because his Managing Director wanted everyone to be vetted. The Personnel Director would obtain a list of new employees. The firm's Economic League code would be written at the top right-hand corner of a sheet of paper, and the following headings would be listed along the top: name, address, date of birth, National Insurance number and occupation. His secretary would type in the details and send them in a plain envelope to a Post Office box address.

The League's response and verdict was given by telephone. For a list of ten workers, the Personnel Director waited twenty-four hours before ringing the local League office and saying: 'This is code . . . calling. Are they clear?' The information was then read out with, in his experience, little comment. Any prospective employee who had been targetted as a trade union or political activist by the League would be rejected by his company. This was confirmed by Barry Field, Director of the Great Southern Group funeral firm, who stated in a confidential memorandum about using the vetting service: 'If there is the slightest suggestion of any information held against the proposed employee from this source you do not engage same.'

The League's seven regional offices (see Appendix for details) no longer use their own files for labour-screening. Instead the names are given either by telephone, telex or FAX machine to the Central Records and Research Department, based at 99a High Street, Thornton Heath, Surrey. In 1986 alone over 200,000 people were checked through the system by subscribing companies.

There are two sets of files held in this office. Firstly, there is what the League calls 'low grade material' or 'raw data' on individuals who are actively involved in politics. These dossiers are not used for employment vetting but are kept for future reference. The second type of file, kept on a card index, contains the names of 'subversives' whose trade union and political record is given to employers. According to the League's Director-General Michael Noar, there are 'approximately 10,000' on the latter, which are used for vetting purposes, and 'probably another 20,000' in the 'raw data' files.

Sources of Information

The data in these files comes from a variety of sources. Much of it comes from newspapers, particularly left-wing journals. League staff mark up the papers and then photocopy articles about individuals and political organisations. The published items on pressure groups and political parties are stored away in separate files which are labelled 'CND', 'Anti-Apartheid', 'Greenpeace', 'Communist Party' etc. If the article is about an individual, a short reference is written on their index card for possible vetting purposes. The newspapers and magazines are then stacked away for reference, and often loaned out to sympathetic Fleet Street journalists.

Advertisements and petitions are another source of material, because occasionally they contain names and addresses. One list kept in League files was an advertisement signed by twenty-nine stars and celebrities in early 1987 calling for a nuclear weapons freeze. Among them were broadcasters Anna Ford and Ludovic Kennedy, comedian Billy Connolly, authors Laurie Lee and Catherine Cookson, composer Sir Michael Tippett and film producer David Puttnam. The League's Director-General, Michael Noar, strongly denied that these names would be used for employment vetting: 'There is no way that we saw all those people as subversives or that they shouldn't be employed. They were signatories to an advertisement calling for a nuclear freeze. It is possible that one of our members compiled that information. But there is no question of putting those names on a blacklist.'

The League also monitors signatures on the nomination forms of individuals they see as subversive candidates at local and general elections. This means that friends and neighbours who support such a candidate could end up on the League's files without their knowledge. Noar admits they keep such information: 'We have cards on all the election candidates of all the political parties. But there is no suggestion that those cards are used for employment vetting at all. They are merely for our own internal information.'

Information on employees is also supplied to the League by Personnel Managers of member companies on an informal basis. Perhaps the League's most controversial method of obtaining information is by infiltrating private political meetings and pressure groups. This is a sophisticated operation, and the League has its own full-time agents for the task. One man who was convinced he was being asked to do surveillance and intelligence work for the League was Bill Anderson. In November 1986 Anderson, then aged fifty-six, took early retirement from his job as a proof-reader on the Scottish *Daily Record* and *Sunday Mail*.

He thought about setting up his own business with his redundancy pay, but on Friday 5 December 1986 he was browsing
through the *Glasgow Herald* when he noticed an interesting job
advertisement. The headline ran: 'Industrial Relations Advisory
Services' and the advertisement began:

'A non-profitmaking organisation whose mission is to improve
employer/employee relations requires an Advisory Services Manager to
monitor problem areas and develop services to Scottish companies.'

Anderson was immediately interested, as he had been a chapel
official in his trade union SOGAT and had some experience of
industrial relations. He wrote off for further details, and received
a letter from the Economic League, of which there had been no
mention in the advertisement, which stated:

'We require [you] to monitor the revolutionary fringe and identify its
supporters and their targets. This entails careful first-hand study and the
maintenance and development of our intelligence network.'

Anderson was appalled. 'I actually thought the job was to act as
a liaison officer between management and unions,' he told the
authors. 'But I was shocked to learn I would be required to set up
an industrial espionage network. I would be spying on active
trade unionists or even anyone interested in joining a trade
union.' He added: 'I take it I would have had to join various trade
unions or go to various meetings, whether they be political or
trade union, and report back to my so-called superiors.'[9]
It did not take Anderson too long to decide to refuse an
interview invitation. 'As a trade unionist I found it repugnant,' he
said. But that was not the end of the matter. After refusing to
become a spy he told his old newspaper, the *Sunday Mail*, about
his experience. They headlined the story 'Super Snoop'. A year
later he was told by Granada TV's *World in Action* that his name
was on a League list compiled by the Scottish office in Glasgow.
'It's unbelievable that such a thing could happen,' replied
Anderson.[10] He then disclosed what had happened when he had
applied for tenancies in local pubs with two breweries: 'I had
received favourable responses over the telephone. I also received
an application form from one particular brewery asking me if I
could put up between £12,000 and £18,000. I said I would be able
to afford more than that. But since then I've had no response,
which leads me to think that very likely I am on the blacklist.'[11]

His suspicions were well-founded. The two breweries in question are both subscribers to the League's services. Anderson now runs a small shop in one of Glasgow's covered markets. But his name remains in the files of the League's North Claremont Street office in Glasgow, the Director of which, Hamish MacGregor, a former CBI Regional Deputy Director, said: 'There is nothing sinister about this. Without political subversives and with better understanding between management and workers, the country would soon be back on its feet.'[12]

One person who did join the League as a spy was Ned Walsh. Until February 1988, when he was exposed by *World in Action*, Walsh had spent the previous twenty-seven years infiltrating pressure groups and trades unions and reporting back to the League's South-East regional office, based at 43 Bridge Street, Leatherhead, Surrey.

Walsh's job as a full-time 'research assistant' involved obtaining intelligence about individuals whom the League saw as dangerous or potential subversives. One targetted organisation was the Anti-Apartheid Movement (AAM), which is deemed a 'vehicle for extremists'.[13] Walsh attended many private AAM meetings pretending to be a delegate from the science and technical workers' union ASTMS. One meeting he infiltrated discussed how to oppose a Government Bill which would prevent local authorities from boycotting South African goods. He wrote a summary of the meeting which contained the names of those who had attended and an account of their strategy. This was sent to the League.

Walsh was able to do this because for many years he was an active member of the AAM's Trade Union Committee. As the AAM does not investigate its supporters, it was difficult for Walsh to be identified as a League spy. 'I understood that he was a full-time trade union official with the ASTMS,' said Liberal Party member Alan Salter. At ASTMS Ken Pilling, his Branch Secretary in South London, said: 'I understood he was a travelling salesman.'[14] That was what Walsh had written on his application form when he had joined the union in 1970.

Another organisation Walsh infiltrated was the Transnational Information Centre (TNIC), an organisation, set up in 1984, which provides information on multi-national companies to the trade union movement. Walsh had been one of the first to join TNIC, and he was a regular attender of seminars at their offices in Ayres Street, London. He seemed particularly interested in

information about individual trade unionists. TNIC official
Barbara Dinham said:

'He asked quite a few questions. [He was] more interested really in
personalities, tracing where various trade unionists that he had known
in the past had since moved to . . . He was so keen on collecting
information but it was difficult to see what he used it for. There was very
little exchange, and for someone who was so keen on collecting
information, he didn't really seem to want to use it.'[15]

As Walsh had told Dinham that he was a full-time ASTMS
official, the TNIC did not suspect that he was secretly feeding
data into Economic League files.

Perhaps his most important post was as minute secretary at
ASTMS National Executive meetings. Walsh sat alongside the
union Chairman, Treasurer and Secretary at the head table taking
notes of what was said. He also kept a record of the correspondence which was read out.

At no time did Walsh ever disclose his links with the Economic
League. It was only after being traced to the League's office in
Leatherhead by the *World in Action* team that his identity was
revealed. But when approached by Granada and given the
opportunity to explain his actions, Walsh ran away. The League
subsequently admitted that they had been employing him since
1961.

Walsh was effectively doing the same job as an MI5 or Special
Branch agent sent into a trade union or political organisation. He
was gathering intelligence on false pretences and feeding it into
files which could be used against individuals during vetting
procedures. The difference, according to former Chief Constable
of Devon and Cornwall Police John Alderson, is that the League
is a law unto itself:

'I would regard the Economic League – which is an organisation
unaccountable, unofficial, funded by business management – prying
into legitimate political activity as absolutely outrageous . . . I think the
whole business of unofficial organisations taking this on themselves is
highly dangerous. We've seen this in Europe before – unofficial
organisations becoming a police force which is unaccountable. It's highly
dangerous and quite improper.'[16]

The League is now essentially a private security company,
specialising in industrial relations, so perhaps it is not surprising
that they employ agents like Walsh to acquire information.
Private detectives have also been hired, notably Peter Hamilton,

the veteran right wing security consultant (see Chapter 10 for profile). During a telephone conversation with fellow private investigator Gary Murray in August 1985, Hamilton said of the League: 'Yes, well, I know them very well of course because I do jobs for them from time to time.' Michael Noar did not deny that the League had used Hamilton: 'I'm not saying that's not true.' But he added: 'We do not have private detectives on the staff nor do we directly employ them, but occasionally we can say [to a member company] "We know that this firm have used this private detective and have said he is reliable so try him out." That's as near as we get to it. It's not our scene.'

Noar says that most of his staff 'are from industry, ICI or whatever . . . I am now trying to recruit much younger people with a straightforward industrial background.' But the League has had former security consultants working for it, notably in the late 1970s in the London region office from which the labour-screening was operated. Former police officers have also joined the League's ranks, and there are at least two ex-policemen currently employed on staff.

It is the League's links with the police which have proved most controversial. These have been very close since the League's early years. In the mid-1930s the Lancashire region of the League worked in co-operation with local police forces. Meetings were held with detectives specialising in political 'subversion' and information was exchanged. On 20 January 1937 Major R. R. Hoare, the League's Manchester Organiser, wrote to the then Director-General John Baker White:

'I had the Manchester police in here yesterday and found them extremely helpful and have now arranged to work in the closest co-operation with them. Among other things, they promised to give me as long as I like looking over their Communist industrial file in their office. I am also keeping in touch with the Salford police, their Communist man having already called at this office.'[17]

This intimate relationship with the police was further revealed in a letter written two days later, on 22 January, from Major Hoare, later the League's Director-General, to the Chief Constable of the Manchester force, thanking him for the help of his staff, particularly Detective Eckersley and Chief-Inspector King. This assistance involved secret surveillance of meetings, as a memorandum to Detective Eckersley revealed: 'I understand there will probably be a meeting of the executive of the unofficial shop stewards' movement at the Albion Hotel on Thursday at 7.45 pm. Can you get this meeting covered, as I consider it of considerable importance.'[18] Major Hoare made it clear that he was receiving information from police reports: 'I understand that the Communist Party are holding a meeting of delegates at the Burlington Café tomorrow,' he wrote to his Director-General, John Baker White, on 20 March 1937. 'I shall get a report from the police without sending one of our own men.'

Fifty years later, in February 1987, further evidence was revealed about the League's close links with the police. *World in Action* secretly filmed and recorded Alan Harvey, Deputy Director of the League's North-East region, talking to two businessmen in a hotel room in Harrogate. Harvey told them:

'We give all our information to the police. In return, they're not exactly unfriendly back. I can spot a number plate quicker than you can blink an eye. But I don't want that to go outside, because it is illegal. We do have people who can look at credit-worthiness, criminality, number plates, this sort of thing . . . You do pay extra if you wanted to know, and it is illegal, whether someone had a criminal background. We can look at criminal records but we can't do criminal investigations. We do have men who we call special men who you might call private detectives . . . If you would come to me and say, "Look, we're going to take on someone to handle the money." I mean, he's got to be as honest as the day is long, and politically clean and be relied on not to even leave his thumbprints on any pound notes. Well, then we send out one of our specialist men who would look at the man's criminal background and his general character, and there will be an extra price on that. It would be something like £150.'[19]

The League angrily denied that they receive information from the police, and disowned themselves from the comments of Harvey, who then resigned after ten years' service. Director-General Michael Noar said: 'We do tend to fish in muddy waters so we are often asked by the police to provide information. But it is a one-way trade, I'm afraid.'[20]

After the programme Home Secretary Douglas Hurd ordered a police investigation into the allegations. The inquiry was conducted by the North Yorkshire police in North Allerton – the very force against whom some of the charges were made by Harvey, who was based at nearby Skipton. The inquiry concentrated on whether the League had access to Police National Computer (PNC) records rather than general information. Two months later the Home Office announced there was 'no indication that the

PNC had been used to obtain criminal record information for the League. Further enquiries and interviews produced no evidence to support the implication that other police information had been passed to the League.'

But in an interview with the authors in December 1987, Noar seemed to contradict his earlier denials that the League received information from the police: 'As far as the police is concerned, of course the police and Special Branch are interested in some of the things that we are interested in. They follow the activities of these groups in much the same way as we do and therefore they do get in touch with us from time to time and talk to us and say "were you at this demonstration or that." Obviously we help them where we can. If we come across things that we think will be of particular interest to them we send it to them. Now obviously, again in the course of discussions, there is an EXCHANGE of information just in the ordinary course of talking' (our emphasis).

The admission that the League has close links with the Special Branch is another indication of their sources of information. As the two agencies have common roles, the relationship is long-standing. In 1937 a confidential list of communists in the Manchester area, provided by the local Special Branch, was sent to the League's Central Council office in London for filing and indexing.[21] Noar maintains that any liaison is now purely informal. In 1981 the Special Branch investigated allegations that the League's records on individuals were based on information provided by senior Special Branch officers.[22] No evidence was found to subtantiate the allegations.

However, John Alderson, who was responsible for Special Branch operations, said: 'It is possible that there could have been an exchange of information, certainly between Special Branch officers and the Economic League . . . I think it's possible because the role of the Special Branch in keeping an eye on industrial subversion would bring it into common ground to some extent with the Economic League. Individual officers would then exchange information about particular people who may be activists which both sides would be interested in.'[23]

Formal links with the Special Branch include providing them with their press-cutting service. The League has also provided full-time officials as speakers to lecture on training courses for military and Special Branch officers, usually on the role of political extremists in society. In the 1960s this was done by Harry Whelton and in the mid-1970s by John Dettmer, then Director-

General and himself a former Army officer. Michael Noar says that the League no longer provides staff to lecture on current affairs at MoD training colleges, but 'we would be happy to do so.'

Similar lectures have been given by League officials at joint services intelligence courses organised by MI5. An RAF security officer who attended one of them in 1970 said that they were held at MI5's then head office in Gower Street, central London. One lecture was on 'Subversion In Industry', and after the talk the RAF officer was 'astonished' to find that the League official had a desk and filing cabinet inside MI5's headquarters.[24]

The Security Service's links with the League seemed to be confirmed when an internal report in May 1984, stated: 'The flow of information into the Research Department [the vetting office], prior to 1978, came from London Region's contacts with OFFICIAL SOURCES . . . In 1978 London Region had four men who had professional security or police backgrounds working in the Research Department' (our emphasis). The report added that the 'official sources' had declined in recent years and that, by 1984, 'there is not a single professionally-trained security or counter-subversive member of the staff in this [vetting] department.'[25]

Michael Noar strongly denied that any League official would have a desk inside MI5, but acknowledged that they did have links with the Security Service: 'There is no question of us being that close but we undoubtedly have contacts with them. Some of our people meet with them on an informal basis and might provide information to them but unfortunately it's usually a one-way trade. But when they do come back with information then they want to alert the League about problems in certain companies.'

Some Industrial Relations Managers and Personnel Officers who have had dealings with the League remain highly suspicious about its sources of information. In 1985 an Industrial Relations Manager at Plessey went with his Personnel Director to a League seminar with executives from other subscribing electronics companies. During the meeting the League official said that a recent defector from the Soviet Union had disclosed 'a lot of information' about trade unionists in Britain. The executives were told that they should be 'on the lookout' for trade unionists who 'had links with the Soviet Union'. The Industrial Relations Manager said: 'I was very surprised. I was aware of their activities but I didn't know they went into such depth.'

Politics

A crucial factor in examining the vetting practices of the League is to analyse the political criteria it uses when branding an individual a 'subversive'. The League insists that it is independent of all political parties, and that it collects information on both left and right wing extremists. Michael Noar says: 'We are supporters of the democratic centre.' He also maintains: 'We are not against trade unionism but we are against trade unionism that is used not to achieve straightforward industrial objectives but is really being used for political objectives.'

However, the League is overwhelmingly funded by large companies, many of them multinational, who are dependent on a *laissez-faire*, capitalist economy for their profitability. These firms support Conservative governments because of their free-market economic policies. Hence, it is no coincidence that at least twenty-six companies who subscribe to the League also make annual donations to the Tory Party (see Appendix for details). None of them give money to the Labour Party.

The League has always made it clear that it supports a 'capitalist free enterprise economy'. This has been its policy since its foundation in 1919. Many Conservatives have thus regarded the League as a supporter. In 1949 Tory M P Quintin Hogg, later Lord Hailsham and a Cabinet Minister as Lord Chancellor, said: 'The Economic League and Aims of Industry . . . are, so far as I can see, bodies with very largely parallel political aims to those professed by most Conservatives and no doubt in close alliance in a practical way with many individual Conservatives.' [26]

This was reflected in the political affiliations of the League's Central Council members, who for many years included Tory M Ps and active Conservative supporters. One of the two Tory M Ps on the Central Council in the mid-1950s was Sir Waldron Smithers, a notorious cold warrior who once told the Commons: 'The comprehensive Welfare State is ruining the character and homes of our people and, instead of being a lifebuoy, will be a millstone round our necks . . . I do not fear the atom bomb or the hydrogen bomb which kill the body, so much as I fear the socialist concept of using the law to relieve individuals of the responsibility of their own welfare and to deprive them of their freedom of choice, which kills the soul.' [27]

Another notable Central Council member was Herbert Hill, Chairman of the Birmingham car components firm Hardy Spicer

Ltd and a strong Tory Party supporter. In September 1964 his employees took strike action over pay. Hill responded by saying his workers were all doing 'frightfully well'. He added: 'They are all being much overpaid for the work they are doing . . . The poor dears have a pretty poor mentality, most of them. They have a pretty poor level of intelligence.'[28]

More recent connections have included Lord Hewlett, a Central Council member who in 1979, as well as being chairman of Anchor Chemical Co. and Borg Warner UK, was President of the Conservative Party. But the most important link is with British United Industrialists (BUI), a right wing group which acts as a clearing house to 'channel' (or launder) corporate donations to the Tory Party. In 1987, BUI's Director Alistair Forbes wrote to companies:

'We believe that a donation to BUI is less emotive than a donation to the Conservative Party appearing as a note to your financial statements. It is for this reason that I'm asking you for a donation to our funds to put us in a position to help the Conservative Party and other free enterprise agencies.'[29]

One of these agencies is the Economic League. For many years BUI has paid substantial sums to the League (£18,000 in 1987). Since 1984 the BUI have been the League's tenants and share the same building at 7 Wine Office Court, a narrow side-alley off Fleet Street. The two organisations have also shared personnel, notably Sir Halford Reddish, a League Vice-President in the late 1970s who also ran BUI for many years.

The Tory Party connections continue to extend to the League's full-time staff. Russell Walters, a member of the Information and Research Department which provides data for labour-screening, is an active Conservative. He has been an executive member of the Tory Party's Selsdon Group and an organiser for the right wing pressure group 'Committee for a Free Britain'. In 1987 he was an unsuccessful candidate for the Vice-Chairmanship of the Young Conservatives.

The League has always attracted staff of Conservative inclinations, particularly ex-Army officers who have retired early. For many years their right wing, establishment view of the world was channelled into the League's non-vetting services, such as their current affairs talks for apprentices. This service was used mainly in the 1960s. Member companies hired League officials to give compulsory lectures on the evils of nationalisation, high wage increases, shorter hours and militant trade unionism to young workers during their induction course. Richard Stokes, former Personnel Director of the pharmaceutical firm Glaxo Holdings plc, was told by one League official that these courses instilled 'a sense of values' in the workers. By this he meant loyalty to the company, patriotism and ensuring that 'they don't challenge authority'. Above all, the League official added, they were taught to reject trade unions because unions were 'controlled by outsiders, financed from abroad'.

It is only fair to say that the proportion of ex-majors and colonels in the League's ranks with views such as these has decreased in recent years. But there is no question that a strong right wing economic stance is taken by the staff. This becomes a vital issue when a company sends in its list of new employees to be politically vetted. Michael Noar maintains:

'What we are trying to do is keep information that might be of interest to an employer from the point of view of political allegiance, political activity of a kind which might be likely to override the person's loyalty to their company. That is membership of, or known support for, an extreme political group or party . . . These would be anti-capitalist parties, all the parties who have a fundamental opposition to a capitalist, free enterprise economy and to ordinary liberal democratic values.'

Noar says the League does not include membership of the Labour Party as a criteria for employment vetting, but rather 'any overt Marxist, communist party because they are clearly opposed to a capitalist free enterprise society.'

However, the League sees other organisations and pressure groups as 'vehicles for subversion'. As an official booklet stated in 1986: 'Anti-Apartheid, CND, Animal Liberation and other "popular causes" offer ideal vehicles for the advance of revolutionary ideas and can be turned against both industry in general and particular companies.'[30] This publication, entitled 'Companies Under Attack', lists a number of groups which either 'conceal an ulterior motive' or 'are unduly influenced by political aims'. They include Oxfam, War on Want, the Anti-Apartheid Movement, Christian Aid, CND, the Low Pay Unit, Campaign Against the Arms Trade and the Child Poverty Action Group.

Active members of these organisations are also placed on registers or 'blacklists', as one former Personnel Manager described them. One former Personnel Director who had access to one of these lists was Richard Stokes. He was approached by an

Economic League official while working for Glaxo, a pharmaceutical company based in Greenford, Middlesex. The purpose of the visit was to persuade Stokes to make Glaxo a subscriber to the League. When a price of £5000 was proposed Stokes hesitated, and said he would have to consult more senior executives. The League official then opened his attaché case and said that he had 'lists of subversives' to which subscribing companies would have access. He went on: 'Well, I'm not really supposed to do this but I can show you some names on the register. It's not a conclusive register but this is a sample.'

He then handed a section of the document to Stokes, who spent about fifteen minutes flicking through the lists. They contained the names of thousands of people, whom the League deemed potentially 'subversive'.

Stokes noticed the names of two people in particular, because he knew both of them. One was Eric Moonman, a Labour MP from 1966 to 1970 and again from 1974 to 1979. Stokes had known him since they were teenagers, when they had both been members of the Liverpool Young Socialists. He was shocked to find Moonman listed, as he had gone on to become a right-wing Labour MP – notably pro-EEC and anti-CND.

The other name Stokes noticed was even more surprising. This was Dame Olga Uvarov, CBE, a distinguished veterinary scientist who also worked for Glaxo. Stokes says of her: 'She was a very responsible and establishment-orientated person who by no stretch of the imagination could be a subversive. In fact, like many immigrants she was extremely pro-Britain and right wing.' He asked the League official why she had been included on the list.

'Well, of course anybody with a Russian name would come under scrutiny,' he replied.

'Does that mean they go on the list automatically?' asked Stokes.

'No it doesn't, but they might get on.'

'You mean, they might get on even though they shouldn't get on.'

'Well, the important thing really was to make sure that they didn't omit any subversives.'[31]

Like many Personnel Directors who question the activities of the Economic League, Stokes believes it is secrecy which is the major problem. 'The trouble is that individuals never know whether they are on a blacklist or not,' he says. 'Once a person is on one of their lists it may be very difficult for him to get another job. My complaint is that they are often inefficient and in-accurate.'[32]

Perhaps a more important aspect of the League's lists is the question of who is actually registered and on what basis. Michael Noar acknowledges that the League keeps 'a record of sub-versives', but denies that it constitutes a blacklist. 'A blacklist to me is a list of people which says "Don't employ these people." Which is not what we say,' commented Noar.

But the names are still on lists for potential use. The political criteria used for their inclusion was revealed by documents obtained by the television programme *World in Action*. These lists were compiled by the League's Scotland office and sent to the national headquarters in London.

The documents show that an individual's opposition to apartheid is enough for them to be included on the League's register. This has been a long-standing policy. Ken Mullier recalls telling John Pryce, a League official in the north-east, that there had been a recent anti-apartheid demonstration in Leeds in 1977. 'I mentioned that many of the demonstrators had signed a petition with their names and addresses,' said Mullier. 'He got very excited and kept asking me how he could obtain the petition. I was a bit naive then and didn't realise why he was so keen.'

The lists compiled in 1987 contain a wide range of individuals. Carol Meikle, former secretary of the Glasgow branch of the Anti-Apartheid Movement, was there, as were less active critics of the South African regime. One was Sydney Scroggie, a blind pensioner from Dundee. He had written a letter to his local newspaper supporting Edinburgh City Council's decision to buy a portrait of Nelson Mandela. It was enough for him to be listed.

Scroggie was amazed to learn that he had been registered: 'There can't really be anybody less subversive politically or economically than myself . . . Being on a list and being noted down as someone who is anti-apartheid, that's rather ridiculous because I'm not really violently anti or pro anything. I am as anti-apartheid as anybody normally is. Nobody particularly likes the system, I suppose.'[33]

Another on the list was teacher Frank Phillips. He was said by the League to be an active supporter of the Anti-Apartheid Movement. But Phillips is adamant that, although he is opposed to apartheid, he has never been a member of any anti-apartheid organisation. 'This is quite unbelievable,' he said. 'I have served my country and Queen. I've done four years in the Royal Air Force. When I went into the University of Edinburgh I served for three years in the Officer Training Corps and another year training young lads at a cadet unit, so it must really mean that if I'm a subversive they're going to have to have a very good look at all the armed forces as well.'[34]

Also on the League's secret anti-apartheid hit-list was Hugh McMahon, a Labour MEP. In 1987 he made a speech in the European Parliament attacking apartheid and the South African government's use of the secret police. Within a week his name had been added to the register.

The Economic League seems to believe that opposing apartheid is a potentially subversive activity. Alan Harvey, a former League official, says: 'People like CND, Friends of the Earth, Anti-Apartheid – they're very useful vehicles for subversives.'[35] This was confirmed in 1986 by an official Economic League publication called 'Companies Under Attack'. The booklet states:

'The Anti-Apartheid Movement (AAM), as is often the case with such extremist-controlled organisations, has a titular head. In AAM's case it is Bishop Trevor Huddleston. This presents a dilemma for ordinary people. A cause with such a head is surely all right? Not to get involved or support the cause is to fail to do something a person thinks is right to do. To get involved is to risk being carried along in a revolutionary campaign masquerading as a bona fide cause.'[36]

Other individuals were marked down for bizarre reasons, according to internal League documents. A notable case was solicitor Derek Ogg. The League branded him 'an anarchist' because he was the Editor of a fringe magazine which was on sale in anarchist bookshops. His publication, *The Scotsmen*, is aimed at the gay community in Edinburgh.

As for Ogg's 'anarchist' credentials:

'My only political involvement has been as a Conservative Party candidate in the regional and district council elections and as Chairman of the Young Conservatives in my constituency for two years. As a solicitor who loves the law and who is known as a "law bore", I've been involved in legal affairs and indeed assisted in drafting part of the legislation for the 1980 Criminal Justice of Scotland Act.'[37]

Ogg does not object to the principle of information being divulged to prospective employers. But he believes that people should have access to the records in order to correct inaccuracies.

Otherwise, he argues, the League will get things wrong. A case in point was Tom Stevenson, who lost his job at the Caterpillar Tractor Company plant in Glasgow after its closure in 1987.

The factory's closure led to its occupation by the employees. Stevenson was elected Treasurer of the Workers' Committee and his name was on the literature which was sent out worldwide. All incoming letters went to his house because Caterpillar had cut off the delivery of mail to the plant.

For these reasons, Stevenson was registered by the League as a 'Communist Party supporter'. This was untrue. 'It's utter nonsense,' he said. 'I have never been involved with any political party of any colour or creed.'[38] The sit-in had been supported by a wide section of the Glasgow community, notably the church and the local Conservative M P. It is true that the Communist Party also backed the action, but, as Stevenson remarked: 'Well, if that's the case we also received support from the Conservative Trades Unionists Association, so they must come under the same category.'[39]

Another 'Communist Party supporter', according to the Economic League, is Hamish Imlach, one of the best-known entertainers in Scotland. Imlach was astonished at the allegation: 'People I do know in the Communist Party think of me as a wishy-washy liberal or lazy.' When asked by *World in Action* why he thought he had been listed, Imlach replied: 'I haven't the faintest idea. I mean, during my performances I do have a go at Margaret Thatcher and the Conservative government.'[40]

Employees campaigning against cut-backs in the National Health Service have also come under scrutiny by the League. One G P, Dr Kenneth Williamson, was listed as the Chairman of a campaign to stop an Oxford hospital for the elderly being closed down. As at the Caterpillar plant, the staff staged a sit-in to protest. An active member of the trade union movement for many years, Dr Williamson became the protestors' public spokesperson. 'I suppose from that my name was noted,' he said, 'but it amazes me to think that anybody involved with something which is as topical as defending the Health Service should be regarded as in any way subversive.'[41]

The Economic League documents obtained by *World in Action* show remarkable intolerance. Many individuals were described simply as 'T M'. This stands for 'troublemaker'.

It seems that anyone involved in any kind of political activity is classified by the League. But one characteristic of the lists is that over 90 per cent of the names included are associated, whether accurately or not, with the left of the political spectrum. The League denies this, maintaining that it is equally interested in right wing 'extremists'.

Yet it listed Andrew Jeffrey, a community worker from Dundee, a business studies graduate who spent several years in industrial management. He was registered because he was investigating the activities of far right groups in his hometown. 'I really cannot imagine anyone less subversive than me,' said Jeffrey. 'I'm really sort of middle-of-the-road, all the way down the line.' [42]

Details of the alleged political affiliations and activities of Labour MPs have also been compiled by the League's Information and Research Department. MPs listed include Kevin Barron (Neil Kinnock's Parliamentary Private Secretary), Peter Archer, Robin Corbett and Donald Anderson (all three of whom are front-bench spokespersons), Richard Caborn and Joe Ashton.

Such actions clearly reveal the League's political stance. But this is due more to its being a creature of its subscribers – big businesses rather than any inherent ideological bias. Without corporate funding, the League simply could not survive in its present form.

Profile of a Subscribing Company

By far the largest and most profitable corporation to use the League's 'information and advisory services' has been International Business Machines (IBM). A huge multinational, IBM controls over 70 per cent of the worlds computer production and employs 403,000 workers, 18,800 of whom are based in Britain. But the company is also notably anti-union, with only 10,000 trade union members worldwide.

This anti-union policy was confirmed by a confidential company memorandum circulated to IBM managers in 1985. The document, written by Donald J. Knox, Director of Personnel, listed four 'sensitive employee relations situations' which managers should report immediately – day or night – to IBM's Personnel Department. These were:

1) Reports, or even rumours, of organised labour activity, directed towards our personnel at any location, including questions raised by our people on the subject of union activity.

2) Any indication of group activity, even without apparent organised influence, when the group's purpose appears to be to improve compensation or any aspect of working conditions. For example, an employee who writes, speaks or claims to speak for . . . fellow employees, or an attempt by one individual to reflect the attitude of a group of employees.

3) Any organised labour activity near one of our locations that, while not aimed directly at IBM, might affect us. For example, picketing directed at other companies which could affect IBM.

4) Jurisdictional disputes involving our employees' work and the work done by outside labour groups.

The memo, headed 'Reporting Sensitive Incidents', concluded by warning: 'All incidents, not simply those deemed important by local management, must be reported. A single incident may appear unimportant when viewed alone, but may be quite significant when connected with other information.'[43] It also instructed managers to make their reports both through line management and to two IBM personnel executives whose home and office telephone numbers were provided.

When the memo was disclosed, amidst union allegations of spying on employees, IBM Manager John Wells said: 'IBM obeys the letter and the spirit of the labour laws around the world and respects the rights of all employees to organise (or not) as provided by national law. The intention of the memorandum was to emphasise . . . the need to be sensitive to employee concerns and to report such concerns in a timely manner, so as not to – even inadvertently – violate labour laws.'[44]

It was in line with IBM's anti-union policy that it paid the Economic League an annual subscription, for political vetting services, of £5,750. That was IBM UK's subscription in 1986, as agreed on the telephone by John Steele, the company's Personnel Director, and John Udal, the League's Liaison Director. IBM was also keen to involve its three regional offices in the labour-screening system, as well as its national headquarters in Portsmouth. This was discussed at a meeting on 9 September 1986 by Steele and Udall.

When IBM's links with the League were revealed in the summer of 1987, the corporation at first tried to cover up. Three times IBM denied using the League's vetting services. John Steele told *Datalink*: 'I don't know if we use the League – I've heard about them but only from what I've read in the papers.'[45] Clearly embarrassed, the company then rushed out an official statement:

'Various sources of information are used to ensure applications of prospective employees are bona-fide. These include: references, educational establishments, examination boards, former employers and the Economic League Information Service Department. All this information, and most importantly the interviews, help in the decision.'

The following week IBM released another statement: 'Our subscription to the League has now lapsed and we do not plan to renew it.' The company denied that their decision had anything to do with the adverse publicity the disclosure had generated. But one IBM executive had no doubts: 'I think it embarrassed us in the sense that the average employee was not aware that this sort of investigation was being carried out.'[46]

The League and Personnel Directors

IBM's support for the League was not surprising, particularly as one of the corporation's former Personnel Directors was Parry Rogers, a strong Economic League supporter. He had joined IBM in 1961 after brief spells at Mars Ltd (a well-known anti-union firm) and Hardy Spicer Ltd. In 1966 he was appointed to the IBM UK Ltd Board, but left in 1974 to become Personnel Director of Plessey Group plc, long-time subscribers to the League. While at Plessey he became President of the Institute of Personnel Management. In 1982 Rogers became a member of the League's Central Council. A keen advocate of League policy, Rogers has also served on the Employment Appeal Tribunal and the Final Selection Board of the Civil Service Commission. He retired in 1986, and is now Chairman of the Institute of Directors. Rogers refused to talk to the authors about his work and his views on personnel vetting.

Not all personnel executives have been so reticent. In 1978 Peter Linklater, Personnel Director of Shell UK, whose then Managing Director Sir David Barron was a former League President, admitted using the League's vetting services. 'They give us pretty good value,' he said. 'We are interested in identifying overt opponents of the system to which we are committed. The last thing we want to do is have political subversives on our payroll or on sites in which we have an interest.'[47]

Other personnel managers are not so happy about companies using the League. In one multinational company the Personnel

Director of a subsidiary continually objected to the system. At one meeting he said he wanted to stop using the League because he 'didn't believe in it'. But he was swiftly castigated by his colleagues, who told him it was a Board decision and he had no choice. A more junior Personnel Officer who worked for the same company simply refused to hand over the names for political vetting, and her manager was forced to ask a clerk to obtain the list. 'I was horrified and I never supplied any names unless I was instructed,' said the Personnel Officer. 'In fact, I often used to deliberately forget to supply names . . . I objected to the policy because it was unnecessary because we check references anyway. We also had a very good relationship with the trade unions. Some union officials even tipped us off if there was going to be any trouble with the workforce.'

Douglas Brooks, a former Personnel Manager for Hoover Ltd, who were long-time subscribers to the League, said: 'I was never happy about it because it smacked of the blacklist. It seemed to me to go too far. I regard it as legitimate for employers to use information about their staff to prevent disruption, but I also believe that vetting can lead to blacklisting because it can be inefficient.'

The League has persistently denied that it compiles blacklists as part of its vetting service to companies. But Christopher George, a former Industrial Relations Manager for Turner and Newall, the building materials multinational, says otherwise. When he worked for the firm in the north-west he received regular lists of people from the Economic League who 'should not be trusted'. George would then underline the names of the individuals who worked for Turner and Newall and send the list down to the Personnel Office. 'It was standard practice in the company,' he recalls, 'and almost a matter of course and normal management activity. It was our job to ensure that the teeming hordes didn't impede management or the company.'

Other Industrial Relations Managers are stronger in their criticism. Ken Mullier, who worked for the construction firm John Mowlem in that capacity from 1976 to 1983, said: 'The Economic League need to collect names. The more names they have on their files, the more effective they can appear to be to the people who subscribe to them . . . It's a secretive system, a blacklist that ensnares people, in many cases totally innocent people. Preventing them from finding work, perhaps for the rest of their working lives.'[48]

Out of Control

Michael Noar says that one of his major priorities on becoming the League's Director-General in June 1986 was to improve and reform its labour-screening procedures. He says that the rules on access to vetting information were tightened up and the system improved. But the reality is that the agency is out of control – all kinds of people are being listed in League files, the secrecy continues and its sources of information are based more on intelligence than industrial techniques.

There also remains an attitude of marked intolerance. As the League stated in 1986: 'Some companies may be in a moral dilemma about excluding people from employment on political grounds. But these are not people who just happen to hold certain political beliefs. They apply their beliefs to their industrial activity, to causing problems at every opportunity, with no regard even for their fellow-workers, who they claim to represent.'[49]

However, a more worrying development is the arbitrary methods of vetting job applicants, specifically the use of family connections, for refusing employment. This became prominent in the mid-1970s when personnel managers were told to be 'suspicious' if the prospective employee had relatives who were communists.

This was revealed in 1987 when Alan Harvey, then Deputy Director of the League's north-east region, told two businessmen:

'The thing is when we feed that [information] in we come back with relatives as well. We did this just the other day. It was a funny name, something like Galfham, peculiar name, and Galfham had gone down with a general march, so we know which political side his bread was buttered on. Now, there was another one like that but the Christian name was different. We said, "Well look, you know, by all means take the guy on if you want. But if it was me I would be a little worried about it because you are risking other people's jobs." If he goes to another company . . . I'm going to have to hand that advice out two or three times. And I'm not keen, that is the distasteful bit. But who do you risk? Do you risk ninety people, 100 people, or even thousands of people – or one job?'[50]

It is this kind of power without responsibility that has made so many people – with diverse political viewpoints – believe that the Economic League should be made publicly accountable for its actions. 'I think they should be accountable,' said former Conservative Employment Minister Jim Lester. 'I think that information that is given without prejudice, but equally without the right kind of correction, can be very dangerous.'[51] John Alderson, former Chief Constable of the Devon and Cornwall police force, agrees: 'We know the accountability of the police. They can be brought to book. People can be sacked and demoted and punished for improper use of their powers. The problem about the Economic League is that it's a grey, unaccountable organisation, accountable only to its firms and shareholders, and it can of course affect people's jobs.'[52]

The concern of individuals who are on the files of the Economic League is not just that the information could be inaccurate, but that its secrecy prevents them from challenging it. As Andrew Jeffrey, registered by the League because of his research into far right politics, says: 'It's really McCarthyism, but ten times worse because McCarthy was at least prepared to stand up in front of a Congressional or Senate hearing and justify his actions. These people are not prepared to justify their actions. They're insidious, they're secret. This is really quite immoral.'[53]

This protective cloak of secrecy continues to safeguard the League's activities. A potential threat to its power was the Data Protection Act, which gave individuals the right to inspect files held on them. But the League met this challenge head-on. It was one of the first companies to register under the Act under the category of 'customer/client administration'. The League's entry reveals, intriguingly, that it will be holding computer data on customers and clients, on current or past employees of other organisations, potential business contacts and current, past or potential elected representatives or other holders of public office. The personal information to be held includes career history, work record, trade union membership and security details. But Michael Noar denies that their vetting files are currently held on computer:

'Our personnel staff records and membership lists are on computer. But one thing I am clear about is that there are no files on outside people and activists on computer. They are all on paper. We have had a number of applications from people under the Act saying "tell us what you're holding about me on computer" . . . The only computer records we have are on our staff.'

The League continues to prosper. Among its next victims could be workers who have applied for jobs on the Channel Tunnel.

Trans Manche Link (TML), the five-company consortium which has won the contract to build the tunnel, has secretly arranged to vet all job applicants with the Economic League. Fax communications show that there has been regular contact between the TML centre in Ashford, Kent, and the League's Central Research Department in Thornton Heath, Surrey.

The operation is being masterminded by David Knight-Dewell, the former head of the League's Research Department, who left in the summer of 1987 to join TML, which comprises Richard Costain Ltd, Balfour Beatty, Tarmac, Taylor Woodrow and Wimpey – all long-time subscribers to the League. So the consortium will have easy access to the League's vetting files.

Costain, at least, is embarrassed about its links with the League. After a 'Services Group' meeting, David Barrett, the company's Industrial Relations Advisor, wrote to the League's head office in London. The letter, marked 'Strictly private and confidential', said that under no circumstances should Costain's membership of the League be divulged without the firm's permission.[54]

It seems that the TML consortium is frightened that industrial action will upset the delicately-balanced finances of the tunnel. The workers themselves will not know they are being politically vetted. That will be a secret, of course.

8

The Engineering and Construction Industry: Building the Blacklist

He tried to explain to his wife and kids,
But they could not understand,
Why he was always out of work,
The blacklisted man.

He tried to tell them what he hoped to achieve,
A whole new world, under a better plan.
But with no money Mary had to leave
The blacklisted man.

He thought on all the places he had been,
Forced to trudge the length of the land.
You can't stay long in your own home town
If you are the blacklisted man.

As he remembered the bygone days,
His thoughts soon turned to them –
Those he had fought and worked along with,
The blacklisted men.

For only in their company
Could he truly believe in their plan,
That he who now blacklists them
Will in turn become the blacklisted man.[1]

For almost ten years Tony McCarthy thought he was blacklisted by his former employers, TI New World Ltd, but he could never prove it.

Since leaving the company in December 1978 McCarthy has never obtained a job through official channels. Despite applying for hundreds of jobs in his home town of Warrington, he has only been successful when tipped off by friends and relatives. When he was told that a former manager had disclosed how TI New World Ltd had blacklisted him he was angry, but not completely surprised.

Being blacklisted has meant a total of two years and four months of unemployment for McCarthy in the past decade after a lifetime of continuous work. It has put pressure on his marriage and meant a loss of dignity and self-confidence.

What is shocking about his case are the circumstances behind it. For sixteen years McCarthy was a model employee. His work record was exemplary. He never had a day off, was never late, and the company register shows no trace of any offence. 'First-rate' was how one former manager described him.

McCarthy was also a senior shop steward. He represented twenty fellow workers in the fettling shop of the factory's foundry section. The company manufactured domestic appliances, and McCarthy's job was to clean and grind cast-iron cookers. It was the hardest, dirtiest work in the factory, and he would go home every evening with his clothes filthy with black sand metal. He and his twenty colleagues were well paid for working in such conditions. By 1978 they were earning £163 for a forty-hour week. This was not new. McCarthy's father had worked in the foundry for fifty years and was equally well paid.

The company was far from happy with these wages, higher than those of some managers. The firm's executives were also concerned that the salaries were reducing profitability. So in 1977 a Time Study Engineer was appointed to observe McCarthy and his colleagues at work for three months. The subsequent report showed that the fettling shop was cost-effective and highly productive.

Soon afterwards McCarthy was summoned to the office of Tony Gough, a Works Manager, who told him he wanted to abolish the firm's bonus payments system. 'What would it cost for me to buy out the bonus scheme in your department?' asked Gough.

This would have meant a large wage cut for his members, so McCarthy was sceptical: 'We can't afford it. You are asking my people to lose £3000 a year.' He added that he was prepared to negotiate, but said the company would have to pay a lump sum of several thousand pounds to compensate the loss of income. Gough became angry. 'You're just being greedy,' he said in exasperation.

The real problem for TI New World was that they were incapable of negotiating with McCarthy. According to management sources, he was simply too good for them. 'McCarthy ran rings round management,' said one former executive. He was intelligent, sharp and articulate, and the employers were at a loss to know what to do.

McCarthy did not get his way by making militant threats or taking industrial action. During the ten years he was shop steward there was not one strike, despite the 1970s being one of the most strike-prone periods in history. All annual wage rises were freely negotiated, with hardly an angry word being exchanged. 'I've never believed in militant trade unions and never supported strikes as a strategy,' said McCarthy. 'If the management was incompetent then that's their fault. I went in there to get the best deal for my members.'

Ironically, whenever there was any disruption in the factory, it was McCarthy and two union colleagues who were called in to negotiate on behalf of management. An executive would sidle up to McCarthy and say: 'Have a word with them. See if you can sort it out.'

But by 1978 New World Ltd, a subsidiary of the engineering group Tube Investments plc, was losing money. In June John Crathorne, the Managing Director, announced that the foundry would have to close because of high costs and the advent of new technology. He said 200 workers would be made redundant, but they would be found jobs elsewhere in the company if other employees left.

McCarthy was one of those to lose his job. At 36, he was facing unemployment for the first time. But he was not too unhappy, as the severance pay was reasonable and he was confident of getting another job. He then began to hear stories about company plans to refuse him future employment. On the day of his departure, Tuesday 22 December 1978, McCarthy approached Crathorne and said: 'I've heard a rumour that if I ever apply again for a job here I would be blacked.'

'That's nonsense,' replied Crathorne. 'I've got nothing against you.'

McCarthy was unconvinced by this response, so he went to see Tony Gough. He again received a reassuring answer: 'Tony, we can't recruit any of you straight away. Just let the dust settle. Wait till Easter and beyond and we'll start taking people on. There's every chance of recruiting some of you again.'

McCarthy spent the next six months unemployed. He then got a job at a local engineering firm. It only lasted seven months, and then he was back on the dole. It was a time of heavy industrial recession, with many engineering firms in the north-west closing down. Work was scarce.

The exception was TI New World, who were making money again, and, by the autumn of 1980, began recruiting new workers. Remembering the firm's past assurances, McCarthy went to see a senior manager. To his astonishment he was told: 'I can only give you a foreman's job.'

'No,' replied McCarthy, 'I just want a job on the factory floor.'

'Well, we can't give you a job there.'

It was the first approach to the company that prompted the management to blacklist McCarthy. It was done on the instructions of Crathorne, the Managing Director, who made it clear that the former shop steward was not to be re-employed on the factory floor. A manager was also told to give McCarthy's name and personal details to the local Economic League office in Warrington.

A former manager told the authors: 'Tony McCarthy was blacklisted by TI New World Ltd because of his union and political activities. I saw him as a competent, intelligent and successful negotiator. He was not a subversive in any way.'

The company could hardly brand him as a dangerous agitator, as he had never been active in or a member of any political party. Nor did he advocate strikes as a tactic. His 'crime' was that he was a skilful trade union negotiator.

TI New World always officially denied that he had been blacklisted. Crathorne told his union: 'There is no real prospect of us being able to offer him a position . . . The company has, for some time, operated a rota system. At the time of writing there are more than 630 applicants on the list.[2] In fact, McCarthy's name had been deliberately excluded from the rota book.

Meanwhile, McCarthy was still struggling to get work. Like other blacklist victims, he would be offered jobs at the interview and then be rejected a few days later.

By 1983 he was getting desperate. He began writing pleading letters to TI New World Ltd. He even gave verbal and written assurances that he would not get involved in trade union activities. 'I felt I was degrading myself,' he said. 'But they were the only place employing and there were no other jobs.' His situation was only really made clear in 1984, when he was told by a manager: 'Tony, I've no objections. I'm perfectly prepared to take you on, but I've got to get it sanctioned upstairs.' He did not get the job and has remained blacked ever since.

Being blacklisted has had serious effects on McCarthy and his family. Apart from the prolonged bouts of unemployment, his only jobs have been on temporary contracts. This has meant no job security, lower wages, few employment rights and no pension scheme.

The loss of income caused much hardship. His wife, Pat, was forced to go out to work in order to meet their mortgage payments. When he was unemployed the couple were often forced to consider selling their house. The lack of money meant no holidays for five years, and at one stage they were living on £20 a week. McCarthy now has to work a fifty-five-hour week to keep his family financially secure.

Unemployment had other consequences. His wife said: 'When you're out of work it's not just the money. It creates other problems. It's the pressure it brings on the marriage.' For Tony McCarthy himself, 'The signing on was the worst part. That was the soul-destroying part of it.'

He now feels the trade union spirit has been kicked out of him, and he is working in a non-union engineering firm in Manchester. 'I will get involved in trade union activities,' he says, 'But after the way I have been treated, I wouldn't get involved at shop-floor level. I would just carry on outside the company.'

McCarthy is an angry man, particularly about the motives behind the blacklisting: 'If I had done something wrong, then I could understand it.' But his main fears, at 45, are about his employment prospects and the future of his daughter Rebecca, 18, and son Nicholas, 15. After all, his name and personal details are on the files of the Economic League at their North-West Area Office in Museum Street, Warrington.

McCarthy is just one of hundreds of victims of the blacklist where it is most rampant – in engineering factories and on construction sites. Employers have resorted to blacklisting with increasing frequency in recent years, as the economic recession has begun to bite.

The traditional, and easiest, form of blacklisting in these industries is for managers to contact the worker's previous employer and ask about his political and trade union activities. This has been a growing practice since the late 1970s, when a number of engineering firms closed down, particularly in the north-west.

Blacklisting was especially apparent after industrial action in protest against factory closures. Employees made redundant often found it extremely difficult to find another job. This happened to those involved in the occupation of the Lawrence Scott engineering firm in Manchester in 1980, and also to those who occupied Gardner and Sons, the diesel engine manufacturer, in Manchester in the same year. The employees were taking action against the company's demand for 590 compulsory redundancies. The occupation lasted just under two months. Eventually the management backed down, and agreed that only 325 jobs would be lost through natural wastage.

The union had won. But activists who took voluntary redundancy found future employment prospects blocked. A notable victim was Barry Redfern, the shop steward in the most militant department of the factory. In 1982 he took voluntary redundancy and obtained a job as a milkman with a food company which was non-union. After a week he was summoned by his manager. 'We've got to let you go,' he said apologetically. 'Your references make you unsuitable.' The manager then gave him a glimpse of the offending reference, which said Redfern had 'the wrong attitude'. Redfern was shocked and angry, particularly as he had no intention of starting a union branch at the company. But there was nothing he could do, as neither his present nor his past employer would give him a copy of the reference. Redfern was unemployed for a year before getting another job.

This was one of many cases that the north-west district of the Amalgamated Engineering Union (AEU) used to take up this form of vetting with the Engineering Employers' Federation (EEF). In June 1984 AEU officials met senior EEF members in Manchester, and the weight of evidence persuaded the Federation to adopt a code of conduct. The EEF refused to recommend that employers be obliged to disclose the contents of references, but their members in South Lancashire, Cheshire and North Wales were warned about political vetting: 'References should be confined to such things as ability, performance, attendance etc; and should avoid such things as trade union membership or activities.'[3]

Many companies have ignored such guidelines. Other employers' organisations have even set up their own vetting systems. One Lancashire branch of the National Federation for the Self-Employed compiled a blacklist of individuals who had appealed against dismissal under the Employment Protection Act. This was revealed in a letter from Alan Thompson the Branch Chairman to local employers:

'We already have a confidential register of employees who have accused their employers of unfair dismissal. This register is available for anyone about to engage new staff as a precaution against falling foul of known 'rip-off' artists on the look-out for a new victim of the [Employment Protection] Act. If you . . . are unfamiliar with all the conditions of this Act, I must tell you that it now includes anyone who employs labour, even part-timers, and makes it virtually impossible to dismiss an employee for any reason except at great cost, because the statutory requirements are practically impossible to fulfil.'

Thompson confirmed that there were a large number of individuals on the blacklist, but refused to say whether it had ever been used of not. He added:

'The list is there in case a member should make inquiries about an application for a job. No one ever sees the list except our officials. When somebody [an employer] inquires he must give us a name, address and National Insurance number. If we have a note they will be given the name of the applicant's previous employer and they can take it up with that previous employer. We make no recommendations for obvious reasons.'[4]

More informal blacklists are used in the construction industry, where vetting of workers is rampant. This is partly due to perennial conflict between union and management on site. But it is also because the mobility of the workforce makes it easier to dismiss employees. Some trade union activists have tried to avoid the blacklist by using their wives' National Insurance numbers. But this is only a temporary measure, which means that employers simply take a few weeks longer to sack them.

Building companies have used a variety of vetting methods. Some firms simply compile their own blacklist of employees and make its contents available to other firms. This was revealed in 1978 when two sacked construction workers obtained blacklists kept by their employers, Whatlings and Frank Laffertys, two Glasgow-based building companies. Both were firms which relied heavily on local government contracts.

On their second day at work with Laffertys at Whitfield Road, Govan, Eamonn Monaghan and Tommy Goldie, both joiners, handed their P45s, National Insurance numbers and holiday credit cards to their foreman, along with a personal data form issued by the company. Twenty minutes later both were dismissed and given redundancy pay. They knew they had been politically vetted. Proof came four days later when a Laffertys manager handed them the actual blacklist used by the firm, which included their names, along with those of thirteen other Glasgow workers.

Monaghan and Goldie then obtained jobs with Whatlings, a fast-expanding construction firm and a member of the CBI. They started work on Monday 12 December at Merryland Street, Govan, on a housebuilding contract for the Government-backed Scottish Special Housing Association. Personal data forms were again handed in. Three hours later the foreman sacked both of them, and admitted they were on 'a list'. This time Monaghan and Goldie refused to accept their dismissal, and after heated negotiations they were reinstated.

Later that day they obtained more hard evidence when a sympathetic manager handed them Whatlings' blacklist. Apart from their own names, it included those of fifty-three other workers from all over Scotland, with their dates of birth, National Insurance numbers and likely areas of employment. The names on the list included those of William McFall and Jimmy McBride, who had just been elected as UCATT Scottish Regional Organisers. For McFall it was proof of what he had always believed: 'We have been waiting a long time to get the list we always knew existed . . . Anywhere I've had to fill in forms I've never got a job.'[5] Of the seventy-two individuals on the two blacklists, sixty-seven were active trade unionists.

Another form of political labour-screening on building sites is carried out by the contractor. Large construction corporations use the Economic League. There is also evidence that the Ministry of Defence has vetted union activists.

In September 1981, two young joiners from the Humberside area were offered employment by John Mowlem Ltd to work on an MoD contract at the RAF Coningsby station in Lincolnshire. 'Mick Stewart' and 'Terry Allison' (not their real names) were hired to help build reinforced concrete hangers for the RAF's Phantom jets.

Both the foreman, Peter Shroud, and the Industrial Relations Manager, Ken Mullier, knew Stewart and Allison to be 'first-class workers'. But two days later the company's projects manager, John Barr, was told by the MoD that they were 'politically unsuitable' and could not be employed. Barr then telephoned Mullier and told him about the MoD's objections. Telegrams were then sent to the two workers' homes withdrawing the offers of employment. By that time Stewart and Allison had resigned from their previous jobs, so they were both suddenly on the dole.

The UCATT officials on site were furious, particularly as neither of the workers were politically active, although Stewart had been a shop steward at the nearby Drax power station. Mowlem was accused of operating a blacklist on the RAF site. At the time Ken Mullier denied it and told the union that the two labourers could not be employed because they were 'not local men'. This, he explained, would breach a local agreement as they would have been 'jumping the queue'.

Mullier now admits that this was a fabrication intended to cover up the MoD's involvement. The real reason, he says, was that the Ministry of Defence had vetoed the appointments. This was done under a long-standing practice which gave the MoD ultimate authority over who the building firms could employ. Every week a list of new workers was sent to MoD's headquarters in London, and it would be returned with their recommendations. If a worker was rejected by the MoD, no reason would be given.

It is the Economic League which does most of the political vetting in the construction and engineering industries. Many firms began subscribing to the League's vetting service in the early 1970s, after the nationwide building strike. Construction workers in London were among the first victims. One executive disclosed how he gave the Economic League a list of eighteen building workers who had applied for jobs with his company: 'Within twenty-four hours they were able to tell me that eight of the men had been prominently involved in disruption at other sites . . . We use the service when we want to find workers for sites in troublesome areas such as north London. So far only two of our London sites have been closed by the strike and we want to keep it that way.'[6]

Construction companies now form the largest group of subscribers to the League, with Tarmac, Taylor Woodrow, Balfour Beatty and Bovis among its most prominent members (see Appendix). These building firms also organised collectively within the League. Known as the 'Services Group', in the mid-1970s they paid out substantial extra sums for 'special work' in the regions. A National Co-ordinator, David Laver, was appointed to run the operation from Asphalt House, Palace Street, London. Laver, who was also Director of the League's South-East Region, sent out bulletins to companies warning them about 'widening extremist activity'.[7] The special service did not amount to much apart from occasional lunches at expensive hotels. As one Personnel Director said: 'It is a complete waste of time and money. But my Chairman, who hasn't a clue that he is paying for nothing, likes the idea.'[8]

Although construction firms no longer receive a special regional service, they continue to meet informally. Personnel and Industrial Relations Directors from about twenty building firms meet with senior Economic League officials twice a year. No agenda is set and the member companies use codes to record their attendance.

The aim of these meetings is for the League to brief the firms about the industrial relations scene in their area. If a major strike is taking place the League officials would identify trade union activists involved by name and provide information on them. On one occasion a list of twenty-six workers was presented with the following caption: 'ALL SUSPECT – EXTREME LEFT. CERTAINLY MILITANT IN BEHAVIOUR'.

In the north-east these gatherings (or 'working lunches' as the League likes to call them) are often held at the Chase Hotel, York. One Industrial Relations Manager who attended them was Ken Mullier, of John Mowlem Ltd. He says that the League nearly always maintained that 'outside subversives' were 'infiltrating' to 'wreck the company'.

Mullier thought this was nonsense, as most disputes in the building industry were about bonus payments – hardly a recipe for revolutionary activity. He saw the Economic League as a source of conflict rather than conciliation: 'They used to say things we wanted to hear at those meetings. At one point I asked one of their officials how long someone stayed on the blacklist. He said two years and if they behaved themselves then they would be taken off.'

Mullier says the League is at fault because of their criteria for blacklisting individuals. 'Their definition of subversion and my definition are quite different. A subversive to me is someone who won't do a day's work. Someone who deliberately sets out to wreck the company.' But the League clearly has a much wider definition. And, as Mowlem's Northern Industrial Relations Manager from 1976 to 1983, Mullier had direct experience of their methods. In 1987 he told Granada TV's *World in Action* how the League's operations affected ordinary people.

Like most building firms, Mowlem kept a list of good workers and a separate one of incompetent and lazy employees. But there was another list – the blacklist – which contained the names of active and militant trade unionists. Mullier always refused to put names on this blacklist. But it was his job to check workers' political views and trade union activities whenever Mowlem won a large contract.

The League has always maintained that it doesn't recommend whether or not an individual should be appointed. 'We don't advise a company not to employ a person,' says Michael Noar, their Director-General. 'We give straightforward factual information. It is then up to the company to make its mind up.'[9]

But Mullier says that some regional League personnel did advise him on whether individuals should or should not be employed. After supplying the League's office in Skipton, North Yorkshire, with a list of names, an official would ring him back and say either 'he's clear' or 'politically unsuitable'. Occasionally, according to Mullier, he would be told: 'I wouldn't touch him with a bargepole.'

A case in point was construction worker Dennis Huggins. He joined Mowlem in 1979 with excellent references. His previous employer, Foy Construction Ltd, said of him: 'We found Mr Huggins to be completely loyal to the company, industrious in his effort and an excellent asset to the company. I feel sure that given the opportunity with another company he will prove to be similar.'

In 1981 he became the TGWU shop steward while working for Mowlem as a concrete ganger on the Beverley bypass in Humberside. It was his first and only period as a union representative. He soon became very effective. He stood no nonsense from management and refused to be patronised. His boss, Ken Mullier, said: 'He was very good at his job, particularly at negotiating better pay and conditions for his members.' This was acheived without strikes.

When the contract with Humberside County Council was finished Huggins was asked to represent the workers at the bypass's official opening. The council also gave him a glowing reference.

But after leaving Mowlem, Huggins suddenly found it virtually impossible to find work. About four months later he telephoned Mullier and asked him: 'Am I blacklisted?' Mullier was annoyed at the suggestion. He told Huggins it was 'nonsense' and slammed the phone down. But the call made Mullier think. He rang the Economic League office in Skipton and asked whether he should employ Dennis Huggins. A few minutes later a League official called back: 'Politically unsuitable,' he said briskly.

Mullier couldn't believe it, particularly as he knew that

Huggins was not politically motivated. 'Are you sure?' he asked.

'We don't make mistakes,' replied the League official impatiently. Mullier was shocked. He told the official that Huggins was a first-class employee – 'top rank'. He asked for a reason for the blacklisting. At first the League official was adamant: 'We don't give out details.' But then he added: 'Well, if you must know, it was your own boss who put him on the list.'

Mullier was angry because he believed that Huggins had been blacklisted purely because he was a very good union negotiator. He arranged for Huggins to be taken off the list. Suddenly, after nine months on the dole, Huggins was able to get work again. He was later asked by *World in Action*: 'What would have happened if you hadn't been taken off the blacklist?'

'I'd most probably be sat at home twiddling my thumbs,' he replied.

'You'd still be there?'

'Still be there.'[10]

Huggins was not the only Mowlem worker to be blacklisted by the Economic League. Roy Turnbull had been employed in 1976 as a labourer on the Metro System in Newcastle. After finishing that job Turnbull was unemployed for a year, and for the next decade he was out of work on numerous occasions. In 1986, for example, he was unemployed for the whole year, with the exception of a brief two-week spell.

The source of Turnbull's problems was that Alan Harvey, the Economic League's Deputy Director in their north-east region, was advising prospective employers that he should not be employed. This was revealed by Granada Television's *World in Action* when they posed as possible clients for the League. When asked about employing Turnbull, Harvey replied: 'Well, he first came to our notice in November 1976. Known to be a member of the Communist Party and regularly attends Communist Party meetings in Middlesbrough. You know, to my mind, there is no question you should turn him down. People would be very foolish to take him on.'[11]

This information was also held by Turnbull's employer, Tom Gallagher, Mowlem's Group Industrial Relations Manager. In a memorandum to Frank James, his assistant and a former policeman, Gallagher wrote: 'With reference to our recent telephone conversation, I enclose a list of names of Communist Party members who attended the meeting we discussed.' This list included the names of seven workers, including Turnbull, with sketchy personal details. On Turnbull's employment application form, Gallagher also wrote: 'Unsuitable politics – not to be offered employment.'

Turnbull was outraged when presented with this evidence of his blacklisting. He has never been a member of the Communist Party. Nor of any political party. He has never even voted in an election. He has also never been to Middlesbrough, let alone attended meetings there. He was not even a member of a trade union. The last time he had joined a union was in 1964, when he was seventeen years old.

Another labourer listed on the Mowlem company memorandum was scaffolder Ken Martin. On his application form Gallagher had written: 'Communist Party member. This man is politically unsuitable. Inform all our site agents in the region that under no circumstances is he to be offered employment.'

The Economic League had the same 'information' on Martin. Perhaps more importantly, they were also recommending that he should be blacklisted. When asked about him by *World in Action*, Alan Harvey said that Martin had attended 'the same meetings as Turnbull and he was converted at the same time as I believe Turnbull was.'

'What – to the Communist Party?'

'To the Communist Party. Known to be a member of the Communist Party. That's as much as we've got on him without going to the Central Records Office.'

'But presumably the advice on him would be the same as for Turnbull?'

'Well, I think you've hit it on the head,' said Harvey.[12] As in Turnbull's case, both Mowlem and the Economic League had got their information completely wrong. 'These people claimed I am a member of the Middlesbrough Communist Party,' said Martin. 'I can put my hand on my heart and say that I've never even been to Middlesbrough. I've never been a union official. I have never been a member of any political party. The wife usually has to drag me out of the house just to vote at elections, although, like many working men, I do vote Labour. The last time I was on strike was in 1971 – and that was a national dispute.'[13]

Martin's main worry was for his family. His young nephew, Robert Martin, also a labourer in the Newcastle area, had also been listed by Mowlem as a 'Communist Party member'. Again, this was untrue, and the family were worried about its implications. Ken Martin's wife, Betty, said: 'This whole thing has got us sick with worry. We have two sons out of work and we are worried that this could stop them from ever getting jobs.'[14]

The Economic League refused to comment officially on these cases. 'I don't want to do that,' said their Director-General Michael Noar. 'I just think it would be dangerous and unhelpful.' On Alan Harvey's blacklisting recommendations, Noar claimed he was 'breaking our own rules.' He maintained that the League merely 'gives straight information out to employers. We don't say "Don't employ these people, they are dangerous." So there is no blacklist . . . What we do is we say "This man wrote this article. If that matters to you, good luck."'

But the evidence shows that the League does advise companies. Apart from Harvey's indiscretions, the South-East Region Office has given similar recommendations. In 1978 the *Guardian* posed as a client, telephoned the League and asked them about Tom Durkin and Kevin Halpin, two veteran trade union activists and Communist Party members. After a brief pause, back came the League's response: 'Oh yes, you've got a couple of right villains there.' The League official then disclosed a mass of detail about the two workers' political views and activities, stretching back to 1951.

'Right. Well, I know what to do,' said the 'client'.

'You don't want to entertain these gentlemen,' said the League official.

'Not if you say so.'

'Yes.'

Durkin had certainly suffered from such prejudices. In the early 1950s he was sacked by building firms so many times that he left the industry and went to work for the Communist Party. When he returned to the industry he had more luck. But he did have one chilling experience while working for an American multinational computer company in London. During the Common Market referendum campaign in 1975 Durkin was summoned by the firm's Chief Security Officer and accused of using company facilities for printing anti-EEC material.

'You've been using our photocopy machines to reproduce these leaflets, haven't you,' said the Security Officer.

'No, I wouldn't be that stupid,' replied Durkin. 'Why do you suspect me?'

'Because I know all about you.'

9

The Car Industry: Molehunt or Witch-hunt?

'We needed to re-establish management authority.'
Michael Edwardes, Chairman of British Leyland 1977–82,
Back From the Brink (Collins, London, 1983)

One day in 1978 George Jones, an Advertising Representative for the *Birmingham Post and Mail*, was approached by the newspaper's Security Officer. 'Do you know a man called Arthur Smith?' he asked. Jones said yes, he had worked with him in the *Financial Times*' Birmingham office, where Smith was the Midlands Correspondent. There the conversation ended, and Jones thought no more about it until a few days later when he received a telephone call. It was from an official working for British Leyland (BL), the State-owned car company. The official said he understood that Jones knew Arthur Smith and invited him to lunch. Jones agreed to the meeting.

When he arrived for the lunch he was met by a British Leyland Public Relations Officer and a man who introduced himself as Eric Gregory, BL's Security Officer. The conversation turned to Smith, and it became clear that these were not routine enquiries. Jones, a former policeman, immediately noticed from the line of Gregory's questions that he was no ordinary Security Officer. 'They were concerned about Arthur Smith's sources [for his BL stories],' recalls Jones, 'and had a deep suspicion about his contacts with the trade unions. They asked whether he had links with any left wing organisations or trade unions. They seemed to think he was out to damage British Leyland. I said the real reason he was publishing these stories was because he was a very good journalist, and it had nothing to do with any covert political activity.'

Smith, who reported on the car industry for the *Financial Times* from 1975 to 1987 and is now an analyst for a stockbroker, later asked a BL executive if information was secretly being collected about him. The manager confirmed that a file had been compiled by BL.

BL's interest in Smith's views is just one example of the car industry's long record of labour screening and political surveillance. Ever since car workers became fully unionised in the mid-1960s, management have increasingly taken the view that any strike action is orchestrated by 'political agitators'.

The car industry has always been a focus of management/union battles on the shop-floor. In the post-war period the production of motor cars was seen as a vital factor in revitalising the British economy, and there was a huge market for new models. The trades unions soon realised this, and saw the opportunity to improve the often appalling working conditions of their members. They were also able to take advantage of the fact that, if one part of the production line stops, the whole plant grinds to a halt.

Until the mid-1960s, managers, mindful of the need for continuous production to meet the demand for cars, tended to placate the unions in order to avoid work stoppages. But as the unions became more powerful, management changed its strategy.

British Leyland

At British Leyland industrial disruption was particularly prevalent at the large Cowley car assembly plant. By 1966 all of the plant's 20,000 workers were trade union members, largely of the TGWU. For the next decade the unions were immensely powerful and influential at the plant – to the extent that management was obliged to have the consent of the shop stewards before it could impose any changes. Moreover, the power of the stewards was backed by a very militant workforce.

In 1965 BL, then the British Motor Corporation (BMC), set up an Industrial Relations Department (IRD) after a recommendation by an independent inquiry into strikes at the company. One of the IRD's first managers was Tom Richardson. He recalls that many of his fellow managers expressed a 'contempt for working people' and were 'very anti-trade union'. He argues that, far from being manipulated by political extremists, the employees had genuine grievances. 'The conditions were terrible for blue-collar workers,' said Richardson. 'They had derisory holidays, no sick pay and laughable pension rights.'

At times, according to Richardson, other managers responded to the shop-floor conflict these conditions generated by implementing petty measures. But after BMC merged with Leyland Motors to become BL in 1968, management's strategy became harsher and more sinister.

Throughout Richardson's four-year tenure at BL, the Managing Director kept a blacklist of left wing trade unionists in his desk drawer. This has been corroborated by a former BL Personnel Director, based at Cowley in the mid-1970s, who said: 'Records were kept and the activities of people were recorded. They [managers] would not have been doing their duty if they didn't do this. But they were mainly trade union activities, not political.'

When a number of Trotskyists became shop stewards, MI5 and Special Branch officers were noticed at Cowley. 'They were buzzing around all the time I was there,' said Richardson. He found them very right wing: 'One of the most senior told me in 1967 that they had absolute proof that Harold Wilson was a Russian agent. My incredulous laughter probably put me on the same list as the then Prime Minister, because the political ignorance displayed within MI5, Special Branch and company has to be experienced to understand its chilling indifference to reality.'

The Security Service and Special Branch's real role at Cowley was to blacklist BL employees who were politically active. Richardson recalls receiving late-night telephone calls and being told that a certain worker was 'a dangerous subversive'. One trade unionist targetted by MI5 was Reg Parsons, then a supporter of the Socialist Labour League. In 1970 Parsons went to a rank-and-file trade unionists' conference in Turin. On his return he told Richardson about the conference. Later that afternoon Richardson was astonished when his Managing Director burst into his office and informed him that MI5 had 'tailed Parsons to a subversive conference in Italy.'

The presence of the Trotskyist shop stewards heightened the tension between management and workers in the early 1970s. The company saw them as challenging their 'right to manage', and industrial relations became increasingly confrontational – combatting the 'extremists' became a priority. 'The company does not intend to allow extremists to run the plant,' said John Kennedy, a Production Manager.[1] In their desire to curb the power of a few militant shop stewards, other trade union activists were also targetted.

It was in this atmosphere that British Leyland developed its contacts with the Economic League. Between 1968 and 1976 the company paid the League 'donations' ranging from £1000 to £3000 a year. But BL went further than this in their plans to politically vet their employees. In 1974 a secret front company was set up to oversee the vetting. On 16 July, 1974 Atom Tractors, a dormant BL subsidiary, was renamed BG Research Services (Bicester) Ltd, and the labour screening began.

To co-ordinate the operation, Eric Gregory, who had taken early retirement as Assistant Chief Constable of Thames Valley Police in 1973, was employed as BL's 'special security advisor'. Gregory's fellow director of BG Research Services was John Bate, another former senior Thames Valley Police officer. Both men described their occupation as 'Personnel Research Services', and this is what BL required of them – except that there was a political dimension.

Since 1974 hundreds of applicants for jobs at BL have been secretly screened by BG Research. The names are sent from the manufacturing plants around the country and checked against the front company's files and lists of political activists. They have also been vetted by the Economic League. Telexes, containing the names, dates of birth and home towns of applicants, are sent to the League's Central Research Department at Thornton Heath, Surrey, for 'clearance'.

BL executives were told that the function of Gregory and BG Research was to work on physical security problems, such as the theft of company property and machinery. Gregory kept a low profile, operating mainly from his private house in Benson, Oxfordshire, and later from Banbury. But in 1976 he did attend an Employees' Participation Council seminar at Hasley Manor, near Warwick, BL's management training centre. During the meeting he was questioned about his job. He said that most of it involved preventing the theft of equipment, particularly spare parts. He was then asked: 'Do you keep records on trade unionists?'

'No, but the management does,' he replied.

'Do you do pre-employment checks?'

'Yes, but not much.'

BG Research has always operated in great secrecy. Its articles of association portray it as a dormant (or sleeping) scaffolding company. The annual accounts disclose an accumulated loss of £18,577 and say the firm has not traded for many years. Although BL, now known as Austin Rover, was publicly owned from 1975 to 1988, the then Industry Secretary, Tony Benn, was not informed about this vetting agency. Prospective BL and Rover employees have also been completely unaware that their political views and activities are being checked out.

The existence of BL's vetting system was confirmed by Sir Pat Lowry, the company's former head of Industrial Relations and Director of Personnel from 1975 to 1981. He said that everyone who applied for a job at BL was vetted through BG Research, but denied that the Economic League was consulted while he was at the company. 'It was felt in BL that it was necessary to do this through a centralised, sophisticated organisation,' said Lowry. 'It was not a "screw the militants" policy. It applied to everyone. We had a responsibility to do this. There was nothing sinister about it. It was part of the general recruiting process.'

Eric Gregory ran this vetting operation until his resignation in October 1979. But BG Research's facilities continued to be used. In 1982 the company expanded, with three new directors – William Chapman, a security advisor, Richard Gilbert, a chartered secretary, and Susan Windridge, an assistant company secretary. Windridge was the key appointment. A young and ambitious BL employee, she ran BG Research as its company secretary. In 1984 the vetting procedures were based at BL's headquarters at 106 Oxford Road, Uxbridge, Middlesex. The following year the corporate links were tightened with the appointment of Brian Hoare, a company executive, who was on BL's Board as well as being a director of BL Staff Trustees Ltd. He resigned in January 1987. Windridge continues to co-ordinate BG Research's activities.

The establishment and use of BL's own vetting agency coincided with the management's stategy of attacking the trades unions in the mid-1970s. The company saw unofficial strikes and production stoppages as a threat to its commercial viability. The then Labour government agreed, and in 1977 appointed Michael Edwardes as BL's chairman. Edwardes's industrial relations plan was clear:

'We needed to re-establish management authority . . . inside the company where our 198,000 employees were relatively leaderless. To regain the management role would mean counteracting shop steward power, which had got out of hand to the point where national union leaders, local union officials and certainly management were being treated in a cavalier fashion by some 200 militant stewards who had filled the vacuum left by management. Not to put too fine a point on it, we needed to take on the militants.'[2]

Edwardes made his move in 1979. That autumn the new Metro car reached the market and new working practices, notably the use of robots, were planned. By then BL's employees' participation scheme had collapsed and managers were adopting a more confrontational style. Key shop stewards were targetted. The most senior steward was Derek Robinson, an AUEW convenor at the Longbridge plant who had worked there for thirty-eight years as a toolmaker. Robinson was a prominent member of the Communist Party and was under regular surveillance by MI5.[3] His most significant position was as chairman of the all-union company-wide Combine Trade Union Committee.

Robinson bitterly criticised the company's new policies on pay, productivity and working practices. He was particularly opposed to the 'Edwardes Plan', which involved substantial redundancies and plant closures. Along with three other stewards, Robinson signed a pamphlet attacking the company plan and calling for active opposition to it. The pamphlet appeared just after a ballot of the workers showing majority support for the plan. BL management argued that Robinson's action 'constituted disruption' and was 'undemocratic', and on Monday, 19 November 1979, Robinson was sacked. The three other shop stewards were not dismissed because, said BL, unlike Robinson they had not received formal warnings about their conduct. Robinson had not in fact been formally warned. He had been verbally chastised by two managers during a strike in March 1979, but no documents had been signed and the AUEW District Officer was not present, as is the established practice.

Robinson's sacking provoked a walk-out by Longbridge workers and subsequent strike action cost the company £50 million in lost production. As the unions – the TGWU and the AUEW – were divided over whether to support Robinson, the initial industrial support collapsed. Robinson remained dismissed and was unemployed for the next two years. He says that he was informed by a Deputy Chairman of the CBI that he was 'unemployable'. Eventually he got a job on the *Morning Star*, and he now teaches on a TUC shop stewards' course at a West Midlands college.

The next shop steward on the hit-list was Alan Thornett, who had become a TGWU Deputy Convenor at Cowley in 1968. A driver in the Transport Department, he was also a member of the

Trotskyist Socialist Labour League. His first major conflict with the company came in 1974 when he led industrial action against management's attempts to impose new work allocations without the agreement of the shop stewards. On 10 April 1974 he attended a meeting with Jeff Whelan, the plant's Personnel Director. 'Whelan produced a dossier on what he referred to as my "activities",' recalls Thornett. 'I was accused of holding a series of unauthorised meetings on the plant with sections of workers, particularly the trim shop.'[4] According to Bill Thomson, a TGWU official who was also at the meeting, Whelan 'alleged that Thornett had no intention of promoting harmony.'[5]

The result of that meeting was that management refused to recognise Thornett as a union representative and ensured that he could not act in any trade union capacity. From then on he was portrayed as a secret infiltrator and dubbed 'the Cowley Mole' by the media and the Economic League – a strange description for someone who had worked at Cowley since 1959.

BL managers continued to refuse to recognise him as a trade union official throughout the 1970s. But he remained active at the plant. During that time a number of trade union activists were sacked for very minor offences. 'BL policy against militants for some time has been to sit and wait for some minor misdemeanor to take place,' said Thornett, 'and then move in to make a major issue of it and use that to sack militants. That's how the policy operated.'[6]

The policy was eventually used against Thornett himself. In 1982 he forgot to renew his HGV licence as a driver of heavy vehicles. This was discovered when he was stopped by the police for a minor parking offence, for which he was fined £5. Failing to renew a driver's licence was a 'nothing issue' at BL, as many other workers at Cowley had committed the same offence and had not even been disciplined. But after seven weeks' deliberation Thornett was sacked. Although his colleagues in the Transport Department voted to strike for his reinstatement, the ballot on a plant-wide basis was lost.

Thornett then took his case for unfair dismissal to an Industrial Tribunal. Just before the public hearing, BL declined to contest the action and offered him £8000 in compensation, which he accepted. Despite being an experienced HGV driver and applying for many jobs, Thornett has remained unemployed ever since.

The following year the extent of BL's vetting procedures was revealed when thirteen Cowley workers were sacked for supplying false references. The employees were all members of the International Marxist Group. It was true that the thirteen had used fabricated references when they applied for their jobs the previous year.

However, it was their membership of the IMG that was stressed privately by BL Executives. Hence the banner headlines about 'moles' and 'infiltrators'. As an anonymous senior manager told the *Evening Standard*: 'We can't afford full-time troublemakers on the shop floor.'[7]

BL maintained that the 'Cowley 13' had been discovered during a 'routine audit'. There was speculation at the time that the Economic League had identified them for BL, but this was not the case. An internal League report, produced nine months later, in May 1984, stated: 'All the "Cowley Moles" were checked by this department and none of them were identified.'[8] Various industrial relations consultants were named as the source of the information. In fact, it came from MI5. The Security Service has had agents inside the Cowley plant since the late 1960s, and it was their disclosures that led to the sackings.

The purge of shop stewards with Trotskyist views has continued unabated at BL, often based on the flimsiest evidence. Deputy Senior Steward Bob Cullen was sacked in 1984 for 'damaging the windscreen wiper of a foreman's car' during an overtime ban. This was said to have happened at Gate 16 of the Cowley plant. But Cullen was on Gate 10 the whole of that morning, and he had twelve witnesses to prove it, including the security man. His union even identified the real culprit – Peter Williams, another steward who looked like Cullen. But management was not impressed. At the disciplinary hearing Cullen was not allowed to call any of the witnesses and three days later he was sacked.

At the subsequent Industrial Tribunal the Chairman, P. W. Haydon, said: 'The hearing at the superintendent's stage can only be described as a farce. No attempt was made at this stage to interview any of the witnesses.' The Tribunal ruled that Cullen had been unfairly dismissed, but his compensation was reduced because he had not publicly identified the real offender. According to Cullen, this was a novel form of justice: 'I didn't know that in proving yourself innocent you had to prove another man guilty.'[9] Cullen applied for over 100 jobs after his dismissal, but remained unemployed until 1987. Meanwhile, Peter Williams, who eventually admitted to having committed the

sacking offence, continues to work at Cowley. He is not a
political activist.

There is no doubt that BL had more than its fair share of
Trotskyists in its workforce, particularly at the Cowley plant.
But as the law is currently constituted, it is not a crime to be a
Marxist. The company's management clearly thought
otherwise. But they went much further than merely weeding
out the militants. BG's Research's role was to check out *all*
prospective Rover employees, so many trade unionists may
have been blacklisted, as the vetting was done in secret.

Austin Rover's long-term industrial relations strategy since
the mid-1970s has been to move to a form of company unionism.
To achieve this, the management has needed to remove the
militant shop stewards and to appeal directly to the workforce
when implementing new working practices. By 1986 this had
been accomplished, and a new recruitment policy was introduced.

Entitled 'Working With Programme', this is a five-year plan
whereby employees are appointed after a two-day in-depth
assessment. According to Andy Barr, Austin Rover's Managing
Director of operations, it is 'a total assessment including interviews, team involvement exercises and practical exercises.' He
added: 'We need to change attitudes, not just behaviour
patterns . . . We are not looking just for manual skills and
dexterity. We want to know whether their aspirations are the
same as the company's. It is a two-way process. What is good
for people is good for the company.'[10] This recruitment system
is already being used at the Cowley plant, and will be installed
throughout the rest of the company by 1991. Such vetting is
aimed at ensuring the new employees support the company's
commercial aims. It also provides the opportunity to screen
political and trade union activists.

Ford

In the autumn of 1983, Paul Roots, the Industrial Relations
Director of Ford UK from 1980 to 1987, was asked about his
company's vetting policies. He gave a vague, but intriguing,
response: 'We rely on a rigid system of selection techniques
covering jobs at all levels. This involves taking up fairly exten-
sive references to ensure that we do not take people who are
unsuitable for whatever reason.'[11]

Like many multinational companies, Ford has always been reticent about its labour screening procedures. Yet there is evidence that Britain's biggest car manufacturer has used vetting techniques to sack trade union activists, although the most aggressive tactics have been used in the company's American divisions.

The Ford Motor Company was founded in 1903 by Henry Ford I in Detroit, a city which had an international reputation for large reserves of cheap labour. Detroit was an open shop, but its companies were violently anti-union. A period of labour unrest in the 1880s had resulted in the city's wealthiest businessmen forming the 'Employers' Association of Detroit'. This organisation sought to combat trade unionism by 'providing the city's hiring offices with blacklists of potential troublemakers.'[12]

Henry Ford was equally keen to suppress trade unions. 'We will never recognise the United Auto Workers or any other union,' said Ford. 'Labour union organisations are the worst things that ever struck the earth.'[13] But the company's ultra-high production targets for its famous Model T cars soon caused international unrest. This was aggravated by job insecurity, since most workers were employed on a day-to-day basis. Henry Ford found many of his employees attracted to trade unions like the Industrial Workers of the World (or 'Wobblies').

Faced with the prospect of unionisation, Ford adopted a progressive reform programme for his workers in 1914 – wages were doubled and the working week shortened. The company also set up a 'Sociological Department', which was supposed to oversee new welfare programmes. But its inspectors spent most of their time investigating employees' moral attitudes by questioning their families, neighbours and friends.

By the mid-1920s Ford had reverted to its hard-line industrial relations as the Model T lost ground in the marketplace. When a new plant was built in Detroit, the infamous 'Service Department' was set up. This was Ford's 3000-strong private police and security force, based at the new River Rouge plant. Its purpose was to prevent any unionisation of the factory by mass surveillance of the workforce. As an American government department noted: 'We find that the Service men . . . were actively engaged in identifying union members and combatting union activities.'[14]

The Service Department's role was illustrated in 1932. On 7 March some 3000 workers on a 'Hunger March' approached the River Rouge plant. Their demands included a six-hour day, free medical care and the right to form trades unions. The Service Department and the local Dearborn police – 'little more, in many respects, than a branch of Ford's own police force.'[15] – responded by firing tear-gas canisters and truncheoning the demonstrators, who fought back. The Service men and Dearborn police then machine-gunned the marchers: four were shot dead and many others were seriously wounded.

Tactics like this ensured that by 1937 Ford remained the only non-union motor manufacturer. One day in May of that year a group of United Auto Workers (UAW) handed out leaflets outside the River Rouge plant. Before long they were attacked by a gang of thugs and professional wrestlers hired by the Service Department. One of the union activists beaten up was William Reuther, later a UAW leader. Reuther had been sacked by Ford and then 'found his name on a blacklist that Ford and other car companies distributed amongst each other.'[16]

Even more brutal operations were run at the Ford plant in Dallas, Texas. There a special squad, led by 'Fats' Perry, was hired for anti-union work, armed with pistols, whips, blackjacks and other weapons. Perry later estimated that his squad handed out at least twenty-five beatings to labour organisers during the summer of 1937. Much of his information about the union activists came from the local police.[17]

The head of the Service Department, ex-boxer Harry Bennett, had more sinister connections. His semi-permanent group of thugs often drew on his criminal underworld contacts. Like Perry's mob, his brief from the company was to identify and neutralise union activists. Bennett did this in close co-operation with the FBI, the USA's equivalent of MI5. As an FBI report stated: 'This office has contacted the Ford Motor Company for the past several weeks to obtain pertinent data from their vast files on communist activities.'[18]

It was not until 1945 that Bennett was sacked and the Service Department disbanded. By then the United Auto Workers was fully organised within Ford. But the company continued to spy on union activists, and in 1953 was employing two FBI undercover agents, Stephen Schemanske and Milton Santwire, to compile intelligence on UAW workers. These agents were paid substantial sums by both Ford and the FBI.[19]

The British division of Ford has also been under surveillance by the security services. During the 1969 pay dispute Cabinet Ministers in the then Labour government received regular reports from MI5 about the views and activities of the union representatives involved.[20] MI5 went further during the Ford strike over pay in 1978 when they tapped the phone of Syd Harraway, the key shop steward at the Dagenham plant in Essex and a member of the Communist Party. A former MI5 officer said: 'I was instructed by my superiors to listen out particularly for any reference to the Ford unions' bottom line in the pay negotiations . . . It was considered of vital importance to obtain the union's private position. This seemed to be economic information from within a legally constituted trade union organisation which the security service had no right to know.'[21]

As with their American counterparts, it was Ford's hard-line attitude to trade union activity that marked their industrial relations practices. As a Labour Relations Manager, L. T. Blakeman, said in November 1962: 'We intend to continue to operate a firm policy under which we shall retain the right to terminate the employment of employees who refuse to play their part and give a fair day's work.'[22]

One union representative who was dismissed in the company's formative years was John McLoughlin, an AUEW shop steward at Briggs Motor Bodies, a Ford subsidiary, at the Dagenham plant. In January 1957 he was sacked along with several other union members for supporting an unofficial strike and being guilty of 'indiscipline'. This resulted in a strike by some 2000 workers at the plant.

During an inquiry into the dismissals set up by Lord Cameron, Blakeman said of the Briggs Works Committee: 'We cannot ignore reports we received that no less than eight of the thirteen committee men are members of the Communist Party. We are not interested in our employees' political beliefs in themselves, but we cannot blind ourselves to the disruptive influence exercised by a powerful clique in our midst.'[23] Another indication of Ford's real reason for sacking McLoughlin and his colleagues came when Lord Cameron made a point of asking, McCarthy-style, all the shop stewards for their political affiliations. McLoughlin refused to answer.

On the basis of his inquiry, Lord Cameron concluded: 'There are good grounds for the company's belief that it has a troublemaking political clique in its midst.'[24] McLoughlin and his colleagues remained sacked.

Ford has never been completely free of industrial disruption. There have been national strikes over pay in 1969, 1978 and 1988, and since 1979 the workforce has been cut from 85,700 to 48,700 in 1986. These redundancies, coupled with poor shop-floor conditions, has made the Dagenham plant in particular a potential source of industrial confrontation.

1986 was especially crucial for Ford, which planned that year to reduce its workforce by a further 1,800. To achieve this it needed a compliant and co-operative trade union organisation inside the factory. But in February the company had to recruit 350 extra workers at its Dagenham plant in order to meet increased orders for the Ford Sierra, which in 1987 became the country's third biggest-selling car.

Two of the new employees were Denny Fitzpatrick and Jane Watt. Both started work on 3 March 1986 and were assigned to the section where car bodies are given waterproofing treatment. They also joined the 4,000-strong 1/1007 branch of the TGWU.

At 7 am on 12 March, just fifteen minutes before the end of her shift, Fitzpatrick was called off the sealer deck production line by her foreman. She was taken to the office of Barry Thomas, the Production Manager, where she was met by Thomas and two Personnel Officers, Chris Last and Karen Barrett. As soon as Fitzpatrick sat down, Thomas read a document out to her. It was her letter of dismissal. Thomas told her that her employment 'was subject to our receiving satisfactory references. Unfortunately, your references have not proved satisfactory to us.' Fitzpatrick immediately asked him to identify these references. Thomas declined to answer and looked to his colleagues, who were sitting on either side of him. One of them, Personnel Officer Chris Last, said: 'We don't divulge confidential information between employers.'

Fitzpatrick was frogmarched out of the factory by the two Personnel Officers. Her union arranged for an appeal against the sacking, which took place the next day. Her case was put by Steve Hart, the TGWU District Official, accompanied by two shop stewards. Normally when Ford sack a worker they are very quick to give a reason. But not this time. The management refused to give any indication of the reference. Fitzpatrick and one of the shop stewards began asking impatiently: 'Which reference?' Chris Last refused to answer except to say: 'I'm sorry, we can't comment. You can't expect us to divulge confidential information.' Her appeal was rejected and she was told to leave the building immediately without returning to the production line.

Despite strong protests from her union and from Labour MPs, Ford UK stuck to their story. 'She was dismissed because her references had not proved satisfactory,' said Sam Toy, the company's Chairman and Managing Director. 'Because references are dealt with in strict confidence, we did not, and are not able to, expand on that. However, we would obviously not have taken the serious step of dismissing an employee unless we believed that we had good reason to do so.'[25]

Presumably Fitzpatrick's references from her previous employer would show a poor record or some act of dishonesty for her to be sacked in such a fashion. But the reference we obtained from British Telecom in Manchester, where she was a telephone engineer, is far from 'unsatisfactory', as it is a standard reference. A computer print-out of Fitzpatrick's sickness and absence record of her six years at BT shows that she was late just three times and was off sick for a total of seven weeks.

Clearly, she was not sacked for professional reasons. Her union believed that it was because she was an active trade unionist and a strong supporter of Socialist Action, a Trotskyist grouping in the Labour Party. It was claimed that British Telecom had secretly given information about her political activities to Ford. As evidence they pointed to a confidential BT vetting questionnaire circulated to managers by the Personnel Office. Under the heading 'Subject No Longer Employed', the document stated: 'If known, what is the name and address of next employer?'

BT declined to comment on whether they had spoken to Ford about Fitzpatrick. So her union decided to obtain evidence that she was blacklisted. A secretary for a London publishing company, Zoe Picton-Howell, wrote to Fitzpatrick's ex-Personnel Manager in Manchester, pretending that Fitzpatrick was applying for a job and needed a reference. A week later Picton-Howell received a telephone call from the BT Personnel Manager: 'She said that she was sending a written reference stating that Denny Fitzpatrick was OK while she was there as far as conduct and efficiency were concerned. But she said she was phoning to tell me to read a *Daily Mail* article for Tuesday 29 April, which described Denny's career since she left British Telecom, and in which she described herself as an ultra-leftist. The woman clearly thought that Denny was the last person on earth who should ever be employed and expected me to think the same. The whole tone of her remarks was that Denny should not be employed.'

Three months later, in July 1986, Fitzpatrick applied for a job as a technician at British Telecom's City of London district. Her interview on Tuesday 1 July went extremely well, and the Manager even suggested work locations for her. She was told to turn up for a medical which, BT confirmed to the authors, means she was offered the job. But before she could attend the medical she received a letter from BT's Personnel Division: 'I regret to have to inform you that your application has not been successful. Consequently, you will not be required to attend a medical examination.'[26] No reason was given.

Two weeks after Fitzpatrick was sacked by Ford, another ex-BT shop steward was summarily dismissed at their Dagenham plant. This was Jane Watt, who had been an Engineer in BT's City of London telephone exchange. At 3 pm on 25 March 1986, five days before the end of her probation period, she was summoned to the Personnel Office. As with Fitzpatrick, she was greeted with the reading out of her sacking letter, which stated: 'During our check of your references we have found significant factual inaccuracies in your application form.' The meeting was adjourned, and reconvened in the Production Manager's office the following morning.

At this meeting Personnel Officer Chris Last told Watt she was being dismissed because she had failed to include in her application form the fact that she had a Sociology degree from Glasgow University. Last explained that the company was not recruiting graduates. Watt was asked to resign. She refused and so she was sacked as from 10 am that morning.[27] Later that day the Personnel Office issued an internal bulletin to Watt's colleagues on the sealer deck which stated: 'The Company has explained that it does not employ graduates on line production work.' But this was contradicted by a later statement from Ed Sketch, the plant's Employee Relations Manager, who said: 'We will not exclude graduates from working here on the production line.'[28]

Clearly, being a graduate was not the real reason for her sacking – Ford has always employed graduates on production work, notably the TGWU District Officer Steve Hart, a former Economics student at Cambridge University. As with Fitzpatrick, the answer lies in her politics, as Watt was also an active member of Socialist Action and a former BT union representative. Ford briefed the Press off the record that the two were 'Red Moles', but let slip the vetting operation. As the *Daily Mail* reported: 'A secret

memo from the women's previous employers alerted Ford
bosses. It revealed that the two, both shop stewards, had
fomented industrial disruption.'[29] The Economic League took a
similar line and stated that Watt and Fitzpatrick were dismissed
'when it was found that they had both been militant shop
stewards in previous employment.'[30] In fact, neither Watt nor
Fitzpatrick had been involved in any strike action at BT. The
League's Director-General, Michael Noar, declined to comment
when asked if his agency had given any information to Ford.

Despite the uncompromising attitude of Ford, Watt believed
she had a strong case. She had obtained her reference from
British Telecom's Personnel Division. It stated: 'Miss Watt was
employed by British Telecom as a technician from 27 April 1981 to
28 February 1986 when she voluntarily resigned. During her
employment her conduct was satisfactory and there was no
reason to doubt her honesty.'[31] There was no mention of not
disclosing information on her application form.

Watt's union, the TGWU, agreed to support her appeal. On
Saturday 29 March 1986, three weeks before the appeal hearing,
her union branch issued a press statement, letters and leaflets
alleging anti-union victimisation and political vetting. The press
release listed Steve Riley, the TGWU Branch Chairman, and his
deputy Mick Gosling, as contacts for further information and
provided their home telephone numbers. For the next week
Gosling's phone rang regularly, but when he picked up the
receiver it would always go dead. On the night of 8 April his
house in north London was broken into. Nothing was stolen. Six
days later, on 14 April, a week before the appeal, Steve Riley's flat
in south London was burgled. It happened between 1 pm
and 2.15 pm, while Riley and his wife were at work. Cash, a video
and a computer were stolen, but it was noticeable that a lot of
paperwork was thrown all over the floor. Riley's files and
briefcase had been opened and his diary had been taken. More
significantly, five sheets of paper with about 100 names and
addresses of mainly trade union contacts had been stolen from
the filing cabinet. These documents had been removed from
among a large number of other papers in the files.

The following week, on 21 April, Ford rejected Watt's appeal
against her sacking. The decision provoked a strong reaction
from her former colleagues on the 'B' shift sealer deck. They
voted 44–10 for an indefinite strike and brought the production
line to a halt. The next morning, in an unprecedented move, the

'A' shift also voted to take action and about half the workforce walked out in protest. But the TGWU District Officer Steve Hart refused to make the strike official, and Watt was left isolated without wider support. She was then unemployed for two months. She resents being labelled an extremist: 'I'm not a subversive or anything like that. I've always been completely open about my politics.'

Throughout this vetting dispute, some union activists were convinced that the State was involved in some way. That may have been true at some stage. But the overriding priority for Ford as a multinational company was economic and commercial, not political. They wanted to ensure that the production line was going to run smoothly and not be disrupted by trade union militancy. This has always been the company's prime concern, ever since Henry Ford I hired gangsters to beat up union organisers in Detroit in the 1930s.

The corporate motives behind the vetting of Fitzpatrick and Watt were revealed when Ford's Industrial Relations Director, Paul Roots, travelled to Coventry four days before Watt was sacked. In his speech to Warwick University, Roots said: 'Quite clearly what the government has done is to clip the wings of the trade unions and weaken their bargaining power . . . That is quite legitimate for supporters of a capitalist system to do. I work for a capitalist company and I am much happier if I am dealing with a weakened trade union movement.'[32]

10

The Private Security Industry and Police Vetting

'The purpose of security in its widest sense is to protect a way of life.'

Peter Hamilton, veteran security consultant.[1]

'Employers don't ask us how we get our information. They have no scruples about that.'

Ian Withers, private investigator,
Christopher Roberts Agency.[2]

On Friday 3 April 1986, a private detective working for IPCS Law and Security Agents Ltd drove from his office at Protection House, Albion Road, North Shields, to Newcastle City Hall. After a drink in a nearby pub he joined the throng of shipyard workers employed by Swan Hunter as they assembled for a mass meeting. He began asking discreet questions, but averted suspicion by pretending to be an employee from another shipyard.

He had infiltrated the meeting for a specific reason. The Swan Hunter workers were considering industrial action over the pay and conditions deal offered by management after the privatisation of the company. At the meeting they decided to call a one-day strike the following Monday and to prevent the launch of the frigate *Coventry*. Their union convenors told them this was a 'do-or-die strike' by the 'poorest-paid warship building force' in Britain.

The detective noted all this down and hurried back to his car, only to find a £6 parking ticket waiting for him. But it was worth it, as Swan Hunter was pleased with his report, for which they paid him £166.20. His inside information enabled the company to launch the frigate at 3 o'clock on the Monday morning without any industrial disruption.

When asked about employing a private investigator, Swan Hunter confirmed the arrangement: 'There are all sorts of things companies have to do in certain circumstances to acquire information . . . All organisations, both trade unions and companies, have a number of methods of keeping themselves abreast of situations.'[3] But the shipbuilding unions believe the information collected was used to compile dossiers on union activists: 'He seemed more interested in who spoke at the meeting rather than what they were saying,' said one union official.

The use by companies of private investigators to collect information on employees has been a common practice for many years. In 1973 it was disclosed at an Old Bailey trial that the Christopher Roberts Private Detective Agency had been employed to check on workers' political activities. The firm had often been used by non-unionised companies to investigate the background of prospective employees to ensure their labour force was not 'infiltrated' by union members.[4] 'Employers don't ask us how we get our information,' said Ian Withers, one of the agency's detectives. 'They have no scruples about that.'[5]

But in recent years these private security agencies have been used much more frequently for employment vetting. 'It's very much on the increase these days,' says Richard Jacques-Turner, who runs an agency with offices in Hull and London. 'I think people now feel that they must vet their potential employees before they employ them to safeguard their company's assets.'[6] Turner has up to 45,000 names on file, with a card index system in Hull and a computer data base in London. He says that his information comes from 'local records, county court judgements, criminal records through the newspapers, reports from various clients and information built up through our associate companies.'[7]

One of Britain's most politically controversial private investigators is Peter Hamilton, who has spent all his working life in the security industry. He began as a security advisor in the mid-1950s, spending three years 'fighting communism in Malaya both in the intelligence and combat sense.'[8] He then became a security advisor to the governments of Cyprus (1958–60) and Southern Rhodesia (1960–62). In 1962 he returned to the UK and became a director and security adviser to Chubb Security Services before leaving in 1978 to set up his own company, Zeus Security Consultants Ltd, which, according to its memorandum of association, would 'investigate the fidelity and character of persons, firms or companies and make confidential reports thereon to customers and others.'

The company files also state that the job of Zeus is 'to provide security services of all kinds to government and other authorities.' This fits in with Hamilton's background as a former Army intelligence officer and 'secondment to the Security Service' (i.e. m I5).[9] He has also done work for the Economic League, Britain's premier vetting agency.

Hamilton denies that his firm has been involved in political vetting. He says that his company does pre-employment checks for firms in the financial sector. 'We steer very clear of political stuff, although if a person is a member of a fascist party or the Communist Party we would notify the company.'

But Hamilton has in fact done political work. In January 1983 he was employed to monitor the objectors and critics at the public inquiry into the Sizewell 'B' nuclear reactor. He was hired to compile information about members of environmental pressure groups, the peace movement, the anti-nuclear lobby and local residents. As soon as the Sizewell inquiry opened, Hamilton passed the work – through another security consultant – to Vic Norris, who runs a company called Contingency Services based in Colchester. A briefing sheet spelled out the nature of the job:

'Client wishes to ascertain identities of principal objectors at the Sizewell atomic power station at Snape Maltings. If possible, obtain list of objectors, their connections with media, political leanings etc.'[10]

Norris was a bizarre choice to do the surveillance work. A convicted child molester and a supporter of the National Front and the British National Party, he also claims to have worked for the government: 'I do the work that the Home Office don't want to do because it's too precarious or dirty,' he says.[11]

Hamilton acknowledged his involvement. He said the operation was set up to find 'subversives who were agitating'. But he refused to reveal who had commissioned him except that it was 'a private client'. He added: 'I can absolutely assure you that this had nothing to do with Whitehall.'[12]

In the autumn of 1983 Zeus changed its name to Peter Hamilton (Security Consultants) Ltd, with a new fellow director in James Grocott, a management consultant. The new company soon acquired an impressive Board of establishment figures such as Major-General Sir Philip Ward and Lord Chalfont, later to be the 'General Consultant'.

Hamilton remains a politically-conscious security consultant. He argues that private security professionals have a role to play in society. 'The purpose of security in its widest sense is to protect a way of life,' he says.[13] For many years he saw deliberate industrial disruption as the main threat to 'established values'. But, although he says 'the motor industry has been ruined by subversion', he now regards 'society as very well balanced'.

Hamilton's remedy provides an interesting insight into his political views: 'Management, on whom our future power and prosperity primarily depend, cannot be effective without a loyal and contented staff and labour force.'[14]

The implication here is that private investigators have a key role to play in ensuring that 'troublemakers' are not employed by companies. But private detective Peter Heims, a former President of the Association of British Investigators, argues that political vetting is a very small part of their work. He says that only about 3 per cent of his company's vetting procedures involves looking for political or trade union 'troublemakers'.

Nevertheless, private investigators continue to be involved in political vetting. They are used not so much in pre-employment checking as in secretly collecting information about trade union activists, which is later used by employers.

The Illegal Checks with the PNC

Perhaps a more disturbing trend in recent years is how private investigators have been gaining illegal access to the Police National Computer (PNC) during their vetting inquiries. The PNC, based in Hendon, north London, has details of the criminal records, including spent convictions, of nearly 5 million people. Set up in 1969, and operational since 1974, it is linked to 800 terminals in police stations throughout Britain and can provide a check within five seconds. It is the largest police intelligence system in Europe, and is organised and run by the Home Office. But there is considerable evidence that confidential criminal records stored on the PNC are being illegally leaked to private investigators.

The most serious aspect of the abuse of the PNC is that it contravenes the 1974 Rehabilitation of Offenders Act. This bill makes it a criminal offence for anybody to disclose spent convictions from official files except in the course of their official duties. A 'spent' conviction is a sentence of under thirty months, which is removed from an individual's criminal record after a rehabilitation period. If the person is not convicted again during the rehabilitation period, which can be up to ten years, the conviction is regarded as 'spent'.

In theory, ex-offenders are protected by the 1974 Act. They are not obliged to disclose their spent conviction when applying for jobs and cannot be sacked for not doing so. In practice, however, there are many loopholes. Doctors, accountants, lawyers, dentists, veterinary surgeons, nurses, opticians, chemists, social workers and teachers are among those not covered by the Act. They must reveal any spent convictions. The police also do not indicate on the criminal record whether or not a conviction is spent.

A major weakness of the system is that this information is being illegally released to private detectives and security officers. This offence carries a maximum fine of £1000. If the person gains access to the PNC by fraud or corruption it can mean six months in prison or a £2000 fine. In addition, unauthorised disclosure of any information from criminal records is an offence under the Official Secrets Act.

The police authorities argue that it is now very difficult for their confidential records to be divulged to a third party. This is because all enquiries are logged and are subject to inspection by the Assistant Chief Constable of each police force. In 1987 the Home Office also transferred all information on manual records systems to the PNC.

But the system continues to be abused by private detectives and company security officers. According to the private detective Gary Murray, a former RAF investigator, this is because of their cosy relationship with senior police officers. Murray, a highly experienced operator who has been a security consultant since 1969, says that illegal access to the PNC is quite simple to obtain. Most security officers and private investigators are former police officers, and so have many police contacts. If the private eye needs to 'do a check' he telephones his local police contact, who needs to be of CID rank. They then meet informally and the name of the person to be vetted is handed over to the senior police officer.

The police officer then returns to his station and goes to the visual display terminal and keyboard which is logged into the PNC. He taps in his access code and his own personal code. He then adds the person's name, address, date of birth, National Insurance number and other personal details. Within five seconds the person's criminal record flashes up on the screen. The information is then passed to the company's Security Officer or the private detective. The vetting operation is complete.

This illegal access to the PNC is not detected, according to Murray, because the vetting is done by senior rather than junior police officers. If a Detective-Inspector wants access to the PNC he can simply say it is part of his 'official duties' on a case. Quite often he does not even need to give a reason.

Murray's allegations have been corroborated by the former senior police officer Leslie Prince. For thirty years Prince worked for West Midlands police in CID, Uniform and Training. He then joined the security industry and held senior posts in retail security before becoming Deputy Chief Investigator with a large electrical company. Prince is quite explicit about vetting:

'Police officers in the United Kingdom have always been involved in the vetting of employees in the private sector. Employers who have taken ex-police officers onto their security staffs have been cognisant of the fact that, in all probability, he or she will have some form of access to criminal records. Although such checks were rarely admitted, the practice has existed for many years and in many companies it has been an integral part of security procedure.

'These checks were usually made under "The Old Pals' Act", and if any reward were received by the police officer it was nothing more than the occasional liquid refreshment. This, of course, was not so in every case and there have been instances of police officers accepting quite lucrative rewards for the gaining of information.'[15]

Prince's confirmation of the corrupt relationship between police officers and private investigators lies at the heart of this type of vetting, for the security departments of most private companies are full of experienced former policemen with impeccable contacts. One Personnel Consultant said it was a deliberate policy to recruit former police officers. They were expected to check the names of employees with the PNC, and also to obtain information about their political sympathies.

Some firms prefer to use outside security companies and private detectives for their vetting procedures. These outfits also have large contingents of ex-Assistant Chief Commissioners and Detective Inspectors. According to Leslie Prince, some of these security firms have collated blacklists and set up vetting schemes called 'Protection Associations':

'A leading security company in the United Kingdom was quick to realise the quandary in which employers were finding themselves with regard to security vetting. For some considerable time this company has been building up a register containing names of persons who have been dismissed, or who have left their previous employment in circumstances "amounting to dishonesty".'[16]

Prince revealed that these names were programmed into a computer, and 'an all-out campaign' was launched to persuade companies to subscribe to their 'Protection Association'. In one vetting scheme, according to Prince, some 25,000 names were on the computer. Subscribing firms pay an annual fee for membership plus an extra amount for each pre-employment search requested. Prince also revealed that the subscribing company is not given any reason or information when a prospective employee is rejected: 'When a search is requested, a reply is received which merely states "suitable" or "unsuitable".'[17]

Apart from the Economic League, these 'Protection Associations' are the only organised schemes for private companies to vet their employees. Not all security companies operate them, of course. Many simply employ officers and consultants with easy access to the PNC and do their own checks.

Vetting by the Private Eyes

It would be misleading to claim that most, even many, private detectives and police officers are regularly securing illegal access to the PNC. Private investigator Gary Murray became disillusioned with this growing practice in the early 1980s. In 1983 he complained to his professional association, the Institute of Professional Investigators (IPI), along with Dennis Byrne, a retired London policeman. Murray and Byrne were both Directors of the IPI, but the rest of the board refused to accept that there was a problem about illegal use of the PNC. This was perhaps not surprising, as at least thirty IPI members were serving police officers and members of civilian and military intelligence.

In 1985 both Murray and Byrne resigned in disgust at the IPI's response. Murray was particularly angry as he has collected considerable evidence of misuse of the PNC during his inquiries. Since 1981 he has tape recorded a number of conversations with private detectives and employers which provide a remarkable insight into this form of vetting.

One of the firms identified by Murray was Securicor, one of Britain's largest security companies. Founded in 1935, Securicor's main business is in cash-carrying and supplying security guards.

But they have also been involved in vetting. In 1963 Security Services Ltd, an associate company of Securicor, informed potential clients that its undercover specialists could be used to report on 'any person who may be suspected of causing dissension or inciting employees to disaffection.'[18]

In more recent years they have also undertaken security vetting. Murray discovered this when he telephoned Securicor's London office on 27 February 1985. Posing as a manager from a scientific company, Murray asked a Securicor official, Charlie Clements, about employing and vetting security guards.

'A recruiting process is done in great depth,' said Clements. 'Certainly at the interviewing stage and then as a secondary stage we screen all applicants and they're screened back for twenty years.'

'Well, how can you be sure that they haven't done six months [in prison]?' asked Murray.

'Well, we employ a very high number of ex-police people . . . We have an enormous number of Security Liaison Officers who do this screening and, I promise you, it is to the highest possible standard.'

'So what you're saying is you're in a position to tell whether "Joe Bloggs", unofficially, has a criminal record.'

'We can. I mean, if he's got a record we will pick it up. We don't accept what he's got on paper. We actually take up his references.'

Murray then decided to find out who actually did the vetting. So the same morning he rang Mark Hurley at the Securicor Carphone company. This time Murray said he needed someone to vet his eleven employees.

'We have a guy who really goes to town on these people,' said Hurley, laughing, 'to find out inside leg measurements and if they've ever been in trouble with the police, and all sorts.'

'He can find out criminal records, can he?' asked Murray.

'Well, um, unofficially.'

Hurley disclosed that their vetting investigator was Mike Anderson, a former policeman who is Managing Director of Cornhill Management Consultants. He charges £60 for every pre-employment check and it takes less than a week.

Ten minutes later Murray rang Anderson's office, based at a stud farm near Stratford-on-Avon. He spoke to a secretary about his prospective employees.

'It was suggested to us,' said Murray, 'that you might be able to unofficially find out if they had criminal records.'

'Yes,' she said, clearing her throat.

'You can?'

'Yes, but we don't talk about that . . .'

'Well, no, of course not,' Murray said.

Murray was not able to contact Anderson himself until 15 March 1985, two weeks later. Anderson confirmed he could get access to criminal records. But he also told Murray that he could check with Ministry of Defence files.

'What about a man with an Army record?' asked Murray. 'How . . .'

'I can do that as well,' said Anderson briskly.

'You can do that?'

'Uh, huh . . . I will need his Army number though.'

Since that conversation took place in 1985, the Home Office and police authorities have stated that they have dealt with the problem of illegal access to the PNC. In November 1987 we asked a private detective about his vetting work. He has run his own agency in Cardiff since 1982. Before that he was a policeman for ten years.

He said: 'A lot of us [private investigators] are ex-coppers so it's natural that we've got, er, links with the force.'

'What sort of jobs do you get your contacts in the police to do for you?'

'Look, if you're a copper you can get things done real quick, get information and so on. What would take me a week will take a bloke on the force a couple of hours. You've got the computer, you've got records, you've got contacts. It's all dead easy if you're a copper.'

He has done pre-employment checks for insurance firms. As well as checks with the PNC, the company wanted information about applicants' political views. 'They did want stuff on politics,' he said, '"Is he a strong trade unionist? Does he have strong leftie views?"'

Private detectives also utilise their links with the Special Branch and MI5 to obtain confidential information. Special Branch officers have easy access to the PNC. Many of them go on to join private companies.

It is this cosy relationship that is often illegally exploited. Gary Murray discovered this when he telephoned Malcolm James, a private investigator based in Windsor, Berkshire. James said he had access to criminal records at Thames Valley Police Station and New Scotland Yard. Murray then asked him: 'How about your friends in the Special Branch. If you had the names could you just sound them out?'

'Well, I've got somebody in Special Branch I know,' replied James. 'I could ask her if she could have a look for me and see.'

This relationship verges on the corrupt, according to former policeman Dennis Byrne, who was Principal of the Institute of Private Investigators in 1983. He claimed that information from Special Branch files has been on sale among IPI members. 'If private investigators have the right contacts, the information is there for them to take,' said Byrne.[19]

Private detectives have also used MI5 for vetting purposes. Gary Murray said he had a particularly close relationship with the Security Services: 'I had access to a number of areas that were useful to them. I did one particular job for them and then they came back and engaged me for other work. They paid me a monthly retainer and expenses.' In return he was able to use MI5 to vet employees: 'I have sat on a park bench with an Operational Controller from MI5 and given him the name of a particular individual and said I wanted details on him. He has written it down in his Ministry of Defence notebook and come back to me with what I wanted.'[20] At first Murray was happy to cultivate his MI5 connections, but he became disillusioned: 'Initially I thought the work needed to be done, but after a while I realised it was a total waste of taxpayers' money. They had a 'money-no-object' attitude. I didn't like some of the things they asked me to do, so I told them to get lost.'[21]

This close relationship between private investigators and MI5 is a long-established one. As with the police and Special Branch, many MI5 employees join private security companies when they leave or retire. A notable case was Commander Rollo Watts, former Head of Operations of the Special Branch, who became Managing Director of Saladin Security. From MI5 Sir Percy Sillitoe, Director-General from 1946 to 1953, later became the first Chairman of Security Express Ltd. After being head of MI5 from 1965 to 1972, Sir Martin Furnival-Jones retired to become Head of Security for Playboy and a consultant to ICI. Other ex-MI5 officers simply set up their own companies, such as Diversified Corporate Services Ltd, formed in 1970.[22]

Veterans of the security industry like Peter Hamilton deny that their firms have access to the PNC: 'We do not take part in sneaky ways of getting police records.' He says that '90 per cent' of information necessary for vetting is public anyway, and records

of criminal activity are available from local and national newspaper reports.

Peter Heims, who is Managing Director of his own security
company, takes a similar view. But he does acknowledge: 'It does
happen in this business and always will happen, unfortunately.'
On contravening the 1974 Rehabilitation of Offenders Act, he
says: 'Imagine the investigator's dilemma when he discovers that
an applicant has a criminal conviction which is pertinent to the
position he is seeking, yet that conviction is "spent" . . . In such
instances I always advise my client to obtain a certain newspaper
giving him the date of edition in which the report of the
conviction appeared. The client can then read a public document
and make up his own mind.'[23]

It would be inaccurate to claim that the police authorities and the
Home Office are not concerned about illegal access to the Police
National Computer. Many officers disapprove of the release of
confidential information from the PNC in order to vet job
applicants. In recent years the rules have been tightened up so
that Assistant Chief Constables can audit all PNC entries, which
are recorded automatically.

But the fact remains that private investigators and security
officers are still conspiring with senior policemen to obtain
criminal records. Officers are regularly being charged under the
Official Secrets Act or the Rehabilitation of Offenders Act for this
offence.

The Home Office cannot blame corrupt private detectives and
security consultants for the situation. If police officers refused to
co-operate, outside access to the PNC would be impossible. The
reality is that senior officers are giving bogus excuses and there is
not enough vigilance from the higher echelons of the force.

The Victims

William Unsworth, aged 32, has been unemployed since October
1985 and is unlikely to have a proper job again for a long time – if
ever. In January 1987 he had a severe stroke and is now prone to
epileptic fits. Since the stroke he finds it very difficult to express
himself and suffers from a poor memory.

One of the main reasons for Unsworth's situation was his
dismissal from his job as a part-time caretaker and cleaner at
Alexander House Day Centre on Liverpool Road, Manchester.

For seven months Unsworth was happy with his job, even though it was for only a few hours a day. He was looking forward to getting married and starting a family. But one day in October 1985 WPC Ruth Best, the local Community Police Constable, walked into the Day Centre and asked to see Dorothy Perry, Unsworth's supervisor. A confidential memorandum written by Perry spelled out what happened next: 'She [WPC Best] informed me that Mr Unsworth should not be working here and that he is currently on suspension by Manchester Crown Court. He has been in prison and some of the charges were for attempted burglary, attempted wounding, theft and handling stolen goods. This has upset me very much.' Unsworth was summoned by Perry and promptly sacked.

It is true that Unsworth had a criminal record. In November 1983 he was convicted for several theft-related offences and given a fifteen-month prison sentence. But it was suspended for two years because the judge said he wanted to give him the chance to prove himself. For the next two years Unsworth did just that, and did not re-offend.

It seems the police had other ideas. Yet they had no legal right to inform his employer about his past suspended sentence. There are some jobs where the police can do this, notably local authority workers. But part-time caretakers and cleaners are not among them.

Unsworth does not blame his employer for losing his job, but says: 'My complaint is how they received the information about my having a criminal record.'

His dismissal came at the worst possible time – just a few days before his wedding and eight months before the birth of his baby son. It caused domestic problems almost immediately – 'She [his wife] had no respect for me after that,' he said. The couple decided to move to Scotland, as Unsworth believed he would never get a job in Manchester, particularly as he had no references. But their life in Scotland did not work out, as he could not find work, and they returned to Manchester.

By October 1986, a year after his dismissal, his marriage had collapsed. The couple separated and his wife returned to her native Scotland. Three months later Unsworth had his stroke. He does not blame the police's action and his sacking for all his problems, but says: 'If that didn't happen then I probably wouldn't have had the stroke.'

Another caretaker to fall victim to police vetting was 'Jim Bruce' (not his real name). In 1978 he applied for a job at the Jack Kane Community Centre in Edinburgh, which is run by Lothian Regional Council. He was interviewed by a panel, who were all impressed by him, and was chosen for the job.

A few days later his local Councillor, Paul Nolan, Chairman of the Jack Kane Community Centre and a member of the interviewing panel, was told that Bruce could not be appointed. He made inquiries and discovered that a Personnel Officer from the Council's Education Department had telephoned the Community Centre's warden. The Personnel Officer said that the Education Department had secretly checked out Bruce with the local Lothian and Border police. On the basis of the police's information the Council decided not to employ him.

Nolan objected strongly, particularly as the vetting had been done 'without (the job applicant's) knowledge or permission and with no right of appeal or way of challenging the information.'[24] He protested even more strongly when told that Bruce's criminal record consisted of two minor theft offences committed when he was 15 years old, twenty years previously. The Education Department eventually backed down and Bruce was offered the job. But the Council refused to officially give a reason why they had initially rejected him. However, the Council did confirm that they vetted applicants with the police without the applicants' knowledge. Nolan was also told that for education posts the police do not give reasons for their decision – simply a recommendation on whether to employ the person or not.

Outside local authorities, in the private sector, the victims of police vetting have far less protection. The case of Anthony Norris is remarkable in that he did not even have a criminal record.

For eight years he had worked for Associated Leisure Hire Ltd in Lancaster as an engineer, before becoming a foreman in 1978. But by 1981 he had become disenchanted with the company, particularly its working atmosphere, so he requested voluntary redundancy. This was refused. Then, in April 1981, he was suddenly demoted and transferred to the electronics section of the company. A few weeks later he was accused of stealing £2.80 from one of the gaming machines and sacked. The police were called in and he was charged. But Norris was innocent, and was acquitted by Lancaster Crown Court. He then took the company to an Industrial Tribunal for unfair dismissal. He won there as well, and in April 1982 was awarded £5000 in compensation.

Norris thought he had cleared his name – both legally and professionally. But his troubles were just beginning. After the tribunal decision he applied for over 100 jobs, mainly in the games machine industry. But, although many of the positions did not require his qualifications and experience, he was unsuccessful every time. On several occasions he was offered a job, but the offer would suddenly be withdrawn within a few days.

Norris was unemployed for three years. He suspected it was because of information passed on by the police, but he could never prove it. In 1985 he was offered a job with the Lancaster firm of Cascade Amusements. He was told by Michael Jevon, the Supervisor, that he was to start work the following Monday morning. Jevon added, however, that he did not have the formal authority to employ him and would need his Managing Director's approval. On the Saturday morning Norris rang Jevon, who told him that his appointment had been confirmed. Norris told him he wanted to be sure as he had a forthcoming interview for a job on the *Queen Elizabeth II*. 'I was told categorically that I had no need to apply for that job,' recalls Norris. But within twenty-four hours Cascade's offer was suddenly withdrawn. Norris was given no reason. He was later told by a Cascade employee that it was because of 'something the police said.' He asked his solicitor, Charles Bottomley, to telephone the company and confirm this. According to Bottomley: 'In a telephone conversation between myself and Mr Jevon it was said that an adverse report had been received from the police and that this was the reason why Mr Norris was not to be appointed. This information corresponded with that given earlier in the day by Ms Bell [manageress of the Lancaster branch] . . . They went on to say that, of course, such information was strictly confidential.'[25]

The owners of Cascade Amusements, United Leisure Ltd, denied that they had received any information from the police. They said Norris was not appointed because, of the three references he supplied, two were out-of-date and one was for part-time work.[26]

Later in 1985 Norris finally obtained a job – with the Post Office. But once again his innocent past haunted him. The Post Office was told he was 'untrustworthy'. When approached by management about this accusation, Norris produced the Industrial Tribunal report which exonerated him. The Post Office was satisfied, and he kept his job.

Norris now steers well clear of the gaming machine business. He has a job repairing domestic appliances in his home town of Morecambe. But being blacklisted for three years had a profound effect on his life. He had to sell his house and his car. He says that his original dismissal from Associated Leisure Hire Ltd and his subsequent unemployment were factors in the break-up of his marriage.

A Law Unto Themselves

The recurring factor that dominates the issue of police vetting is the absence of vigilance and accountability, which allows confidential information to be used illegally. This was starkly illustrated in 1980, when a police blacklist was leaked to *Time Out*. The thirty-one-page document, compiled by Scotland Yard, was entitled 'Assistant Chief Commissioner's Consolidated Instructions'. It contained 221 names with the following order on its introductory page: 'Officers are advised to exercise caution should they have cause during their official duties to deal with any of the persons or firms listed below.' A telephone number for 'further information' on the names was attached to the front of the dossier. It could also be used to add other people to the blacklist.

The document included the names of twenty former police officers. Also listed was Dr Denis Howard Glyn, a GP from Roehampton, whose only previous conviction was in 1962 for obstruction during a CND march. Dr Glyn had also made two complaints about his local police. Another person included was a solicitor who worked for a well known south London law firm. He said he was 'flabbergasted' to be listed: 'I deal with the police every day. Presumably they make a note of all the times I call them. This could seriously prejudice my clients.'[27]

Among the groups included in the document were Release, the drugs and legal advice agency, and St Mungo Community Trust, a charity for the homeless. Many of the firms on the blacklist were private detective companies and security agencies like Nationwide Investigations and Finlay's Bureau of Investigation. Ron Studden of Nationwide said he was 'not at all surprised' to be included: 'I knew it [the list] existed unofficially but I couldn't confirm it. It's part of the job – the police collect all sorts of information, officially and unofficially. It's a *1984* situation.'[28]

The problem, of course, is what the police do with that

information. At the moment a number of senior police officers are illegally releasing it to employers for vetting purposes. Although the Home Office has tightened up the security arrangements on gaining access to the Police National Computer, a central flaw remains in police forces' lack of public accountability for their actions. A possible remedy could be the establishment of an independent judicial body of inquiry, so that an individual's complaint about police vetting could be thoroughly investigated. Only then might individuals receive the protection to which they should be entitled.

Conclusion

> 'If we are to exclude all those who have ever been drunk, had financial difficulties, told a lie, had sex outside marriage or had a cousin living in Eastern Europe, who would remain?'
>
> 'Privacy Under Attack', National Council for Civil Liberties pamphlet, 1968.

It was a remark by GCHQ worker, Mike Grindley, to the authors that perhaps crystallised the danger of secret political vetting. 'Just because I read the *Morning Star* doesn't make me a communist,' he said, 'anymore than reading the *Financial Times* makes someone a capitalist.'

Grindley summed up the prejudice that has permeated much of the information-gathering by Personnel Managers, Security Officers and private investigators during vetting procedures in Britain today.

The essence of blacklisting is that people can be deprived of their livelihood not because of their actions, or even intentions, but for their beliefs. In many cases this could be for their suspected – not actual – beliefs, or even because of the views of their friends or relatives.

Blacklisting takes place in all Western democracies, but in Britain it is uniquely secretive, information being obtained and recorded without the individual's knowledge. Not only does this secrecy lead to inaccurate information (partly because of its second-hand nature), it denies victims the chance to face their accusers. Victims in Britain have no opportunity to see their file and correct any misinformation or factual errors – as they do in many other countries. Moreover, the burden of proof is borne by the victim, without legal protection. In a country that is so proud of its democratic tradition and liberties this is a remarkable situation.

Not all blacklisting in Britain is secret. Positive vetting of civil servants is open, and most workers in the nuclear industry and defence companies are aware of the personnel security procedures.

Even some private corporations freely admit that they would refuse employment to people with radical political views. One such company is Gladeside-Ardent Ltd, a publishing firm based in Dorking, Surrey. In 1986 their publication for business executives, *Leadership*, declared that their holding company's announcement that 'they will not employ any known CND member is to be applauded. Let us hope that other companies follow suit.' The magazine added: 'Many feel that these people must be regarded as disloyal, treacherous and anti-democratic traitors unworthy of any trust or responsibility. They should learn that in the same way that nuclear missiles are a proven deterrent to any potential aggressor, membership of CND can be a deterrent to employers.'[1]

Such honesty is rare. Most employers choose instead to hide behind the elaborate smokescreen of the Economic League, the Security Services and various private agencies. Even when employees can prove they have been blacklisted they have little protection and few obvious courses of action.

The Legal Situation

As Britain is a country without a written constitution, there are no statutory rights protecting the civil liberties of the individual. A person who has been blacklisted has no legal rights. It is quite lawful in the United Kingdom for a company to refuse to employ an individual because of his political views or trade union activities. Although an employer can be prosecuted for similar discrimination on the grounds of race and sex, there is no legislation to combat blacklisting.

It *is* illegal under the 1975 Employment Protection Act to *dismiss* an employee because of his trade union activities. But the Act only applies to those who have been sacked for their trade union activities *during* their period of employment. There is no legal protection for individuals who are refused a job because of information about their political views used against them *before* being formally appointed. This was confirmed by the case of Philip Beyer, a bricklayer and an activist in the building workers' union UCATT. Birmingham City Council admitted that he had been blacklisted, but the Employment Appeal Tribunal ruling stated: 'There is nothing in the legislation which we have to administer which lays down that an employer may not refuse to employ a man unless he has reasonable grounds for refusing.'[2]

The Labour government which implemented the 1975 Employment Protection Act always refused to extend it to victimised workers. Harold Walker, the Employment Minister of State, said in 1978: 'I deplore the practice of blacklisting, but I am not convinced that the best way of proceeding is to legislate against it.'[3] On 28 March 1979 the Employment Secretary Albert Booth said that 'union pressure and public opinion' would have more effect than Government action in dealing with blacklisting.[4]

There is still no legal protection for victims of the blacklist. This was spelled out by Patrick Nicholls, a Junior Employment Minister, who said in February 1988 that firms had the right to refuse employment to workers with a trade union background: 'The only fetters that we put on the right of an employer to discriminate against somebody, even before he has employed him, are based on either sex and race. We regard that as correct . . . We do not believe that an employer should be fettered if he decides to employ someone because he is or is not a member of a trade union.'[5] Clearly, such a discrepancy needs to be addressed, and legislation should be introduced to ensure that people could not be refused a job because of their trade union activities *before* starting work as well as after their appointment.

Meanwhile, staff who have been vetted shortly after being appointed can, theoretically, claim reinstatement and compensation by taking their employer to an Industrial Tribunal. Since 1980 over 4000 workers have used this procedure after claiming they were sacked for their trade union activities. But there are major obstacles for applicants going through this process. The most important defect of Industrial Tribunals is their lack of legal sanction. Even if they rule that an employee has been unfairly dismissed, the company can still legally refuse to re-employ them.

The Industrial Tribunal system has always been weighted against employees. But in recent years a series of subtle changes have moved the balance of power even further towards the employer. These include not allowing employees to seek redress at an Industrial Tribunal until they have worked for a firm for two years and the introduction of pre-hearing assessments in order to discourage tribunal claims, as well as the removal of the onus of proof from employers during unfair dismissal cases. In addition to increased legal powers, there should also be more onus on the employer to justify its actions. Ordinary employees could also be more involved in the recruitment process, with elected representatives from the workforce attending job interviews, contributing to discussions about appointments and having access to references.

The most a vindicated victim of blacklisting can hope for is financial compensation. Employers usually offer this about half an hour before the Industrial Tribunal hearing in order to escape from the public gaze. Some employees refuse, most accept. But the amount is relatively small, the average award being £1000 plus redundancy payments. Many employees are now turning to the Advisory, Conciliation and Arbitration Service (ACAS), an independent body set up by the last Labour government, to settle their disputes. This has proved financially more beneficial for aggrieved workers. But the main drawback for employees is that the ACAS solution is negotiated in secret, so the company is not held publicly accountable for its actions.

Another form of redress for victims of the blacklist is appeal to the European Commission of Human Rights. This is a laborious process, but there are signs that the Commission is now taking the issue of security vetting more seriously.

This was shown by their attitude in the case of Torstan Leander, a Swedish carpenter who was offered a job at a naval museum next to a military security zone. After a few days at work he was sacked because of information on a secret police register which was consulted during a security check. Leander complained that the compilation of such information about him, and the refusal to disclose it to him, violated his right to privacy. The European Commission did not ask to see all the papers in the case and found against him on the official complaints. But in July 1985 it did refer his complaint to the European Court of Human Rights.

Their action is significant, as it will serve as a precedent for future vetting cases. Britain's National Council for Civil Liberties is currently taking two cases to the European Commission, those of Isabel Hilton, who was vetted by MI5 when applying for a BBC job (see Chapter Five) and 'John Simpson', refused a job by the defence firm MEL after security procedures (see Chapter Three). Their appeals should be heard late in 1988 or early in 1989.

It would not be necessary for British citizens to resort to the European Commission if the government made their security vetting procedures more open and consistent. While civil servants are positively vetted, many employees in defence companies are being secretly vetted, thus breaking government rules. By being open about security procedures, not only would the information collected about the individual be more accurate, but bad personnel relations with employees would be avoided.

The European Commission has become a last resort principally because Britain provides little protection or redress for individuals who are prevented from earning a livelihood because of their political views.

But vetting does not only affect people because of their trade union activities or political views. Since July 1986 thousands of local authority employees whose jobs involve working with children – teachers, social workers, caretakers etc – have been officially vetted using police criminal records. This has been done for a laudable reason – to prevent child abuse. But it means that even more people are being secretly vetted without the opportunity to correct wrong or irrelevant information.

Data Protection but no Access to the Files

Files are already kept on individuals by doctors, teachers and university vice-chancellors. Under present law most of them are secret and inaccessible, even though they may be entirely inaccurate. This is in stark contrast to the United States, where Freedom of Information and Privacy laws give American citizens the right to inspect files held on them by Federal Agencies, including the CIA and the FBI (though bureaucratic obstacles have to be overcome there too).

It was not until late 1987 that a law was implemented in Britain which gave people access to certain kinds of information held on them. Under the Data Protection Act, individuals have the right to see what files are kept on them by Britain's 250,000 companies, government departments and other data users. If they don't like the way organisations are collecting or using the information on computer they can complain to the Data Registrar or the courts. Individuals can also have inaccurate computer records corrected or deleted.

That is the theory. But there are serious flaws and loopholes in the system which make its effectiveness almost negligible. For example, computer users can pass data on to another organisation, but the individual who is the subject of the file has no right to know where it has gone. Computer users are not required to disclose for what purpose they are compiling the information.

Under one of the unconditional exemptions from the Act, the government can refuse to disclose personal data held 'for the purpose of safeguarding national security'. Such a claim by the government can be challenged. But a certificate from a Cabinet Minister, the Attorney-General or the Lord Advocate, saying that data must be protected in the interest of national security will, according to the Act, be sufficient grounds to reject the appeal. There are shades here of the terms of the purge procedures announced by the Government in 1985.

Another problem is that transfers of information by registered data users, such as the Department of Employment, to unregistered users, such as the Special Branch or M15, will not be shown on the Register and will remain secret. The Data Protection Registrar, Sir Eric Howe, is not able to issue enforcement notices against the security and intelligence agencies and, unlike commissioners in countries such as Sweden, he will not be able to inspect their files. 'National security' is an exemption to the general principle that data users must not disclose information 'in any manner incompatible with (the) purpose for which it is held.' But even if M15 was registered and gave the information to another registered user, the data would still be protected under the general 'national security' umbrella.

Another major defect of the Data Protection Act is that any citizen who asks for information and does not obtain it will not know whether this is because there are no records or because the computer user regards it as exempt. We can see the problem by examining what happens if a person wants to find out whether their telephone is being tapped. The 1985 Interception of Communications Act (which, like the Data Protection Bill, was introduced only after pressure from the European Court of Human Rights) set up a tribunal to which the public can refer. The tribunal can investigate whether a tap has been wrongly authorised, i.e. whether the criteria for the issue of a warrant was observed. But it cannot take any action in the event of an *illegal* tap – one that is made without any warrant at all. So individuals will not be informed that their telephone is being tapped in the case of a properly authorised warrant or an illegal tap. The same kind of loophole has reduced the impact of the Data Protection Act.

If Directors of companies fail to register with the Data Protection Registrar they face heavy fines, particularly if they are convicted in the High Court. But important institutions, notably government departments, are exempt from prosecution. As Dr John Woulds, the Assistant Data Protection Registrar responsible for central government's use of computer information, has said:

'It is true we cannot prosecute a government department. We can issue an enforcement notice to a department, requiring them to comply with a particular data protection principle, but that's really as far as we can take it . . . The Registrar can only really present a complaint to a department and require it to respond. If it doesn't there is not a great deal we can do.'[6]

By far the most important defect of the Data Protection Act is its exclusion of access to card-index and manual files. This means that employers and organisations can get round the Act simply by storing on paper information they do not wish the public to see.

Government Initiatives

As the government and employers continue to expand their vetting practices, political concern has increased about the lack of protection for the individual. Jim Lester, a Conservative Junior Employment Minister from 1979 to 1981, believes that managers should have the right to ensure that a potential employee is 'going to work well for the company and have no other ulterior motive for going into his employment.'

But he believes that secret vetting has serious dangers: 'I think the basic fear is whatever files they accumulate, isn't from direct interview with the person concerned. It's from other information, from other sources, and it can be wrong. And of course people do change. If one took politics for instance. I think quite a lot of members of Her Majesty's Government in the past were Communist Party members in the 1930s, and certainly have got nothing to do with them now.'[7]

Senior Labour M Ps are also taking the issue of blacklisting more seriously. In February 1988 Michael Meacher, the Shadow Employment Secretary, called on the government to change the law to protect victims of blacklisting. Describing the Economic League's practices as 'McCarthyite and insidious,' Meacher said that employers should be forced by law to inform job applicants that they are being politically vetted and give them the opportunity to check information on file for accuracy.[8]

The growing demands for government action have centred on extending the rights of individuals to see information held on them. This has received cross-party support. In February 1987 148 M Ps, including fifty-four Conservatives, backed an Access To Personal Files Bill which would give people the right to inspect their school, housing and employment files. But the government was quick to restrict its power and range. For example, the Liberal and Tory sponsors of the private member's bill were forced to drop the clause on access to employment records.

The government justified its actions by arguing that M Ps should wait to see how the Data Protection Act would work before extending access. But its main explanation for opposing the inclusion of employment files in the Bill was 'lack of resources'. Home Office Minister David Waddington said: 'Extending the right of access to personal information costs money and resources . . . There is no doubt that the practicalities of granting access to manual records are of a different scale from those involved in granting access to computerised records.'[9]

But the shortcomings of the Data Protection Act (and the activities of the Economic League) have made many M Ps impatient for action. In April 1988 the Blacklists (Access to Information) Bill was introduced in the Commons by Maria Fyfe, Labour M P for Glasgow Maryhill. The Bill is aimed at giving access to all information on blacklists maintained by employers, including paper files. M Ps voted by 138 to 49 to give this Bill its first reading.

On a short-term basis, individuals who suspect they have been blacklisted can ask their constituency M Ps to take up their case. This can occasionally be effective, particularly if the M P has the right political and security connections.

Another way to combat blacklisting and secret political vetting, particularly in private industry, is for key managers to change their attitudes, especially Personnel Directors and Officers and Industrial Relations Managers. Many Personnel Officers are, of course, honest, professional and strongly opposed to blacklisting. Some simply refuse to carry it out, but there are just as many who meekly carry out company policy without protest. It may be naive and idealistic to believe that Personnel Managers will take a stand on this issue. After all, they are risking their own livelihood if they refuse to obey or oppose company policy. But many B B C executives have taken a stand and have been successful in preventing individuals from being blacklisted.

The Institute of Personnel Management (IPM), which represents most Personnel Directors, does have guidelines on 'Standards of Professional Conduct' and a 'Recruitment Code' for its members. Part of the code states: 'The practice of taking up references before making a job offer is largely restricted to the public sector. Employers should make it clear that they will not approach current or previous employers without the candidate's permission.' However, this code is being broken every day of the year by many IPM members. Indeed, one highly experienced former Personnel Director, an IPM member for over twenty years, did not even know that the IPM had a code of conduct!

There is no indication at all that the IPM is going to do anything about the practice of blacklisting by its members. Unless the government introduces rigorous reforms (an unlikely prospect), it will be up to the officials themselves to take a stand. When this suggestion was put to them, most Personnel Directors told the authors that they were 'just doing their job' and 'following orders'. They argued that using the Economic League, for example, was a Board decision, and they were only implementing company policy. But one former Personnel Director changed his mind during our conversations. After admitting to having blacklisted an employee for political reasons, he said during our next meeting: 'I've thought a lot about the morality of what we talked about. What we did was wrong. I can say I was just following orders but that's just an excuse.' It certainly is.

Vetting first crept into Britain in a peculiarly English way in the early 1950s. It was managed at first by an establishment which did not want show-trials or martyrs, and during the post-war period, the closely supervised system of vetting in Britain was not as potentially threatening as it has since become. There were unwritten ground rules which, though fragile and undoubtedly sometimes broken, limited the dangers of secret monitoring. This situation prevailed until the early 1970s, when industrial militancy and lack of government control encouraged elements of MI5 to abuse their power.

Now, an increasingly authoritarian administration, with a huge majority in the House of Commons, is laying down different ground rules. The old liberal establishment, with its ethos based on consensus (though always determined to maintain the status quo), is on the defensive. The government, and particularly Mrs Thatcher herself, has shown a fierce intolerance of opposition and dissent. In 1984 the Prime Minister branded 140,000 striking miners as 'the enemy within'. The internal enemy, she said, was just as dangerous as any external threat.[10] Cabinet Ministers have claimed that left wing councils and some pressure groups encourage law-breaking. It is in this political atmosphere that vetting and blacklisting has flourished and gone unchallenged. It is not only political radicals and trade union activists who have been affected. Critics of the government's health, education and social policies have also been sacked or muzzled. The atmosphere at present is one of confrontation and polarisation: 'Those who are not with us are against us.' In this climate definitions of security easily merge into vaguer and far wider criteria of political dissent – criteria which allow practices such as blacklisting to flourish unchallenged, disrupting and damaging the lives of untold numbers of people in Britain today.

Appendix One

The following companies subscribe to the Economic League. Where the company is part of a larger group, the name of the parent company appears in brackets. The symbol * indicates that the company also donates to the Conservative Party. The symbol † indicates that the company donates to British United Industrialists, a 'clearing house' organisation which channels funds to the Conservative Party.

Acme Signs & Displays (Sign & Metal Industries)
Addle Shaw & Sons & Latham
Alcan Enfield Alloys Ltd (British Alcan Aluminium, Delta Group)
Alder & Mackay
Allmay & Layfield
Alpine Double Glazing (Henlys Group)
AMEC Construction Services
Amey Roadstone (Consolidated Goldfields)
A. Anderson & Sons Electrical Engineers (Staveley Industries)
Ardon Contractors
Associated Engineering (Turner & Newall)
*Associated Fisheries
Augustus Barnett (Bass plc)
W. & T. Avery (GEC)
Babcock Power Engineering (FKI Babcock)

Balfour Beatty Construction (BICC)
Barclays Bank
Barfab Reinforcement
Henry Barratt
Bass Charrington
Baxter Fell International
BEC
Beecham Products (Beecham Group)
Benson Turner Ltd
†BICC
Biggs Wall Ltd (Charter Consolidated)
BMARC Grantham
Bomag (GB)
Bovis Construction (Peninsular & Oriental)
Bradford & District Newspapers (Pearson plc)
H. Branner & Co
Bridon plc
British Aluminium
British Engines Ltd

British Investment Trust (Black
  Diamond Pensions)
British Ropes (Bridon plc)
Brooke Bond (Unilever)
Bryant Construction
Brymbo Steel
D. T. Bullock Construction
  (Whittaker Ellis Bullock)
*Cape Boards Ltd (Charter
  Consolidated)
*Cape Industrial Products
  (Charter Consolidated)
Cementmakers' Federation
Chanton Engineering Ltd
Charlton Leslie Construction
  (BTR)
Cholride Industrial Batteries
Ciba Geigy plc
Clothing & Allied Products In-
  dustrial Training Board
Coalite Group
Coldflow (IMI)
Commercial Union Assurance
Compair Broomwade (Siebe)
Compaq Computer Corpora-
  tion
Compass Services
Consolidated Goldfields
Corals Racing (Bass plc)
*Richard Costain Ltd
Coutts & Co (National West-
  minster Bank)
Crabtree Vickers (Vickers)
Derek Crouch (Ryan Interna-
  tional)
Dalepak Foods
Davidsons Ltd
Delta Enfield Cables Ltd
Dickinson Robinson Group
Distillers Co (Guinness plc)
Doncasters Sheffield (Inco
  Europe)

R. M. Douglas Construction
  Ltd
Dowsett Engineering Con-
  struction Ltd (Trafalgar
  House plc)
Dowty Communications Divis-
  ion
Dunlop (BTR)
Dupont Plastic Gas Pipes
Eastman Kitchens (Magnet &
  Southerns)
English China Clays Interna-
  tional Ltd
English Electric (GEC)
Evans Medical Ltd (Glaxo
  Holdings)
Faber Prest Holdings
Fairclough Building
  (AMEC)
Fairey Group
Fairport Engineering Ltd
Fasco
Herbert Ferryman Ltd (AAH
  Holdings)
Fitch Lovell
Fluor
Formica Ltd
Fry Construction
Furness Withey
Galliford Sears
James Galt & Co
Geest Holdings
General Combustion plc
General Electric Company
  (GEC)
GES
Gillingham Woodcraft (Magnet
  & Southerns)
Glass Bulbs Ltd (THORN EMI,
  GEC)
*Glaxo Holdings plc
M. J. Gleeson

J. R. Govett

Grand Metropolitan Contract Services

Thomas Grice & Co

Group 4 Total Security (Group 4 Securities)

†Guardian Royal Exchange

*Guest, Keen & Nettlefolds (GKN plc)

*H. & J. Quick Group plc

Matthew Hall Engineering

*Hambros plc

Hanson Engineering

*Hanson Trust plc

Harlands of Hull

P. C. Harrington Contracts

T. C. Harrison Ltd

Hartwells of Oxford

P. Hassall Ltd (Raine Industries)

Hawker Siddeley Group

Hazleton UK

Heinz Ltd

Helix

†Hepworth Ceramic Holdings

*Hewden Stuart Crane Ltd

Hotpoint (GEC)

Howard Doris Construction (John Howard Group)

Howson Algraphy (Vickers)

Hunters Foods

Huwood Ltd (FKI Babcock)

Hyphen Fitted Furniture (Magnet & Southerns)

Ilfords (Ciba Geigy plc)

Inner Guard Ltd

Insulated Buildings Ltd

Interiors

J. & W. Wood Products

JGM Building Services

John Jones Excavation (Norwest Holst)

Jones Lang Wooton

Samuel Jones Ltd

K. Wool Products

Keeton Sons & Co (Rostend)

Kings Investigation Bureau Ltd

Kleinwort Charter Investment Trust plc

*Kleinwort Overseas IT plc

Komatsu UK Ltd

John Laing Construction Ltd

Walter Lawrence

Laycock Engineering (GKN)

†Legal & General Group plc

Lincold Woodworking (Magnet & Southerns)

Lindsay Oil Refinery (Total Oil, Petrofind UK)

Lister Petter (Hawker Siddeley)

Walter Llewelyn

Lloyds Bank

London Brick (Hanson Trust plc)

Y. J. Lovell Construction

M. & G. Group Holdings

*Sir Alfred McAlpine Ltd

Sir Robert McAlpine & Sons Ltd

McCarthy & Stone

McLaughlin and Harvey

Magnet Joinery (Magnet & Southerns)

Magnet Metals (Magnet & Southerns)

Main Gas Appliances (Myson)

Markham Systems Ltd

Marley Group

Marples International

Massey Ferguson

Maxwell UK

Metal Box
Midland Bank
Miller Buckley
MJN Newcastle
A. Monk & Co plc
Mono Pumps Ltd (Gallaher)
†Morgan Crucible Co plc
*Morgan Grenfell Group plc
*John Mowlem & Co Ltd
Harry Neal Ltd
T. & E. Neville
Newman Tonks Building Products
Nico Construction Ltd
North British Distillery
North Sea Ferries Hull (Peninsular & Oriental)
Norwest Holst Ltd
Nove Leather
Edmund Nuttall
Geoffrey Osborne Ltd
T. S. Overy
Penrith Door Company (Magnet & Southerns)
Phoenix Insurance
Phoenix Steel Tube Co (Senior Engineering)
Pilkingtons
*Plessey Group plc
Powell-Pigott Ltd (Newman Tonks)
Power Steels
Powers Samas
Precision Cast Parts Corporation
Press Offshore Ltd (AMEC)
Racal Guardall (Scotland) Ltd
*Ransome Sims & Jefferies plc
RCO Contract Services
†Reckitt & Coleman
Redland Engineering
Reliance Security Services

Renshaw Peel Ltd
Ross Foods Ltd (Dalgety)
Rosser & Russell Building Services (Grand Metropolitan)
*Royal Insurance plc
Ruberoid
*Rush & Tomkins Group plc
Scandura Ltd (BBA Group)
Schrieber Furniture (GEC)
Shell Petroleum Co
Shepherd Building Group
Shepherd Hill & Co
Sinclair & Collis (Hanson Trust)
Skefco (SKF UK)
*Slough Estates plc
Slough Newspaper Printers (Pearson plc)
W. H. Smith Electrical Engineers Group (Staveley Industries)
*Smiths Industries plc
Spear & Jackson (James Neill Holdings)
Sprungrove Ltd
Standard Continuous
Staveley Industries plc
E. C. Stenson
Charles Stevens Funeral Directors
Stockholders Investment Trust
Stocksbridge Engineering Steels
Storeys of Lancaster
Streed Ltd
Sulzter (UK) Ltd
*Sun Alliance & London Insurance
Bernard Sunley & Sons

Symbol Biscuits (Allied Lyons)
A. E. Syms
Syntax Pharmaceuticals
Tabuchi Electric u k Ltd
Tallent Engineering (Charles Colston Group)
*Tarmac Construction plc
Taskman Security Services
*Tate & Lyle Sugars
*Taylor Woodrow plc
Daniel Thwaites
T I Domestic Appliances
Tilbury Contracting
Total Oil Marine plc
*Trafalgar House plc
Trans Manche Link
C. Percy Trentham Ltd
Trico Folberth Ltd
Tube Investments plc
Turner & Newall
Turriff Corporation

Tysons (Contractors) plc
Union Discount Co of London plc
Uniroyal Engelbert Tyres Ltd
United Molasses (Tate & Lyle)
Variant T M Ltd
Vaud Breweries
Venesta International Components
Vickers Instrument Company
Victor International Plastics (Cope Allman International)
Walsall Conduits (G E C)
Wandel & Galtermann & Co Ltd
Samuel Webster & Wilsons Ltd (Grand Metropolitan)
Westminster Contractors Ltd
Whitbread
John E. Wiltshier Group
*George Wimpey plc

The following companies are known to have subscribed to the Economic League in the recent past.

Akroyd & Smithers
Alexanders Discount
Arbuthnot Savory Milln
Automotive Products
Baker Perkins
Bankers Investment Trust (I T)
Barrow Hepburn
B A T Industries
Berkeley Hambro Property
Birmid Qualcast
Boddington's Breweries
Border & Southern Stockholders (I T)

Thomas Borthwick
C. T. Bowring
Braithwaite Engineering
Brintons
British & Commonwealth Holdings
British Vita
Burmah Oil
Capital & Counties Properties
Cawoods Holdings
Cedar (I T)
Charter & Trust Agency
Chrysler u k (now Talbot)

Matthew Clark & Son
Clayton Dewandre Holdings
Coates Brothers
Common Brothers
Cookson Group plc
Courtaulds
Crane Frueheuf
De la Rue
Dominion & General Trust
Dow Scandia
Eagle Star
East Lancashire Paper
Edbro
Electra (IT)
English & New York Trust
Everards Brewery
J. H. Fenner
Fleming Far East Trust
Fleming Technology (IT)
Foreign & Colonial (IT)
Gerrard & National Discount
Glasgow & Stockholders Trust
Greene King
Green's Economiser
Hardys & Hanson
Hiram Walker & Sons
Homfray & Co
Imperial Group plc
John I. Jacobs
Johnson Matthey
Jones Woodhead & Sons
Kleinwort Benson Lonsdale
Lake View (IT)
Lindustries
London Prudential (IT)
Low & Bonar
Lyon & Lyon
McKechnie

National Westminster Bank
Neepsend
NEI
Norwich Union
Pegler Hattersley
Pentland (IT)
Plaxton
Pochins
Powell Duffryn
Provincial Insurance
Rank Hovis McDougall
Readicut International
Frederic Robinson
Rockware Group
Sanderson Kayser
Scottish & Newcastle Breweries
Scottish National Trust
Senior Engineering
Singer & Friedlander
Swan Hunter
Tanks Consolidated (IT)
Thermal Syndicate
Trans Oceanic Trust
Transport Development Group
TR City of London Trust
TR Natural Resources
TR Pacific Basin (IT)
Wadkin
Wagon Industrial Holdings
Wardley Group
Weir Group
Wests Group International
Wilkinson Match
William Baird
William Jackson & Son
Wilmot Breedon

Sources: Annual Reports and Accounts, Labour Research Department, *World in Action*.

Appendix Two: Economic League Personnel

(*: Member of the Policy and Finance Committee)

Staff

Director-General: Michael Noar
Joined the League as Director-General on 1 June 1986. Before that he was Director of External Relations of the Federation of Civil Engineering Contractors from 1976 to 1986.
Director of Research: Jack Winder
Also Director of the League's Midlands Region
Secretary and Director of Information: Thom Robinson
Joined the League on 12 May 1987. He is also a Director of Policy Research Associates Ltd, a right wing political research consultancy.
Liaison Director: John Udal

Central Council Members

*Sir Gerald Thorley
President of the Economic League. Also Director of Fitch Lovell plc. Former chairman of Allied Breweries Ltd, British Sugar plc and MEPC plc.
John S. Dettmer
Vice-President of the Economic League. Former Army officer. He was Director-General of the League from 1959 to 1977. Now Director of H. C. Freeman Ltd.
Major-General Thomas Brodie
Vice-President of the Economic League and President of the

Eastern Region. He worked for the League between 1957 and 1984.

Peter Savill
: Vice-President of the Economic League. He joined the League in 1959 and has been Director of the North-West and Midlands regions. He was Director-General from 1977 to 1985.

*John Lawrence-Mills
: Chairman of the Economic League. Director of Allied Lyons Second Pension Trust Ltd, Business In The Community and the North London Business Development Agency.

David Andrews-Jones
: Personnel Manager. In the early 1970s he was head of the Industrial Relations Division at Metal Box. Before that he was in personnel management at ICI.

Peter Ashworth
: Company Director. He is Director of Greenall Whitley plc, Symonds English Wine Co Ltd and Hereford English Wine Co Ltd.

*Major Walter Bridge
: Chairman of the League's Eastern Region. A brewer, he is Director of Greene King & Sons plc.

Lord Cayzer
: Chairman of British and Commonwealth Shipping Co plc, British Air Transport (Holdings) Ltd, Caledonian Investments plc, Scottish Investments Ltd and several other companies.

James Coull
: Company Director. He is currently Director of Christian Coull Consultancies Ltd and former Director of British Syphon Industries Ltd.

Lord Dowding
: Former Wing-Commander in the RAF.

*Peter Edwards
: Business consultant. President of the League's North-East Region and a Director of Hunting Petroleum Services plc and Granville & Co Ltd

*Denis Fahey
: Company Director. President of the League's Midlands Region and a Director of Deancroft Fahey Ltd and Rexshire Ltd.

*Robin Fremantle
: Management Consultant. He is Chairman of the League's Scottish Region and a Director of Management Securities Investments Ltd (MSI Ltd).

Graham Hale
    Company Director. He is a Director of Forward Chemicals Ltd,
    Rexodan Ltd and Fortham Ltd.
*Antony Hampton
    Chairman of Hampton's Wholefoods Ltd and President of
    Record Marples Tools Ltd. He was President of the Engineer-
    ing Employers' Federation from 1980 to 1982.
*Joseph Harding
    Chairman of the League's South-East Region.
*Sir Maxwell Harper Gow
    President of the League's Scottish Region since 1985. Vice-
    Chairman and a Director of Christian Salvesen plc and on the
    Council of the Institute of Directors. Director of at least
    twenty-eight other companies, mainly Scottish financial in-
    stitutions.
*Richard Hunting
    Manager. Director of at least eighteen companies.
*Harry Jakeman
    Company Personnel Manager. Chairman of the Western
    Region and appointed a Director of the League on 2 July
    1987.
Sir Michael Nall
    Former Lieutenant-Commander in the Royal Navy.
Lawrence Orchard
Jimson Parsons
    Director of Robin Marlar & Associates
*Edward Rea
    Company Director. Chairman of the League's South Wales
    Region. Also a Director of the South Wales Electricity Board,
    Wales Region TSB and Intercosmetics GB Ltd.
*Dr Alan Robertson
    Company Chairman.
*Ronald Rowles
    Business Consultant. Former 'Chief Executive of Operations'
    for the League. In the early 1970s he was Director of Industrial
    Relations and Personnel at British Leyland Triumph Motor
    Company. Before that he worked for Frys and Cadburys.
    Director of Chevron Foods Ltd and Robin Marlar Ltd and
    Chairman of Smith Warehousing & Transport Group.
*C. D. Runge
*Brian Whitehouse
    Personnel Executive. Chairman of the League's North-East

Region. Former Group Personnel Manager of James Neill
Holdings Ltd.

*Robert Willan
Company Director. Chairman of the League's North-West
Region. Director of RR and J. Willan Ltd, Federated Employers
Press Ltd, Willan Home Improvements Ltd and Manchester
Chamber of Commerce & Industry.

Appendix Three: Economic League Offices

*National Headquarters and
Eastern Region*: 7 Wine Office
Court, Fleet Street, London
EC4. *Tel*: 01–3537672.
Director-General: Michael Noar.
Director of Eastern Region:
P. F. Leach.

*Central Records and Research De-
partment*: 99a High Street,
Thornton Heath, Surrey.

Midland Region: 108c Alcester
Road, Birmingham B13. *Tel*:
021–4491594. *Director*: Jack
Winder.

North-Eastern Region: High
Street House, Newmarket
Street, Skipton, North
Yorkshire BD23. *Tel*: 0756–
68021. *Director*: S. J. Brom-
ley.

North-Western Region: 18
Museum Street, Warrington
WA1. *Tel*: 0925–54391 or
0925–54616. *Director*: Roland
Brett.

Scotland: 15 North Claremont
Street, Glasgow G3. *Tel*:
041–3329108. *Director*: Hamish
Macgregor.

South-East Region: 43 Bridge
Street, Leatherhead, Surrey
KT22. *Tel*: 0372–378963. *Dir-
ector*: A. L. Weeks.

Western Region: Bakers Row,
Cardiff CF1. *Tel*: 0222–382428.
Director: E. Dover.

Bibliography

John Baker White, *True Blue* (Muller, London, 1970)

Huw Beynon, *Working for Ford* (Penguin, Harmondsworth, 1984)

Tony Bunyan, *The Political Police in Britain* (Julian Friedmann, London, 1976)

Duncan Campbell and Steve Connor, *On the Record* (Michael Joseph, London, 1986)

Barbara Castle, *The Castle Diaries 1964–70* (Weidenfeld and Nicolson, London, 1984)

David Caute, *The Great Fear* (Secker and Warburg, London, 1978)

Barry Cox, *Civil Liberties in Britain* (Penguin, Harmondsworth, 1975)

Michael Edwardes, *Back From the Brink* (Collins, London, 1983)

Edward Frow, *Engineering Struggles* (Working Class Movement Library, Manchester, 1982)

Peter Hamilton, *Espionage and Subversion in an Industrial Society* (Hutchinson, London, 1968)

Peter Heims, *Countering Industrial Espionage* (20th Century Education Ltd, London, 1982)

Stuart Hood, *On Television* (Pluto Press, London, 1980)

Diane Johnson, *Dashiell Hammett: A Life* (Random House, New York, 1983)

Robert Lacey, *Ford* (Heinemann, London, 1986)

Chapman Pincher, *Inside Story* (Sidgwick and Jackson, London, 1978)

Michael Redgrave, *In My Mind's Eye* (Weidenfeld and Nicolson, London 1983)

Charles Stuart, (ed.) *The Reith Diaries* (Collins, London, 1975)

Anthony Thompson, *Big Brother in Britain Today* (Michael Joseph, London, 1970)

Alan Thornett, *From Militancy to Marxism* (Left View, London, 1987)

Ian Trethowan, *Split Screen* (Hamish Hamilton, London, 1984)

Sidney and Beatrice Webb, *The History of Trade Unionism* (Longmans Green & Co, London, 1950)

Notes

Introduction

1. *Guardian*, 12 May 1987 and 15 June 1987.
2. *Guardian*, 31 December 1987.
3. The Grunwick dispute in 1977 was a prolonged struggle by a largely Asian workforce to win trade union recognition at a north London film-processing company. Dromey was there in his capacity as Secretary of both Brent Trades Council and the South-East Regional Council of the TUC.
4. *MI5's Official Secrets*, *20/20 Vision* documentary, Channel 4, 8 March 1985.
5. Lord Denning's Report, Command Paper 2152, HMSO, 1963.
6. House of Lords, 26 February 1975.
7. Letter from Leon Brittan to Peter Jones, 15 August 1985.
8. Statement on the Recommendations of the Security Commission by Mrs Thatcher, May 1982, Command Paper 8540, HMSO, 1985.
9. Private meeting between Mrs Thatcher and Civil Service trades unions, 23 February 1984.
10. Letter from Larry Gostin to Mrs Thatcher, 4 April 1985.
11. House of Commons, 25 January 1988.
12. Sidney and Beatrice Webb, *The History of Trade Unionism* (Longmans Green & Co, London, 1950).
13. Philip Bagwell, *The History of the National Union of Railwaymen* (Allen and Unwin, London, 1963).
14. House of Commons, 23 July 1840.
15. *Daily Telegraph*, 20 March 1953.
16. Barry Cox, *Civil Liberties in Britain* (Penguin, Harmondsworth, 1975).
17. *New Statesman*, 6 June 1980.
18. Diane Johnson, *Dashiell Hammett: A Life* (Random House, New York, 1983).
19. David Caute, *The Great Fear* (Secker and Warburg, London, 1978).
20. *Dark Victory*, Episode 5 of *The RKO Story*, BBC TV, September 1987.
21. From *A Journal of the Plague Years* (Atheneum, New York, 1973).
22. *The RKO Story, op.cit.*
23. *Washington Post*, 30 September 1987.
24. *New York Times*, 2 February 1952.

25. *The Secret File on Citizen K*, BBC2, 11 June 1987.
26. *Common Cause*, January/February 1986.
27. *Washington Post*, 10 September 1979.
28. *Los Angeles Times*, 12 February 1985.
29. *The Secret File on Citizen K, op. cit.*
30. *New York Times*, 29 March 1984.
31. *Washington Post*, 18 February 1984.
32. *New York Times*, 29 March 1984.
33. Letter to Labour MP Ron Brown, 21 April 1987.
34. 'National Campaign Against the *Berufsverbot*' Newsletter No.3, 1983.
35. Letter to Labour MP Ron Brown, 21 April 1987.
36. 'National Campaign Against the *Berufsverbot*' Newsletter No.1, 1987.

Chapter 1 – The Civil Service Since 1945

1. Clive Ponting, a senior Ministry of Defence official, was acquitted in 1985 of charges under the Official Secrets Act. He had been charged with sending official documents relating to the sinking of the Argentine cruiser, the *General Belgrano*, during the Falklands conflict, to the Labour MP, Tam Dalyell.
2. The government, without any warning or consultation, announced a ban on union membership at GCHQ, its electronic information-gathering centre based in Cheltenham, on 25 January 1984.
3. First Special Report from the Defence Committee, Session 1982–83, HMSO, May 1983.
4. *Ibid.*, p.77.
5. A questionnaire asking for details of their political affiliations was sent to applicants for the Youth Training Scheme. Sir George Young, then a Junior Environment Minister, questioned the need for such a system of vetting (*Tribune*, 1 June 1984). In 1986, ASTMS, the white-collar union, discovered that some YTS Inspectors argued that their recruits were employed 'in connection with work that is vital to the security of the State.'
6. *Bulletin of Atomic Scientists*, June 1950.
7. Peter Hennessy and Gail Brownfeld, 'Britain's Cold War Security Purge: The Origins of Positive Vetting' (*The Historical Journal*, Cambridge University Press, December 1982).
8. Report of the Conference of Privy Councillors, Command Paper 9715, HMSO, 1956.
9. Letter to the *Economist*, 13 December 1986.
10. 'Security Procedures in the Public Service', Command Paper 1681, HMSO, 1962.
11. Statement on the Recommendations of the Security Commission. Command Paper 8540, HMSO, 1982.
12. First Special Report from the Defence Committee, *op. cit.*
13. *Ibid.*
14. House of Commons Paper 59, 24 November 1982.

15. Command Paper 9514, HMSO, May 1985.
16. *Ibid.*
17. John Vassall was gaoled for eighteen years in 1962 for passing secrets to the Russians. Both he and four of his superiors were interviewed by an investigating officer.
18. Duncan Campbell, *New Statesman*, 1 November 1985.
19. *Guardian*, 6 March 1984.

Chapter 2: The Civil Service and the Nuclear Industry

1. House of Commons, 4 February 1985.
2. The Inland Revenue Staff Federation was the first union in the Civil Service to vote to set up a political fund. Other unions followed as concern grew about how the government would use its broad, and vague, definition of the term 'political' in its employment legislation.
3. National Council for Civil Liberties booklet, *Civil Rights for Civil Servants*.
4. Defence Committee, *op. cit.*
5. *Guardian*, 6 March 1984.
6. Letter from Rex Davie to the FDA, 13 July 1983.
7. Channel 4's *20/20 Vision* programme, *MI5's Official Secrets*, in which Cathy Massiter, a former MI5 officer, was interviewed, in 1985. The programme was initially banned by the Independent Broadcasting Authority.
8. Sue Corby, FDA Assistant General Secretary, to Peter Jones, Secretary of the Council of Civil Service Unions, 16 October 1984.
9. 1982 Security Commission report, *op. cit.*
10. Ministry of Defence official, Defence Committee, *op. cit.*
11. R. W. Ayres, 'Plutonium Recycling', in *Harvard Civil Rights – Civil Liberties Law Review*, Volume 10, 1975.
12. Royal Commission on Environmental Pollution, Sixth Report, 'Nuclear Power and the Environment', 1976, Cmnd. 6618. HMSO.
13. *Taming the Dragon: Swords and Ploughshares*, BBC2, 15 October 1986.
14. *Observer*, 24 August 1986.
15. *New Statesman*, 22 July 1983.

Chapter 3: Defence Companies

1. Note by Ian Townsend attached to a summary of the 'Staff Employment Handbook', 1 October 1984.
2. Letter to Bill Benyon, Tory MP for Milton Keynes, 5 February 1987.
3. 'Security Procedures in the Public Service', Lord Radcliffe Report, 1962. HMSO Cmnd 1681.
4. Statement by Mrs Thatcher on the recommendations of the Security Commission, May 1982. HMSO Cmnd 8540.
5. Evidence given to the House of Commons Defence Committee on 9

March 1983 on Positive Vetting Procedures in HM Services and the Ministry of Defence. HMSO 242.

6. House of Lords, 21 June 1956.
7. *Computer Talk*, 23 June 1986.
8. *Electronics Times*, 10 October 1985.
9. Letter to British Aerospace, 21 October 1985.
10. Letter from A. G. Tween, Personnel Officer of MEL, 13 September 1985.
11. Letter from Colin Gills, Personnel Officer of MEL, 22 October 1985.
12. Letter to Colin Gills, 28 March 1986.
13. Letter from Colin Gills, 18 April 1986.
14. *Computer Talk*, 23 June 1986.
15. *Guardian*, 3 January 1987.
16. Supplied by Peter Warren, *Electronics Press*, 13 April 1987.
17. *Today*, 28 January 1987.

Chapter 4: British Telecom

1. Confidential memorandum from BT Personnel Office, 13 May 1985.
2. Letter to Alan Chamberlain, Secretary of the British Telecom Unions Committee (BTUC), 18 October 1985.
3. Minutes of meeting between BT and trades unions on 16 June 1986 to discuss 'Security Procedures'.
4. Letter from Malcolm Argent, Company Secretary, to Alan Chamberlain, 19 December 1986.
5. Letter from Alan Chamberlain to Malcolm Argent, 5 November 1986.
6. Letter from Ken England, Head of Security Division, to Alan Chamberlain, 12 June 1987.
7. Letter from Ken England to Alan Chamberlain, 12 June 1987.
8. Letter from Malcolm Argent to Alan Chamberlain, 19 December 1986.
9. Letter from Alan Chamberlain to Malcolm Argent, 10 April 1986.
10. Minutes of meeting between BT and trades unions, 16 June 1986.
11. Letter from Major Oehlers to Alan Chamberlain, 16 October 1987.
12. Letter from Malcolm Argent to Alan Chamberlain, 26 January 1988.
13. Letter from Ben Marshall, British Telecom Executives, to Alan Chamberlain, 8 October 1986.
14. Agreement signed between NCU and BTI Marine Division, 17 June 1986.
15. Memo from Len Gillard to John Starmer, outgoing Chairman of the NCU Networks Committee, 5 June 1986.
16. Letter from John Starmer, 5 June 1986.
17. *Ibid*.
18. *Computer Talk*, 25 May 1987.
19. Letter from Richard Hammock, City of London District Personnel Manager, to S. E. Blake, Chair of NCU City Branch, 3 March 1987.
20. Letter from John Deason to Maureen Dresser, Head of Personnel Services in City District, 13 May 1987.

21. Memo from Richard Hammock, Personnel Manager of City District, to a number of district managers and executives, 20 May 1987.
22. 'Extremists Plot BT Union Coup' – *London Standard*, 28 April 1987.
23. *Time Out*, 17 February 1988.
24. *Daily Telegraph*, 7 October 1985.

Chapter 5: MI5 and the BBC

1. *Sunday Times*, 25 May 1986.
2. *Observer*, 18 August 1985.
3. Charles Stuart (ed.), *The Reith Diaries* (Collins, London, 1975).
4. *Guardian*, 22 August 1985.
5. *Observer*, 18 August 1985.
6. Michael Redgrave, *In My Mind's Eye* (Weidenfeld and Nicolson, London, 1983).
7. *Observer*, 18 August 1985.
8. From Alaric Jacob's diary, published in the *Observer*, 25 August 1985.
9. Stuart Hood, *On Television* (Pluto Press, London, 1980).
10. Ian Trethowan, *Split Screen* (Hamish Hamilton, London, 1984).
11. *Independent*, 29 September 1987.
12. *Observer*, 4 October 1987.
13. *Daily Telegraph*, 28 September 1987.
14. *Guardian*, 26 September 1985.
15. *Observer*, 18 August 1985.
16. *Ibid*.
17. Letter from Christopher Storey to Yvette Vanson, 13 November 1979.
18. BBC Radio Shropshire, 20 August 1985.
19. *Observer*, 18 August 1985.
20. *Broadcast*, 29 February 1985.
21. *Guardian*, 26 September 1985.
22. *Guardian*, 2 September 1985.
23. Departmental Committee on Section 2 of the Official Secrets Act, 1911, Franks Commission, Volume 2.
24. *Evening Standard*, 20 May 1977.
25. House of Commons, 20 November 1985.
26. Letter to Tam Dalyell, 15 September 1985.
27. *Guardian*, 26 September 1985.
28. *Ibid*.
29. *It's Your World*, BBC World Service, October 1985.
30. Letter from Christopher Martin to National Union of Journalists, 28 October 1985.
31. *Guardian*, 20 August 1985.

Chapter 6: MI5 and The Special Branch

1. This information comes from Joe Haines, former Press Secretary to the Labour Prime Minister Harold Wilson, writing in the *Daily*

the Labour Prime Minister Harold Wilson, writing in the Daily Mirror, 1 August 1986.

2. *Guardian*, 17 April 1984.
3. Barbara Castle, *The Castle Diaries 1964–70* (Weidenfeld and Nicolson, London, 1984).
4. *Ibid.*
5. Chapman Pincher, *Inside Story* (Sidgwick and Jackson, London, 1978).
6. *Ibid.*
7. *Observer*, 17 July 1977.
8. Duncan Campbell and Steve Connor, *On the Record* (Michael Joseph, London, 1986).
9. *Observer*, 12 May 1984.
10. House of Commons, 15 January 1988.
11. *New Statesman*, 5 December 1986.
12. *New Society*, 31 May 1984.
13. House of Commons, 11 December 1979.
14. Evidence to the House of Commons Treasury and Civil Service Select Committee, 12 February 1986.
15. Lord Denning's report on the Profumo Affair, Command Paper 2152, HMSO, 1963.
16. House of Commons, 3 December 1986.
17. *MI5's Official Secrets*, *20/20 Vision* documentary for Channel 4, 8 March 1985.
18. *Ibid.*
19. *The Spy Who Never Was*, *World in Action*, Granada Television, 16 July 1984.
20. *Observer*, 3 January 1988.
21. *Time Out*, 25 July 1980.
22. Sir Harold Scott, *Scotland Yard* (Penguin, Harmondsworth, 1957). Quoted in Tony Bunyan, *The Political Police in Britain* (Julian Friedmann, London, 1976).
23. Letter from Leon Brittan to John Prescott, 25 January 1985.
24. *Observer*, 28 February 1982.
25. *The Times*, 18 March 1970.
26. *File on Four*, BBC Radio 4, 10 August 1982.
27. Duncan Campbell and Steve Connor, *op. cit.*
28. *Observer*, 31 January 1982.
29. Evidence to House of Commons Home Affairs Select Committee, 16 January 1985.
30. *Panorama*, BBC Television, 2 March 1981.
31. *Ibid.*
32. Evidence to the House of Commons Home Affairs Select Committee, 12 December 1984.
33. *Panorama*, *op. cit.*

Chapter 7: The Economic League

1. *Morning Star*, 31 January 1976.
2. Economic League Annual Review, 1986.
3. B. R. Mitchell and P. Deane, *Abstract of British Historical Statistics* (1962).
4. 'Fifty Fighting Years', Economic League publication, 1969.
5. John Baker White, *True Blue*, (Muller, London, 1970).
6. Annual Report, 1925.
7. Annual Report, 1931.
8. 'Two Minute News Review', Economic League newsletter sent out to member companies, March 1987.
9. *World in Action*, Granada Television, 1 February 1988.
10. *Ibid*.
11. *Ibid*.
12. *Sunday Mail*, 21 December 1986.
13. Confirmed to the authors by Michael Noar, Director-General of the Economic League, December 1987.
14. *World in Action*, *op. cit*.
15. *Ibid*.
16. *Ibid*.
17. *Times Law Report*, 14 June 1937.
18. *Daily Worker*, 12 June 1937.
19. *World in Action*, 16 February 1987.
20. *London Standard*, 3 March 1987.
21. Arthur McIvor, 'The Economic League – 1919–39' (Research Working Paper, Polytechnic of Central London, September 1983).
22. *Daily Telegraph*, 26 January 1981.
23. *World in Action*, 8 February 1988.
24. Duncan Campbell and Steve Connor, *op. cit*.
25. 'The Need For A Change In Direction', internal Economic League report, May 1984.
26. House of Commons, 15 December 1949.
27. House of Commons, 7 May 1953.
28. *The Times*, 2 October 1964.
29. *Daily Mirror*, 4 June 1987.
30. 'Companies Under Attack – Political Disruption In Industry', Economic League booklet, November 1986.
31. *World in Action*, 16 February 1987.
32. *London Standard*, 3 March 1987.
33. *World in Action*, 1 February 1988.
34. *Ibid*.
35. *World in Action*, 16 February 1987.
36. 'Companies Under Attack – Political Disruption in Industry', *op. cit*.
37. *World in Action*, 8 February 1988.
38. *Ibid*.

39. *Ibid*.
40. *Ibid*.
41. *Ibid*.
42. *Ibid*.
43. *Electronics Times*, 5 September 1985.
44. *Ibid.*, 24 October 1985.
45. *Datalink*, 29 June 1987.
46. *London Daily News*, 30 June 1987.
47. *Guardian*, 29 June 1978.
48. *World in Action*, 16 February 1987.
49. 'Companies Under Attack – Political Disruption In Industry', *op. cit.*
50. *World in Action*, 16 February 1987.
51. *Ibid.*, 8 February 1988.
52. *Ibid*.
53. *Ibid*.
54. *Time Out*, 24 February 1988.

Chapter 8: The Engineering and Construction Industry

1. As read to the 1982 national delegate conference of the Union of Construction, Allied Trades and Technicians (UCATT) by J. Keane, representing Finsbury Park, north London.
2. Letter from John Crathorne to Reg Preston, General Secretary of the National Union of Domestic Appliance Workers, 21 April 1983.
3. Minutes of meeting between the Engineering Employers Federation (EEF) and the Amalgamated Engineering Union (AEU) on 'Employment References', 21 June 1984.
4. *Daily Telegraph*, 23 October 1978.
5. *Morning Star*, 19 December 1978.
6. *Daily Mail*, 12 September 1972.
7. Letter to senior executives of the 'Services Group' companies, 5 November 1975.
8. 'The Need for a Change of Direction', internal Economic League report, May 1984.
9. *Financial Times*, 31 December 1986.
10. *World in Action*, Granada Television, 16 February 1987.
11. *Ibid*.
12. *Ibid*.
13. *Newcastle Evening Chronicle*, 18 February 1987.
14. *Ibid*.

Chapter 9: The Car Industry

1. From a leaflet distributed by management in 1974 during a dispute over 'mutuality', whereby new work allocations could not be introduced without the permission of shop stewards.
2. Michael Edwardes, *Back From The Brink* (Collins, London, 1983).
3. *MI5's Official Secrets*, *20/20 Vision* documentary for Channel 4, 8

March 1985.

4. Alan Thornett, *From Militancy to Marxism* (Left View, London, 1987).
5. *Ibid.*
6. *Open Space*, вв c2, 12 January 1984.
7. *Evening Standard*, 28 December 1983.
8. 'The Need For a Change in Direction', Economic League internal report, May 1984.
9. *Oxford Star*, 22 August 1985.
10. *Financial Times*, 20 June 1986.
11. *Daily Telegraph*, 12 August 1983.
12. Robert Lacey, *Ford* (Heinemann, London, 1986).
13. Huw Beynon, *Working for Ford* (Penguin, Harmondsworth, 1984).
14. 'Decisions and Orders of the National Labor Relations Board', Volume 23 (u s Government Printing Office, Washington DC, 1941). Quoted in Huw Beynon, *op. cit.*
15. Robert Lacey, *op. cit.*
16. *Ibid.*
17. *Ibid.*
18. *Ibid.*
19. David Caute, *The Great Fear* (Secker and Warburg, London, 1978).
20. Barbara Castle, *The Castle Diaries 1964–70* (Weidenfeld and Nicolson, London, 1984).
21. *MI5's Official Secrets*, *op. cit.*
22. Edward Frow, 'Engineering Struggles' (Working Class Movement Library, Manchester, 1982).
23. *Guardian*, 12 March 1957.
24. *Guardian*, 12 April 1957.
25. Letter to Labour m p Jo Richardson, 17 April 1986.
26. Letter to Denny Fitzpatrick, 10 July 1986.
27. Official minutes of meeting, 26 March 1986.
28. Letter to Steve Hart, т g w u District Officer, 21 April 1986.
29. *Daily Mail*, 23 April 1986.
30. 'Companies Under Attack – Political Disruption in Industry', Economic League booklet, November 1986.
31. Letter from Mr M. H. Roberts, Administration Manager, British Telecom, City of London District, 30 July 1986.
32. Speech to School of Industrial and Business Studies, Warwick University Industrial Relations Research Unit, 21 March 1986.

Chapter 10: The Private Security Industry

1. From 'Security: Attitudes and Techniques for Management' (published in 1968 by Hutchinson for Chubb Security, on their 150th anniversary).
2. Anthony Thompson, *Big Brother in Britain Today* (Michael Joseph, London, 1970).
3. *Tribune*, 25 April 1986 and 9 May 1986.

4. Tony Bunyan, *The Political Police in Britain* (Julian Friedmann, London, 1976).
5. Anthony Thompson, *op. cit.*
6. *World in Action*, Granada Television, 9 February 1987.
7. *Ibid.*
8. Peter Hamilton, *Espionage and Subversion in an Industrial Society* (Hutchinson, London, 1968).
9. This information comes from Hamilton's own biographical summary.
10. *Observer*, 27 January 1985.
11. *Ibid.*
12. *Ibid.*
13. Peter Hamilton, *op. cit.*
14. *Ibid.*
15. *Police Review*, 16 April 1982.
16. *Ibid.*
17. *Ibid.*
18. Anthony Thompson, *op. cit.*
19. *Observer*, 3 February 1985.
20. *Ibid.*
21. *Ibid.*
22. *New Statesman*, 22 February 1980.
23. Peter Heims, *Countering Industrial Espionage* (20th Century Education Ltd, London, 1982).
24. *Scotsman*, 6 March 1978.
25. Letters from Clarkson, Whittaker & Shellcross, on behalf of Anthony Norris, to Keely, Smith & Jobson, on behalf of United Leisure Ltd, on 9 July 1985 and 15 July 1985.
26. Letter from Keely, Smith & Jobson, on behalf of United Leisure Ltd, to Clarkson, Whittaker & Shellcross, on behalf of Anthony Norris, 5 July 1985.
27. *Time Out*, 27 March 1980.
28. *Ibid.*

Conclusion

1. *Leadership*, Volume 2, Number 6, 1986.
2. *City of Birmingham District Council* v *Beyer* (1977) IRLR (EAT).
3. House of Commons, 5 July 1978.
4. Cited in the Report of the TUC Annual Congress, 3–7 September 1979.
5. House of Commons, 8 February 1988.
6. *Computer Talk*, 16 February 1987.
7. *World in Action*, Granada Television, 8 February 1988.
8. *Observer*, 21 February 1988.
9. House of Commons, 24 April 1987.
10. *The Times*, 20 July 1984.

Index

0252-726964 (S)
764-5268 (W) ⎤ A.
549-9815 (H) ⎦
736-6163 (AI)